# IDEALISTS

Hans
Scherfig

# IDEALISTS

Translated from the Danish
by Frank Hugus

*With Illustrations by the Author*

Fjord Press
Seattle
1991

Title of Danish edition: *Idealister*
Originally published in 1944 by Albert Bonniers Förlag,
Stockholm, and in 1945 by Gyldendalske Boghandel, Nordisk
Forlag, Copenhagen

Grateful acknowledgment is given to the National Endowment
for the Arts and the Danish Ministry of Cultural Affairs for
their generous support.

Published and distributed by:
Fjord Press
P.O. Box 16501
Seattle, Washington 98116
(206) 625-9363

Editors: Tiina Nunnally & Steven T. Murray
Design & typography: Fjord Press
Cover design: Jane Fleming & Art Chantry
Front cover & text illustrations: Hans Scherfig
Back cover photograph: Courtesy of the Scherfig family
Printed by Thomson-Shore, Dexter, Michigan

Library of Congress Cataloging in Publication Data:

Scherfig, Hans, 1905–1979
    [Idealister. English]
    Idealists / Hans Scherfig ; translated from the Danish by
Frank Hugus ; with illustrations by the author. — 1st ed.
        p.    cm.
    Translation of: Idealister.
    ISBN 0-940242-05-2 (cloth : acid-free paper) : $19.95. — ISBN
0-940242-02-8 (paper : acid-free paper) : $9.95.
    I. Title.
PT8175.S36I313   1991      839.8'1372 — dc20      90-85820

Printed on acid-free paper

Printed in the United States of America
*First edition*

# IDEALISTS

# THE MURDER

## [ 1 ]

A MAN IS LYING in a canopy bed getting ready to fall asleep.

He has closed the bed-curtains, which are made of good, heavy damask from his own store. And he is resting comfortably between fine linen sheets on a first-rate Puma mattress, with a soft, lightweight, ribbed eiderdown comforter on top of him. Both the Puma mattress and the ribbed eiderdown comforter are from his own factory and the sheets from his own textile mill.

He is an energetic man who has successfully worked his way up and has established his own vast business all across Denmark. He was once a simple wool peddler who walked the country roads of Jutland with his bundle. Now he is a wholesale dealer, a manufacturer, and a country squire, and he sleeps in a canopy bed in a historic castle.

An army of wool dealers travels around the country selling undershirts for him. And when the shirts have worn out and turned into old rags, they are collected and purchased by an equally large army of rag pickers and junk dealers. And the rags are sent to the cloth factory near Præstø, where they are ripped and shredded in ingenious machines. Upholstery fabric, wool shirts, bits of curtains, old silk stockings, and tattered rags are turned into a uniform fluff of fibers, which can again be spun, woven, and dyed and made into a blue fabric, which is then stitched into those renowned, strong-as-iron navy trousers.

Unassuming little shops in Denmark's provincial towns sell his stockings, ribbons, mittens, tablecloths, curtains, and lace. His unpretentious little Christmas calendar—with its Bible verses, helpful adages, market days, and gestation tables— hangs in thousands of homes.

He lives in a castle with ramparts and moats, where an illegitimate son of Christian IV once played hospitable host to the officers of the Swedish military and where the Swedish king himself, Karl X Gustav, once spent the night.

He owns fields and marshes and vast forests where Svend Gjønge and his Danish partisans once hid out and harassed the Swedish enemy with constant attacks on their supply columns.

He is an enterprising man who buys up farms and incorporates them into his own estate. And the law that prohibits the merging of smaller farms doesn't apply as long as he makes certain to install a farm hand as manager and one calf as livestock on his annexed properties.

He is a powerful man who holds the reins in his hand and presides over the well-being of many people. But he is modest and unassuming and humble in the face of a Providence that has made things go so well for him. He has been a good man to the church and has helped and supported the congregations and has built evangelical meeting houses here and there on his estate. And he has a small prayer stool in his bedroom; morning and evening he kneels on its canvas cushion embroidered with a white dove on a blue background and gives thanks and humbles himself before his God.

He lies there in the darkness in his historic canopy bed, reviewing the events of the day. Once King Karl Gustav of Sweden lay in this same bed thinking things over. Perhaps war will break out in the world again. Perhaps he would be wise to begin buying up horses in good time, while they are cheap.

And he also thinks about a mausoleum that he has had built for himself in a corner of the village cemetery. A burial mound in the old style, lined with glazed tiles, with bronze doors and wrought-iron grilles and a marble sarcophagus. Someday he will lie there in state awaiting Judgment Day and the last trumpet.

" 'Every task, however simple, sets the soul that does it free.' But I beseech Thee, dear God: let me live and work for many more years to come!" And why shouldn't he live?

Out there in the darkness someone is breathing. He hears a person breathing very softly. He turns cold with fear, and his thoughts stand still. His evening prayer has come to a halt. He listens out into the darkness; there is someone breathing outside his bed-curtains.

He has no voice left and no saliva in his mouth. He wants to

say, "Julie, is that you?" But nothing comes of it. Besides, it couldn't be Julie. His wife sleeps in another room. They have quarreled again and made a scene, and she threatened to leave. She's so terribly high-strung, his aristocratic wife. "Oh, God! I probably haven't been very good to her, have I? Forgive me! No! No!—Take it easy, now. Take it nice and easy."

Someone is breathing out in the room. Very softly. There is someone in the room. And he gathers his strength and slowly sits up in bed. And the excellent Puma spring mattress does not squeak.

Slowly he gets out of bed and moves out into the room. And out in the darkness he bumps into someone.

They don't say a thing. They make no sound. And they are unable to find each other in the darkness.

He stumbles over his prayer stool and picks it up and flings it at something. And he himself is hit by something else. The two struggle around in the darkness without being able to see. Then he is held tightly, and someone's arms are wrapped around him. And now he would like to be able to scream for help. But hands are squeezing his throat. His ears are ringing. He thinks about his mausoleum, and much more. And he has strange dreams and nightmares in the few seconds before he dies.

# [ 2 ]

THE NEXT MORNING Squire Skjern-Svendsen's corpse is found by a servant. The servant's name is Lukas. A strangely taciturn man with a pale, expressionless face.

He looks at the dead man, touching him tentatively, but is not surprised or shaken. And he takes the dead man's wallet out of the jacket hanging in the wardrobe and removes several bills. He doesn't take all the bills, just a few of them. After that he packs up some of the castle's silver in a small suitcase and stores it out of the way before calling the police to tell them that the squire has been murdered.

The police arrive in force. First the local police officer and the county sheriff. Later the homicide squad arrives from Copenhagen. The flying squad, with Police Superintendent Odense himself in charge. The men from the homicide squad are arrogant gentlemen who treat the local police officer with disdain.

Later on, other cars arrive with doctors and reporters and press photographers. The old castle is filled with busy people making telephone calls, snapping pictures, taking measurements, and writing things down.

The local clergyman, Pastor Nørregaard-Olsen, shows up too. He was a personal friend of the deceased, and he hastily improvises a brief devotional service before the body is transported to the Institute of Forensic Medicine. "So now he is dead, our beloved friend. Now he has gone to his rest, he who never allowed himself any repose. Thus it had to end, this energy, this love of work. In the midst of the day's labors, in the midst of his loving diligence, he was summoned to that great repose.

"If we can say anything about Squire Skjern-Svendsen that would characterize him, it would have to be this: He was a good man. A good man. This is a term that we can all understand. Can anything better be said of a person? He was a good man.

"And I would add: He was a faithful man. A faithful friend. In the few years that we have lived here, we have had the good fortune to see him frequently at our parsonage. Faithfulness was his nature. He was faithful to those near and dear to him. He was faithful to the place that he called home. Faithful to his fatherland. He was a Dane. From his good Danish heart he contributed to our work and did not let his left hand know what his right hand was doing.

"He was like a father to us. And now it's as though we have become fatherless. He had a father's authority and sternness. He was a distinguished person in practical matters. But behind his authoritative, reticent nature, there beat a warm and loving Christian heart.

"First and foremost he belonged to the Kingdom of God. And he never forgot this amid the struggles and turmoil of practical matters. He understood fully the art of tranquility. Tranquility with himself. And tranquility with God. Behold, friends! Behold this prayer stool! Behold this simple little cushion with its white dove which his own loving mother embroidered with her tired, working hands many years ago! It was on this cushion that he knelt. This great businessman. This authoritative captain of industry. In prayer to the Almighty. Tranquil and humble before his Savior.

"That is what C. C. Skjern-Svendsen was like. And we say of him: He was a good man. Where he is now, listening to us, we thank him. We thank him affectionately for all that he brought about and did for us. His memory will live on as long as the congregation of the Lord gathers together around the word of God in this parish.

" 'Judge not!' it is written. And it is not for us to judge the evildoer who committed this abomination. His responsibility will be awesome when he ultimately has to account for himself before the Almighty, who sees that which is hidden from men and who shall come to judge the quick and the dead."

Only a few people attend this short, moving devotional service. Several kitchen maids. Several policemen. A page boy. And the pale, taciturn servant Lukas who was the first one to discover the murder. Everyone is moved. The women are crying.

The squire's wife is not present. She drove off in her car during the night, and no one knows where to look for her to bring her the sad news.

The police work quickly and systematically. They dust with powder and photograph fingerprints and measure footprints. Modern technical methods are brought into play, and the local police officer is completely shunted aside, regarded with smiles and arrogance by the skilled experts from Copenhagen. "You've certainly never seen anything like this before, have you, Hansen? There probably aren't very many murders in your district, ha ha!"

"No, we're pretty peaceable out here," Hansen says. And he looks on with interest while the homicide experts are working.

"That's right. Just take a look, Hansen," they tell him. "It'll do you good to learn something for future reference. Then you'll be able to take care of it alone next time somebody is murdered out here."

The press photographers take pictures of the castle, the moat, the room where it happened, and the historic canopy bed where

Karl Gustav once spent the night a long time ago. And the reporters interrogate people on their own, questioning them to get little human-interest anecdotes about the deceased.

Over at the inn, a reporter and photographer are sitting eating ham and eggs. "Ham is the only damn thing you can ever get at these inns!" says the reporter.

"We really weren't prepared for guests today," the waiter tells him. "No strangers come out this way in November."

"No, they're never prepared for guests at an inn!" says the reporter. "I know all about that."

The inn is historic. A local artist has painted scenes of the exploits of the Gjønge chieftain on its walls. "The Gjønge partisans hung out in these parts, you know," the waiter says.

"That's good," says the reporter. "Let's just put that in too. It all takes up space." And as he is chewing his smoked ham, he writes at breakneck speed. "The important thing is to create an atmosphere," he says.

"Are you writing all that about Svend Gjønge?" the photographer asks him.

"Heck no. I'm in the middle of describing a brief, touching episode that says more about how beloved the deceased was than a whole lot of official speeches."

"But there *weren't* any touching episodes."

"Oh yes, there certainly were. You just have to have a little imagination." He lets the photographer read his notes.

" 'We encounter a little old lady at the castle's imposing wrought-iron gate. Old and bent over, she stands there and pulls her shawl around her, shivering from the cold in the biting November wind.' What the hell little old lady was that?"

"There's always got to be somebody like that. Just read on. It's one of those beautiful little details from real life."

" 'The old woman can't be persuaded to go home. She wants to have one last glimpse of her beloved squire when they carry him out. Her ancient face is furrowed with tears. "Oh, sweet Jesus! Now he's dead, our dear father," she says. And later, as we drive off in the dark evening, we can still see that little old lady with her tear-stained face standing there swaying back and forth.' Yes, but we didn't see any old women, did we? What kind of crap is this you're making up?"

"Let me worry about that. It's a nice touch, isn't it? Say, waiter, can you tell me something about the castle? Isn't it haunted?"

"I never heard anything about that—I think things were pretty dead up there," says the waiter.

"Hmm, well I'll just write it down anyway. People really like that kind of stuff. An old fortress like that with an atmosphere reeking of the past is a great background for a murder. 'How often have hands gripped daggers here at Frydenholm? How often has the poisoned cup cut short a glorious life? The atmosphere is gloomy and ominous in this red fortress. Here the very stones can speak. The old masters of Frydenholm had the nasty habit of walling up their unfaithful wives. And now these unhappy women have come back to haunt it. Unable to find rest, they sigh and wring their hands at the midnight hour.' That's not bad, is it?"

"It's fabulous," says the photographer.

"What was he actually like, the squire?"

"It's hard to say," the waiter tells him. "He lived up there almost all alone. He had hardly any servants. He was real tight-fisted. The head servant up there was once in prison. And the previous head servant was too. The squire only had people around him who had been convicts. He found them through the Prisoners' Aid Society. He had them right where he wanted them."

"But we can't write stuff like that in our paper."

"The maids say that every night he would go sniffing around the pantry measuring the cheeses and liver pâté. They also say that he sometimes stole some of his own silver and hid it in his servant's room so he would be able to catch him and put him on the spot. His servant told me himself that every night he had to ransack his own suitcase to check whether the squire had slipped some silver spoons into it. The squire was a peculiar man."

"But wasn't he well liked in these parts?"

"Oh yeah, people buttered him up all right. When he turned 60 last year, everybody had to send him flowers, of course. And they bought the flowers at his own nursery, which has a small shop over there. But as soon as the flowers arrived at the castle, the squire sent them back to the store so they could be bought and sent to him a few more times. That way he got flowers and made money too."

"Our paper isn't interested in that kind of gossip," the reporter says. "Can't you tell us something else? He lived a happy married life with his beautiful wife, the former Countess Rosenkop-Frydenskjold, didn't he?"

"His wife is supposed to be a pretty hysterical person. They quarreled and fought, the maids say. The squire tried to have his wife put away in an insane asylum. But it didn't work."

"Wasn't the squire a pretty charitable person?"

"Oh yeah, he built the evangelical meeting house here, after all. He was a fundamentalist, you know. And he built a real nice burial mound for himself too. It has electric lights and artwork and marble in it. And that sort of thing does create jobs."

"Is this a pretty fundamentalist area?"

"Oh boy, is it. That's why hardly anybody comes to the inn anymore."

"Damned if it's very pleasant here either. Why don't you stoke up the fire in the stove a little more? It's so clammy and cold and disgusting here, I can hardly hold on to my pencil!"

"I'll put in a little more wood right now, sir. But we really weren't prepared for guests today at all. It could be such a nice inn. And it's historic too, you know. And it *is* such a pretty area."

"Let's write a little about the area then. A typically Danish area, right? Outside the village you notice the old medieval roadside crucifix. It looks spooky, by the way. What does it commemorate?"

"It doesn't commemorate anything. It was set up last year. It was donated by an anonymous benefactor. A whole bunch of those things have been put up all over southern Sjælland. I think it looks pretty hideous, with a naked man like that on a cross. There used to be an advertisement of a man shaving there. But the fundamentalists out here were scandalized because he had his suspenders hanging down and was about to lose his pants. So they got the Nature Conservancy to make a stink and have him removed. But is a naked man any better?"

"Well, it does look fairly interesting. It's just like in foreign countries. And it's probably something for tourists. Maybe it was that Danielsen fellow who paid for it."

"Maybe it was. Danielsen's always showing up when something has to be paid for. But he would have done better to give us a statue of the Gjønge chieftain. He hid out in these woods. And he and the other members of the Gjønge band came to this inn."

"But this inn isn't really old, is it?"

"Well, no. But I'm sure there was an inn here in the days of the Gjønge chieftain too. Anyway, this is a historic inn."

And the reporter keeps on writing. And while he's writing, a woman peers in the window, pressing her nose against the glass and grinning idiotically. She has a dozen or so barrettes in her straight yellow hair. She sticks out her skinny bare arms like an insect. Even though it's raining and the wind is blowing, she has a short-sleeved blue dress on. And she knocks on the windowpane and grins and says, "Hee hee!"

"Who *is* that female?" asks the reporter. "Can't you tell her to go away?"

"That's only Jenny," the waiter says. "She won't do anything. She's just sort of feeble-minded."

Jenny keeps on laughing, half-stifled, sticking out her skinny bare arms.

"This is sure one hell of a creepy place!" says the reporter.

# [ 3 ]

AT THE PARSONAGE, Pastor Nørregaard-Olsen has lowered the large Danish flag to half-mast. Other people soon follow suit. The school, the evangelical meeting house, the dairy shop, the grocery stores, and the farms. Even Rasmus Larsen, who was once called "Red Ras," a socialist who spoke out against the squires and employers, has lowered his Danish flag to half-mast at his big new house.

The village is in mourning. A village in southern Sjælland in the wind and rain of November. With its church and inn and

red-brick evangelical meeting house and whitewashed, thatch-roofed farmhouses and small, crooked clay-walled houses.

The houses have geraniums and pretty curtains in the windows. And there are willow trees along the road and small picket fences and bare black fruit trees in the yards. And the flags at half-mast snap in the wind and tug at their ropes.

Inside the houses people are sitting and talking about what happened. "It's sure to be a fine funeral, like none we've ever seen, and he did get his burial mound finished in good time. But what about his wife? She's run off. Maybe she's the one who killed him. They certainly didn't get along very well, and she was an odd person who was capable of anything. Anyway, she won't be mourning for him, because she does have her boyfriend in Copenhagen, they say."

"But then his servant, Lukas, could be the murderer too. He's done time before. Or maybe it was the page boy, who came from a reformatory. It really was strange of the squire to surround himself with criminals."

"Or maybe Panty Marius murdered him. Because Panty Marius has had dealings with the police too. And he has peculiar inclinations, sneaking around at night and stealing women's panties hanging out to dry. Then he cuts holes in the panties with a pair of scissors and has his fun that way. He's just like one of those sex murderers."

A lot of things are new and different these days. People aren't content and hard-working anymore, the way they were in the old days. Now they just make one demand after another and want higher wages. They'd rather live on relief than do any work. But where's the money going to come from? It's the young people who are the worst, running off to dances and parties and throwing their money away on lemon soda and cigarettes.

But fortunately the new pastor has managed to get the Athletic Association disbanded and is attempting to rally the young people around something loftier in the Youth Division — the YD. The young YDers ride their bicycles smartly off down the road in their uniforms, singing cheerful songs, and have the courage to acknowledge their God.

But maybe the pastor's going a little too far, kneeling with the young people out in public in the parking lot in front of the parsonage and inciting them into a frenzy. In fact, there are people who don't really like their daughters to take part in the nighttime YD worship services at the church. Why couldn't they hold them during the day just as well?

The old church stands there whitewashed and Danish, with its stepped gables and cemetery wall and crosses and gravestones and poplars and weeping willows. And Squire Skjern-Svendsen's new mausoleum, which he'll be moving into now.

On the other side of the cemetery wall, where there used to be an advertisement for razor blades, a medieval crucifix has been set up for the enjoyment of tourists. Across from it is the inn, which is historic and empty and depressing, with the exploits of the Gjønge chieftain painted on its walls.

And behind the inn, where there is a bend in the road, stands the red-brick manor with its wrought-iron gate, park, ramparts, and moats. It looks like the highway ends here.

Twice a day a yellow bus drives through the village, stops at the inn, turns around, and drives back. Other vehicles arrive as well; people watch them and pay attention as they drive by. A stylish little cream-colored sports car was here yesterday. And they know it belongs to a man who was here to see the squire's wife. God only knows what those two talk about and what's going on between them. It might even be possible that the wife's boyfriend had an interest in having the squire killed.

There are a lot of possibilities and plenty of mystery. While the reporters are sitting in the cold inn eating smoked ham and fried eggs and soaking up impressions and writing about little old ladies, the police experts are working up at the castle. The servant Lukas, the page boy, and the maids are interrogated thoroughly and instructed not to leave the building. Powder is sprinkled around, fingerprints are photographed, and strange and ingenious analyses are made. The police have a number of different leads to go on.

This much they can tell the reporters: Two cars left town at the fateful hour. One of them was a long blue car with the license number H 2215. Squire Skjern-Svendsen's wife drove off in it. They don't know where she went. The other was a little cream-colored sports convertible, which appears to have been from Copenhagen. The police would appreciate information from anyone who has seen these two vehicles.

# [ 4 ]

THE NEWSPAPERS OF November 23, 1938 are full of stories about the murder of squire and industrialist C. C. Skjern-Svendsen. As well as lengthy obituaries.

"The story of C. C. Skjern-Svendsen's life was a fairy tale that might have been written by Hans Christian Andersen. It was a fairy tale about the poor boy who became one of his country's most eminent citizens. The little shepherd boy from Jutland who became a landed baron and industrial tycoon. A fairy tale about poverty and self-denial, about unflagging diligence and thrift, that led to triumph and success. For young people especially, C. C. Skjern-Svendsen's life stands as a brilliant example of the Dane of today. The man who achieved his goal because he had the will and the dogged determination.

"Carl Christian Skjern-Svendsen was born in Thy in 1877. His father was a poor wool peddler who wandered along the sandy roads of Jutland on foot carrying a bundle of those good old-fashioned homespun woolen goods which his busy wife spun and knitted at home in their small, low-ceilinged cottage beneath the heather-covered roof. There were a lot of children in that small home. Carl Christian was the fifth in a family of nine children. Like so many of our country's other great men, little Carl Christian had to go out onto the heath and herd sheep at an early age. Out there in the deserted but glorious landscape, he dreamed his dreams of a brilliant future and a life of great deeds in the service of his fatherland. Out there too he became acquainted with sheep like no one else, and he grew to love them. He became a connoisseur of wool, that good Danish wool, which could be spun and woven into Danish textiles and which spread the word far and wide about what Danish initiative and enterprise can achieve.

"As a young man, he picked up his wanderer's staff and set out into the wide world. Like his father he journeyed along country roads with a bundle of woolen goods slung over his shoulder. It was a varied and eventful life. Carl Christian, however, never took part in the crude behavior of itinerant vendors. In his entire life C. C. Skjern-Svendsen never tasted liquor. 'When the others went to the inn,' he himself once said, 'I would sit down on the flowering edge of a roadside ditch, preferably in the vicinity of a spring. And there I would eat my wholesome Danish rye bread and drink clear, healthful water with it.' The small amounts of money that he earned from his trade he kept in an old box, and when the box was full, the money was put in the savings bank. His motto was: 'It's not what you earn that makes you rich, it's what you save.' Carl Christian understood the art of saving.

"In 1898 he was able to open his own business in a provincial town on the island of Sjælland. It was a modest little shop where housewives could buy trim and ribbons and those sturdy petticoats of pure Jutland wool. The little shop grew, and soon a branch had to be opened in another town. After several years, Skjern-Svendsen had dry-goods stores in practically every provincial town on Sjælland. It wasn't long before he acquired the Præstø textile mill, which he later remodeled and expanded. Next came knitwear factories in Store-Heddinge and Køge, a button factory in Vordingborg, the Næstved cotton mill, and much more. At the same time he founded the Textile Bank, whose director he was for a number of years. He was a cofounder and member of the board of directors of the Præstø Lending Institution, the Southern Sjælland Mortgage Bank, and a number of other provincial banks.

"In the years during the World War, he acquired Halling Manor in northern Jutland and the historic manor Frydenholm near Præstø. He had the latter manor restored and remodeled and took up residence there. He was not a farmer himself, but he was intensely interested in the operation of his estates and supervised everything personally.

"In outward appearance Skjern-Svendsen was a modest and reserved man. He was never in the limelight but preferred to live in obscurity and do things quietly. He was a tireless worker who never spared himself. He was an idealist. He created his vast fortune solely for the sake of society. He took delight in starting a project and watching it grow and flourish around him, in creating employment for his fellow countrymen. He donated

large gifts to his home region, but always in secret. He did not
wish any thanks for what he did. When the mysterious Danielsen appeared on the scene last year, many people thought that
Danielsen was none other than Squire Skjern-Svendsen. And it
must be admitted that the method Danielsen employed would
have been Skjern-Svendsen's style. Modesty was his most nota-
ble characteristic. Reticence and quiet diligence far from all
publicity—that was what Skjern-Svendsen valued. He was a
good Danish man. A worthy representative of the best in our
people. He had no enemies. His unfortunate death is a mystery
to all who knew him. There can be no doubt that the perpetrator
of this bestial crime is deranged. It is hoped that Police Superintendent Odense will soon manage to render this criminal
harmless.

"Skjern-Svendsen is survived by his wife Julie, née Countess
Rosenkop-Frydenskjold. As mentioned elsewhere in this newspaper, Mrs. Skjern-Svendsen was taking a ride in her car on the
very evening when her husband was murdered. Mrs. Skjern-
Svendsen has still not been located. It will be a sad task to
convey the dreadful news to her.

"Their marriage was childless but an uncommonly happy
one. It was quite a fairy tale in its own right when the countess
from the manor wed the poor shepherd boy. It attracted a great
deal of attention as a symbol of our democratic age. A romantic
love story, worthy of Hans Christian Andersen, about the princess and the shepherd boy. In this sad hour the couple's numerous friends will embrace Countess Julie with their deepest
sympathy."

"C. C. Skjern-Svendsen was very interested in the evangelical
movement. He was given a strict Christian upbringing in his
poor childhood home. And when wealth came to him, he donated significant sums to the church and evangelical work. He
provided the backing for the construction of a number of evangelical meeting houses and assembly halls in southern Sjælland.
When Frydenholm's old church was faced with an extensive
restoration project, it was C. C. Skjern-Svendsen who provided
the necessary funds."

"It is commonly assumed that it was C. C. Skjern-Svendsen who financed the erection of the popular roadside crucifixes which blend in so beautifully and naturally with the Danish scenery and which are admired by all tourists. As everyone knows, the donor was anonymous, but this modesty would have been completely in the spirit of C. C. Skjern-Svendsen. Nothing, however, is known for certain."

"C. C. Skjern-Svendsen never forgot his impoverished childhood or his childhood home in the country. He had a memorial four meters tall erected in the small cemetery in northern Jutland where his parents are buried. The monument, which is made of Bornholm granite, bears four bronze reliefs with allegorical motifs. It can be seen far and wide in the flat landscape, and it is said that fishermen at sea can use it as a navigational aid."

"C. C. Skjern-Svendsen was intensely interested in our country's history and in its wealth of ancient monuments. Frydenholm Manor near Præstø, which has been in the possession of the Rosenkop-Frydenskjold family for several generations, is a historic castle where the Swedish Colonel Sparre and his dragoons were quartered during the Swedish War. The Swedish king, Karl Gustav himself, slept in Frydenholm Castle for one night. Squire Skjern-Svendsen had the old castle restored and returned to its original state down to the smallest details. The squire even had the 'wooden horse,' a torture instrument which irreverent peasants burned 150 years ago, recreated and set up in its old place in the courtyard of the castle.

"He also had several of the estate's prehistoric burial mounds repaired. It was his desire that he might one day rest in an ancient Danish barrow himself. In the cemetery at Frydenholm he had an exact copy of an original prehistoric burial mound built and furnished as a mausoleum. This singularly beautiful burial mound had just been completed. Much too prematurely, he will now be putting his final resting place to use."

"Numerous anecdotes are recounted about C. C. Skjern-Svendsen, whose Jutland humor never deserted him. He was famous for his quick and incisive replies. Once, for instance, when a young man approached him to borrow some money, Skjern-Svendsen said: 'I've never borrowed money from anyone and I've never lent out money. Perhaps that's the secret of my success in the world.' "

"Squire Skjern-Svendsen had a great interest in the cause of horticulture. In conjunction with Frydenholm Manor he operated a large nursery, a model nursery whose products frequently won fine prizes at horticultural exhibitions. He was a pioneer in many areas of horticulture. Our readers will surely remember the pictures previously published in this newspaper of Denmark's largest squash and the giant potato that weighed 4½ kilograms. Both the squash and the potato were from Frydenholm's nursery."

"Exactly one year ago C. C. Skjern-Svendsen celebrated his sixtieth birthday. Modest and reserved as he was, he requested that there be no tributes and on the day itself remained sequestered at his estate. Nonetheless, it was inevitable that people would send him good wishes from many quarters. It must certainly have been a great satisfaction for him to be proclaimed Knight of the Dannebrog. In an interview in this newspaper on the occasion of his sixtieth birthday he remarked whimsically: 'Sixty isn't really old, you know. I've just gotten started. I count on living to be at least a hundred years old. We live a long time in my family. My father, who was a veteran of the Dano-Prussian War of 1848, lived to be 97. My grandfather was 101 years old. I have high hopes of being active for another half century.' Unfortunately, things were to turn out otherwise."

# HOMUNCULUS

# [ 5 ]

SIX MONTHS BEFORE Squire Skjern-Svendsen was murdered in November, a series of events took place, more or less directly connected with the murder.

One day in the spring of 1938 a man walks into an office and donates a very large sum of money to the Cancer Society.

He is a short, gray-haired gentleman with kindly blue eyes. He is wearing a shabby, old-fashioned fur coat and carrying a large paper bundle under his arm. He walks up to the counter modestly and unobtrusively, takes his hat off, and asks if this is where they accept contributions for the fight against cancer. He then starts pulling the string off the bundle. "Here you are," he says. "Here's some money. It's a little something my wife and I saved up. There should be 10,000 kroner. Perhaps you would be so kind as to count it."

The clerk begins to count the large stacks of bills. It takes quite a while; he has to moisten his fingers several times. "That's correct," he finally says. "Ten thousand kroner. Let me write you out a receipt. May I ask your name?"

"My name is Danielsen," replies the short gentleman with the kindly blue eyes.

"Danielsen. Is that all?"

"Yes, that's sufficient." Then he puts the receipt in his pocket, picks up his hat, says goodbye, and walks out of the office with a friendly smile on his face.

On the afternoon of the same day—before the evening papers have reported the incident—the short, gray-haired gentleman walks into another office where they accept contributions for the fight against tuberculosis. Here too he has with him a large paper bundle with string around it. Here too he introduces himself as Danielsen. "Here's a small sum that my wife and I saved up. Perhaps you would be so kind as to count it. There should be 10,000 kroner."

And as the clerk counts, Danielsen gives him a friendly look with his kindly blue eyes.

The evening papers carry the story about the mysterious Danielsen, who donated a fortune to the fight against cancer in such an unobtrusive and modest manner. The next day the morning papers report further that Danielsen has also shown up somewhere else and has contributed an equally large sum to the fight against tuberculosis.

People realize that Danielsen must be an assumed name. But they know nothing more about this strange benefactor than the matching descriptions given by the staffs of the two offices. He was a short, unassuming, elderly gentleman. He had a shabby, old-fashioned fur coat on. He had gray hair and kindly light-blue eyes. Now people are waiting expectantly for the anonymous benefactor to appear again and give away enormous bundles of money for charitable purposes.

And while some people are guessing and speculating about who Danielsen might really be, other people are putting ads in the newspapers asking the mysterious millionaire to come forward and render help to a number of different causes.

"WHERE IS DANIELSEN? I have devised an epoch-making invention but lack the capital to develop it. Here is something for Danielsen to do! Enormous profits guaranteed. Reply to Box . . ." Or: "ISN'T THERE A DANIELSEN who will help me? My wife is ill, and I am unemployed. For a small initial investment of 2,000 kroner I could acquire a small nursery which I am very interested in and which would yield a good profit because it has a good location and I have always been interested in horticulture. If interested, write Box . . ."

There are people whose children have artistic talent who call upon the unknown Danielsen to finance their education. There are people who have come up with new economic and religious systems that would abolish all unemployment and poverty in a single stroke, if Danielsen would chip in a little cash to get them started. There is a man who lacks only a motorcycle to be a completely happy and useful human being. There is a family that fervently desires a little house in the country. There are people who would like to do some traveling and offer to accompany the aging Danielsen. There are the sick and destitute who know of no other recourse than to appeal to Danielsen for help.

Danielsen is no longer just a name. It is a universal designation for benefactors.

"This is where a Danielsen ought to step in," writes one newspaper, "so that our town could finally get that swimming pool it has needed for such a long time."

"Perhaps there is a Danielsen," writes another paper, "who would take it upon himself to pay for the monument to Hans Christian Andersen which the capital city has needed for so long and which would be a worthy memorial to our great author and an unforgettable sight for foreign tourists."

Or they lament the fact that a project has to be shelved and add: "But perhaps a Danielsen will step in and put the necessary means at our disposal."

Danielsen has become a new term in the language. But no one knows who the man is. They know only that he is a short, gray-haired gentleman with kindly blue eyes and that he goes around carrying lots of money in large paper bundles.

The word Danielsen is a concept. It means great and unexpected profits. Sudden fortune. Opportunity. If only we knew a Danielsen!

Apart from the fact that Danielsen's generosity might have been of some use to people with cancer or tuberculosis, it would soon be apparent that his actions would have great and fateful consequences for other people as well. His generosity prompts other actions which affect people's lives and cause disorder and disruption. And these actions propagate others, their effects spreading outward into infinity. And neither Danielsen nor anyone else can undo them.

# [ 6 ]

ONE DAY DURING that same spring of 1938, an old man walks
into the main university building and inquires after a professor
of philosophy.

"The professor isn't here," he is told. "But it's possible that
you might find him over in the psychology laboratory."

"Where is that?"

"It's over in the Studiegaard building. Through the archway
on St. Pedersstræde, across the courtyard, and up the stairs to
the fourth floor."

"Thank you," says the old man.

With great dignity he walks calmly across Frue Plads. People
turn around and stare at him because of his singular appearance.
He is wearing an extremely long black overcoat and has a long
gray sorcerer's beard. His nose is very large. And his eyes are
black and flashing.

He finds his way to Studiegaard and slowly climbs the many
steps to the top floor. On the top floor there are two white doors
with glass panes in them. *Geography Laboratory* is printed on one
of them. And *Psychology Laboratory* on the other. The old man
tries the brass handle of the door to the psychology laboratory,
but the door is locked.

Then he discovers a button and pushes it, and hears a bell ring
somewhere inside. He rings the bell a number of times, and after
a while a younger man comes out in his stocking feet.

"Why are you ringing the bell like that?" he screams. "Why
are you disturbing me? Why don't you let yourself in?"

"The door was locked," says the old man.

"Well, why don't you have your key with you? Do I always
have to be the doorman?"

"I don't have a key. I'm sure I could open this door without
using a key, but I considered it more polite to ring the bell."

"If you don't have a key, you don't have any access to the
laboratory either! You can pick up a key and a card over in the

administrative offices for a deposit of 5 kroner. I can't let you in if you don't have a key."

"Who are you, young man?" the old man asks, glaring at him with his black flashing eyes. The man in his stocking feet recoils before his gaze.

"I am Ph.D. candidate Hansen," he says.

"I see. And what do you do here?"

"What do I do here? I belong here. I'm the professor's assistant. I'm in the middle of some experiments. You're interrupting me, as a matter of fact."

"Why have you taken your shoes off?"

"I told you: I'm in the middle of some experiments. They concern the localization of sounds. The subject must not hear my footsteps."

"You're going to write a doctoral dissertation?"

"Yes, I would certainly like to, if I can have some peace and quiet to do it. But what do you want here? Who are you?"

"I am Kados," says the old man.

"What is it you want here, Mr. Kados?"

"I would like to speak with the professor."

"The professor isn't here."

"When is he coming back?"

"I don't know. It might be a while."

"Then I'll wait till he comes."

"But I'm working here."

"That doesn't matter. You just go right ahead and work."

Kados walks into the laboratory where Ph.D. candidate Hansen is conducting his sound-localization experiments. In the middle of the floor is a chair with a blindfolded subject seated on it. The Ph.D. candidate walks stealthily around him in his stocking feet making noises. The subject is supposed to try to determine the path that the Ph.D. candidate has taken. And the path indicated by the subject is then plotted as a curve. Up to this point, some 50 subjects have taken turns guessing the Ph.D. candidate's route through the room. The numerous curves show extremely interesting differences and deviations in the perception of sound. When another 50 people have guessed, a lot of very valuable data will have been gathered for judging individuals' divergent perceptions of sound localization. And Ph.D. candidate Hansen will be Doctor Hansen. And when the professor retires, he will become Professor Hansen.

Kados solemnly watches what is going on. The Ph.D. candidate is unnerved by his presence, and as he walks stealthily around his subject making the prearranged noises, he looks out of the corner of his eye at Kados.

It's a long time before the professor arrives. Kados sits stiff and motionless on a chair watching things happen. The Ph.D. candidate becomes more and more nervous and is unable to concentrate on his project. He dismisses his subject and calls it a day. He is annoyed. He puts on his shoes and looks spitefully at the old man.

Then somebody comes up the stairs and sticks a key in the outer door. "That's the professor," says Ph.D. candidate Hansen.

"I know," says Kados.

Ph.D. candidate Hansen goes out to meet the professor and tells him there is a man who would like to speak with the professor, and the professor must excuse him for letting him in even though he didn't have a key. "I told him he was supposed to get a key and a card at the administrative offices, but he walked right in."

"You wish to speak with me?" the professor asks.

"Yes," Kados replies. He looks firmly at Ph.D. candidate Hansen and says, "You may leave!" And the Ph.D. candidate obeys and is annoyed with himself for doing so and for submitting to the old man's stronger will.

# [ 7 ]

"WHO ARE YOU?" asks the professor.

"I am Kados."

"Kados? Isn't that a symbolic name? A Masonic degree or something like that?"

"It is my name."

"I see. And what is it that you would like to speak with me about, Mr. Kados?"

"I would like you to let me have a room."

"A room? What kind of a room would that be? We really don't have too much space here. What would you be using the room for?"

"It only has to be an empty room with windows facing west. And then there has to be a good stove in it."

"Yes, but we have central heating in all our rooms, you know."

"There has to be a stove in it, a slow-combustion oven."

"That's something we don't really have. Why can't you make do with central heating? It's spring now anyway."

"I need a stove. A 'furnace of fire.' An athanor."

"Is this going to be for chemical experiments? In that case you'd really better go out and see the chemists. They're out at the Polytechnical Institute on Sølvgade. We don't have that kind of laboratory here. What is it you want with an oven?"

"I wish to produce salamanders."

"Salamanders? Well, in that case you'll have to go over and see the zoologists. They're right across from us. On Krystalgade."

"I am not speaking of those amphibians that ignorant people have named after salamanders. I am speaking of Fire Salamanders. Elemental beings. The elementary spirits that function in fire just as the Undines function in water and the Sylphs in the air and the Gnomes in the earth."

"Ah, so that's it. No, we can't get involved in that here. We don't put much faith in the existence of those sorts of creatures."

"Well, aren't you a Doctor of *Philosophy?*"

"Yes, of course. We work with psychology here."

"How can anyone believe that it is possible to be a doctor of *philosophy* without being in contact with the elementals? The extent to which they can help us certainly ought to be common knowledge, just as we can sometimes help them, for that matter."

"But we don't get involved with those kinds of things here. Our work is strictly practical. We conduct psychotechnical experiments to find out what young people are suited for so that we can guide them before they enter commercial life. We don't have anything to do with fire spirits and that sort of thing."

"Has all our ancient knowledge been lost then? Haven't you ever studied the scholars of the past? How does one actually become a professor of philosophy nowadays?"

"Why yes, of course I have devoted a little time to historical matters. And I think I know what salamanders are. But we don't really believe in salamanders anymore."

"Then I'll show you a salamander! Get me a room and a good athanor, and I'll produce a living salamander!"

"I didn't really know that one could *produce* that sort of thing. I thought that salamanders were spirits."

"But haven't you ever read what Theophrastus Bombastus Paracelsus wrote in his work *De Generatione Rerum Naturalium?*"

"No, to be honest I never have."

"Perhaps you don't even know of Bombastus Paracelsus at all?"

"Oh yes, I've read about him. It seems he was a charlatan. Wasn't he?"

"Haven't you heard of the being that Paracelsus fostered in a bottle?"

"Yes, I think there was something about a homunculus in a bottle. Could that have been a salamander?"

"Yes, exactly. And Paracelsus explains very precisely how one is supposed to go about it. It's just a matter of understanding his figurative language."

"That sounds terribly interesting. I'll have to see about reading that book someday."

"You should do that. And it's about time you did. You can borrow the first edition from me. It's become quite rare. Hardly anyone but me owns it in this country. It's not available in your university library."

"That's very interesting. It must be valuable."

"I suppose you haven't heard of Sigbrit's salamander either."

"Sigbrit? What Sigbrit?"

" 'Mother Sigbrit.' Christian II's advisor. Dyveke's mother. You must have heard about her, since you went to the university."

"Oh, *that* Sigbrit. I didn't really know that she was involved with salamanders too."

"I won't deny that I am somewhat surprised at the ignorance at this university. It is common knowledge, after all, that Sigbrit had a round-bottomed flask with a salamander inside it hanging in her window. One day, when the flask fell to the floor and broke with a loud bang because the matter inside it had been exposed to the air, a violent thunderstorm swept over Copenhagen. Later, when people heard about the bottle, everybody said that it was Sigbrit's spirit that had escaped and had taken revenge for its long imprisonment with this unprecedented storm."

"I really and truly never heard about that. It's very strange. Where do you know this from?"

"From Hans Svaning. And from Hans Gram. Don't university professors ever read books?"

"Oh yes, we read quite a bit, in fact. But I'm sure we could learn a great deal from you, Mr. Kados. I hope you will visit me sometime and tell me more. Unfortunately, I'm very busy right now. I'm sorry I can't help you with a room and an athanor. As I said, we don't have that sort of thing here anyway. But perhaps you could try the chemists out at the Institute."

"So you refuse to let me have a place and a furnace of fire?"

"I'm afraid I can't, whether I want to or not. But do try the chemists."

"But there's no time to waste. Tomorrow is New Year's!"

"New Year's? But it's a long time until New Year's. It's only March now, you know."

"I see that you regard me as crazy because you are ignorant yourself. Perhaps you haven't even heard about Julius Cæsar's insane destruction of the calendar, which he changed to start in January in spite of all common sense. The real year naturally begins on March 21. The day on which we enter the sign of Aries."

"Well, now that you mention it, I do remember that Cæsar got the calendar straightened out. It must have been in a horrible mess before that."

"It was Cæsar, along with that confounded Sosigenes of Alexandria, who committed the crime of putting the New Year in January at the first new moon."

"Isn't it irrelevant whether we celebrate New Year's in January or in March?"

"It is certainly not irrelevant. We are out of step with the rhythm of the universe. We cannot accomplish anything sensible unless we take into account the aspects revealed to us by the Zodiac, or 'The Circle of Signs.' "

"But why can't you make your salamanders in April or May?"

"At the beginning of April it would still work. But in May, no. May is Taurus until the 21st. On New Year's Day, March 21st, on the other hand, we enter Aries—the Ram—which is ruled by the planet Mars. The planet of fire. And if I am to produce beings of fire, it must happen under the sign of Mars."

"So that's the way it is. Well, it really is a shame that I can't help you. But if there's anything I can do some other time, Mr. Kados, just come to me. I'll always be interested in talking with you."

"Yes, as a curiosity. As a diversion. As an object of your ridicule. I don't need you, Professor. You might need me, but I can't waste my time instructing you. Master the elementary incipient knowledge, then we can talk."

"Now you mustn't be angry, Mr. Kados. You mustn't take it like that. It really has been interesting talking with you."

"I'm not angry. If I were angry, you would be in serious trouble. In the face of ignorance and simplemindedness I have only sympathy. Goodbye, Professor."

"Goodbye, Mr. Kados. I'll show you out."

"I can find my way all right. I can also go through a door without getting a key and depositing 5 kroner at the administrative offices. There was a little Ph.D. candidate here earlier. He's gone now. Tell him that he himself doesn't know what he is."

Slowly and with dignity Kados walks down the steps of Studiegaard. Scratching his head, the professor watches him go. "I'll be damned," he says. "In 1938!"

# [ 8 ]

ONE DAY A MAN appears at the Physiological Institute of the Rockefeller Foundation near Fælled Park. This happens at about the same time that the mysterious Danielsen is going around giving away large sums of money to fight cancer and tuberculosis. And it happens at about the same time that Kados is calling upon the university and requesting that a room be put at his disposal for the production of fire salamanders. That is, at the time we enter the sign of the Ram and are ruled by the planet Mars.

Like Kados, this man realizes the significance of the cosmic constellation. His mission is similar to that of Kados. And he is working on similar problems.

But he doesn't look a bit like a sorcerer. He is a tall, stylish man. Supple, slim, and sporty-looking. Blond and broad-shouldered, with trustworthy blue eyes. He arrives in a small cream-colored convertible and parks it beside the numerous doctors' cars in front of the institute. Lightly and agilely he springs up the stairs to the institute. He knows exactly where to go and whom to talk to.

All around the institute serious men in white coats are working in laboratories. They observe plants in little flowerpots and let them develop differently under different conditions. They undernourish some of the plants and grow them in shaded areas so that the plants get thin and stunted and pale like proletarian children. They give other plants sunlight plus liberal amounts of rich nourishment so that they grow and swell up like vitamin-enriched butterballs. They inject things into mice and rabbits, and take blood samples and analyze them, and peer into microscopes. They cut the heads off frogs and make them twitch their legs by swabbing them with a little acid. They cultivate living tissue from a dead chicken and let it grow and grow *ad infinitum* year after year. And every week they have to carve off some of the growing tissue to prevent the entire institute from filling up with chicken flesh. They turn roosters into hens and make them lay eggs and hatch chicks. And they turn hens into roosters and make them crow and strut around and act feisty and cocky. Unusual and sensational things are going on inside the institute. And if the esteemed scientists are ready to seize the initiative and give a warm reception to the new idea that is now making its way up the stairs, even more unusual and epoch-making things will soon be going on.

The stranger has managed to get all the way in to see the

professor in charge of the institute. He introduces himself: Dr. Robert Riege.

The professor is an older man with a bald head and a drooping mustache and gold-rimmed glasses. He putters around in his laboratory peering at green frogs in jars and white rabbits and brown guinea pigs in small wire cages. He puffs on his pipe and scatters his ashes and deposits his used matches here and there on the glass-topped tables and steel racks.

"Please, Dr. Riege, have a seat. I am actually quite familiar with your name. You received your doctorate abroad, didn't you?"

Dr. Riege is sitting on a metal chair opposite a table covered with test tubes in racks, some pipes, and a large tobacco humidor. Somewhat nervously he watches the professor puttering around the laboratory.

"Yes, I did," says Dr. Riege. "And I'm well aware that people here in Denmark don't recognize doctorates other than those granted by Copenhagen or Aarhus. Nevertheless, science also exists outside Denmark."

"Yes, of course," says the professor. "I don't wish to belittle your foreign doctorate in any way. I didn't mean anything derogatory. But the fact of the matter is that certain places abroad use the designation 'doctor' for something that most nearly corresponds to what we call a B.A."

"I also have a B.A.," says Dr. Riege.

"Yes, so you do. I remember you well. At one point you were studying medicine. But you interrupted your studies, didn't you?"

"Yes. I had the pleasure of being a student of yours once, Professor. But you're right, I didn't graduate. I went abroad to study."

"I see. And now you're practicing psychoanalysis, aren't you? It seems to me I once read something by you in some journal. Where might that have been?"

"I edit the journal *Sex News*. That's what you probably picked up, or heard about. The scientific establishment hasn't shown any appreciable interest in my work."

"Ah yes, we *are* becoming specialists and professional idiots," says the professor. "We don't have time for much more than our own specialties. But you're in practice as a psychoanalyst, aren't you? Can you make a living doing that?"

"I left Freud and psychoanalysis a long time ago. I admit, that's what gave me the impetus and got me started, but now every reasonable modern psychologist regards Freud as obsolete."

"Well then, what is it you deal with in your journal? It would appear to me that it has something to do with psychoanalysis."

"I am a sex cosmologist."

"I see. So there's something that goes by that name, is there?"

"Yes, there is. Even though the scientific establishment apparently hasn't noticed our existence. Some other time it will be my pleasure to explain to you what sex cosmology deals with, Professor. But I'm not going to waste your time with long explanations now. I'll send you some copies of *Sex News* so you can read them if you have time."

"Thank you, that would be very kind of you, Dr. Riege. That would interest me. And what do you wish of me today?"

"It's a matter of the utmost importance. Of a significance that can hardly be overstated. Quite simply, it involves the solution to everything that you and a thousand other scientists the world over are working on."

"That would be quite a feat indeed. It sounds very exciting."

"It's not *exciting!*" says Dr. Riege, standing up and stepping into the middle of the room. "It's more than that. It's epoch-making! Revolutionary! More so than any of the disciples of the scientific establishment could imagine!"

"Well, well. Go on! Go on!"

"It will take some time to explain. What I would like to request of you for the time being is to have a laboratory put at my disposal here for approximately one year."

"My goodness, that's a rather large request! And what would you use this laboratory for?"

"I know that you cultivate living tissue in a nutrient solution here. That you are studying the growth and formation of cells. And that, among other things, you hope by some coincidence to pick up the trail of that growth phenomenon called cancer. For me there's nothing puzzling about cancer. Bion research has long since explained how what we call cancer comes into being. And I know how to cause it and how to cure it."

"Damnation! That's quite a feat. I see, so it's the riddle of cancer that you've solved. Dear me. I'm afraid quite a few people have done that. But people just keep on dying of cancer anyway." The professor sniffs and knocks out his pipe so that the ashes drift down over a pair of white rabbits with pink ears.

"I don't doubt that you will find this quite ridiculous. But the fact is, I solved what you call the riddle of cancer a long time ago. It's actually quite simple and straightforward. And if the esteemed cancer researchers had taken the trouble to acquaint themselves with what I have published, you, Professor, wouldn't be so surprised at what I have to say. But of course that's the way it is: the scientific establishment doesn't like to admit its mistakes. It just keeps right on wearing blinders and doesn't look to either side."

"Those are harsh words, Dr. Riege. Don't you think you're exaggerating slightly? It certainly does seem to me that science has constantly revised its own results over the course of time. One system after another has been discarded. One view of the world has replaced another. I honestly think that no one is more willing to acknowledge mistakes than science is. We have to be skeptical and critical."

"Yes, so skeptical and critical that you don't want to recognize anything new! And won't recognize anything that goes against something else once it has been established!"

"Now I don't think you would say things like that if you were more familiar with the scientific method. But you haven't come to see me to discuss the legitimacy of science, have you? You want to have a laboratory put at your disposal for a year in order to solve the riddle of cancer?"

Dr. Riege has sat back down on the metal chair. He is fiddling nervously with the jars on the table. In one of the jars a green frog is swimming up and down making bubbles. Dr. Riege looks at it and says slowly and calmly, "I solved that 'riddle' a long time ago. The cancer foundation might just as well save its grant money. And this mysterious Danielsen can use his money for something else. What I want a laboratory for is something far more important. If I can get the proper working conditions, I will undertake to produce living tissue from inorganic, so-called inanimate, matter. I will make a living being from chemical matter! I will activate what you regard as lifeless minerals in such a way that they breathe and take nourishment and reproduce!" Dr. Riege pounds the table so the test tubes rattle and the frog dives down to the bottom of its cylindrical jar in fright. "I will put inorganic matter into the kinds of oscillations and vibrations that will cause it to alter its form into what you call organic tissue. Quite simply, I will create a living being that can think and make decisions and create things by itself!"

The professor folds his hands behind his bald head and stares at Dr. Riege. "I see. That's what you're going to do?" he says. "You're going to create a homunculus just like the one Dr. Faustus made. And which the venerable Dr. Paracelsus gave instructions about?"

"I haven't read Dr. Paracelsus's instructions. But it's certain that he had knowledge about something that has been lost to science. He too spent his life in a struggle against the scientific establishment of his time, you know. I don't expect you to let yourself be convinced by my explanation. Only a small circle is interested in what I'm working on. But let me have a suitable laboratory where I can work in peace for a year, then I'll show you the results! What I have succeeded in discovering is nothing less than the solution to the riddle of life itself!"

"That would be quite a feat!" says the professor.


# [ 9 ]


"EVEN THE SCIENTIFIC establishment would not deny that thought is decisive for the body's physiological condition, would it?" says Dr. Riege, pointing a long finger at the professor. The professor feels as if a pistol is being aimed at him.

"Thought alone can produce bodily changes," Dr. Riege says. "We turn pale with anger and red with shame. Our hair stands on end from terror, and the tear-duct secretions of our eyes are accelerated by sorrow. Our mouths water at the notion of food. Saint Francis of Assisi had stigmata; the mere thought of the sufferings of the Savior produced bleeding wounds on the palms of his hands. Psychological conditions determine the condition of the blood. In the case of disturbances of a psychological nature, the disturbance is transferred through the blood to the body and produces abnormal and irregular growth. In a word: cancer. All physical illnesses have psychological causes. What is illness other than the bodily manifestation of psychological energy?"

"Hmm," says the professor, peering at a guinea pig that looks sick and miserable.

"And what physicists call energy is quite simply sexuality. Energy or life-energy or the primordial force is the same thing as sexuality. Electricity and magnetism, radio waves and vibrations are sexuality. The power of thought alone can kill even at a great distance.

"But thought can also create life. Thought builds up the body. Nervous energy is not, as you believe, a product of the blood. Rather, the circulatory system is the reflection of the nervous system. The form of life-energy and the tempo of its oscillations determine the condition of the mind.

"Thought is the creator of life. Thought can bring about fertilization. What is the Virgin Birth other than the result of fertilization by thought? What we call the Holy Spirit is thought or desire."

"This is fantastic," says the professor, stuffing a new pipe and lighting it and tossing the match down to the guinea pig.

"I don't know how else you and science would explain the Virgin Birth or the Annunciation and Conception. I will leave out the very latest investigations concerning the Virgin Birth and chromosome counts, which of course you must be familiar with, and which sex cosmology has predicted."

"Your sex cosmology seems to be a rather comprehensive field."

"Sex cosmology is universal. The scientific establishment does its work in isolated compartments. Sex cosmology, on the other hand, embraces everything. Not merely psychology, but also sociology, economics, politics, pedagogy, biology, physical chemistry. And of course astronomy and mineralogy as well."

"Why not theology too?" asks the professor.

"Yes, why not theology too? Ho, ho! Astronomy shows us the world as part of solar systems with planets that revolve around a central sun. And these solar systems in turn are arranged in the Milky Way system, which in turn is part of still larger systems. Physics shows that all matter consists of atoms, which in turn consist of electrons that revolve around a central nucleus, which presumably can be divided into even smaller systems. In a word: the macrocosm and microcosm. Every part of ourselves, every bit of fingernail, every hair of our beards, consists of rotating solar systems. Stone, earth, water, air—everything is a rotating world. There is no difference between the inanimate and the animate, between organic and inorganic matter. And everything is permeated by sexuality, which we can also call energy or electricity or primordial force. This sexuality has its rhythm, which is the rhythm of the entire world."

Dr. Riege is speaking ecstatically. His eyes are shining. He gesticulates and points at the professor. He picks up the jar with the green frog and lifts it high in the air.

"Will you put my frog down!" says the professor. "It must not be shaken. You must not touch the glassware on this table, Dr. Riege!"

"Charging. Tension. Discharging. Relaxation! This is the rhythm of everything in existence," shouts Dr. Riege. "Everything in the world. Minerals, plants, animals and human beings, planets, suns—everything strives for orgasm, which is the same thing that we call happiness. To liberate the bound sexual energy is the same thing as liberating the world! In German the Savior is called *Erlöser*—he who 'lets loose'!"

Dr. Riege has froth around his mouth, which he licks away with a red, pointed tongue. The professor can see that he is charged and tensed up and he has an eerie feeling that Dr. Riege might just discharge at any moment. He looks anxiously at the agitated man and the rabbits and the guinea pigs and the green frog. He lights his pipe, which keeps going out, and looks for some place to toss his match. The room is full of bowls and flasks and tubes and jars and apparatus, but there isn't a single ashtray, so ashes and matches are stuck anywhere there is room for them.

"Hmm. So, we got our theology after all," says the professor.

"All religions in all ages have symbolized the same thing. Release. Orgasm. The figurative languages of religions are symbols for the same thing as the mathematical signs. The zero is the symbol for the female egg, or the womb. The number one is the symbol for the phallus, sperm, the male force. In Egyptian hieroglyphic writing, the egg is the symbol of the womb giving birth. In India, Brahma is called *Kalahamsa,* which means the swan in eternity or the swan in the egg. The Egyptians represent the sun god Ra as having been begotten in the egg. The Hindus explain the Creation as God's introduction of the procreating spermatozoon into the egg of the world. The symbolic picture for this is a circle with a dot in the middle. This simple and beautiful motif has often been used by abstract painters. The Egyptians called it Seb's Egg, since Seb is the earthly principle. The planets are shaped like eggs. And the orbits of the planets are ellipses, or eggs. The theosophists feel that every human being is surrounded by a sphere called the 'auric egg.' And I am inclined to believe that they are right. The Greeks said that Apollo was born from Leda's egg after Zeus in the form of a swan had impregnated her. Among the Egyptians, Zeus is called Shu. The egg is the symbol of the elder Horus who lies unmanifest in his egg — bound sexual energy. The younger Horus is manifest and is the savior or redeemer of his father Osiris. This is the Christ myth in another guise."

As he speaks, he stands like a lecturer, leaning on the back of the metal chair. The professor has sat down. And as he listens to the doctor's lecture, he pats a white rabbit and scratches it between the ears. "Ah yes," he says. "It looks as if sexual psychology has turned into occultism. I wonder what old Freud would have said about that. He certainly must be turning over in his grave."

"Freud is obsolete and abandoned. We don't want to keep attributing everything to Freud. Universal sex cosmology has been able to use a few of Freud's observations as corroboration, just as it has found corroboration in the results of so many other researchers working in isolation. Your work too, Professor. As far as I'm concerned, you may call sex cosmology occultism if you like, insofar as occult means 'what is hidden,' and it is the purpose of sex cosmology to expose what is hidden. To awaken the slumbering forces. To loose the pent-up and inhibited life-energy, or sexuality, in every area."

"And now you want to make a homunculus?" says the professor. He has put the white rabbit on his lap, and both of them sit looking expectantly at Dr. Riege, who appears to be charged up and tensed, ready to go off at any moment. "You want to make an artificial, chemical person? I have to admit it would amuse me to hear what procedures you are going to follow. Can you tell me somewhat succinctly? I'll certainly keep quiet about it, and I won't steal your formula."

"The procedure is very easy to explain. And I have absolutely no fear whatsoever that you would take advantage of it. It would simply make me happy if your attitude toward these serious problems would be a little more sympathetic. But I don't expect that."

"I really am very curious. Please do tell me, Dr. Riege!"

# [ 10 ]

Dr. Riege tells him. And as he tells him, he paces back and forth across the floor.

The professor sits quietly on his chair, following him with his eyes. He sits holding the white rabbit on his lap. And once in a while he scratches the rabbit between its pink ears with the tip of his pipe, spilling ashes and tobacco juice on the rabbit's white fur.

The jars around the room are bubbling. Yeast cultures and tissues grow and develop. And the green frog goes up and down in its cylindrical jar like a Cartesian devil.

"In this institute you do a great deal of work with the phenomenon of growth," says Dr. Riege. "You have cultivated tissue and made it live and grow, severed from the parent organism. But you don't have a real explanation of what growth is."

"But you do, I'm sure," says the professor.

"Yes, that's precisely what I have. Both plant and animal cells

as well as minerals possess the capability for growth. Plant cells contain the same energy, or sexuality, that also functions in minerals and functions in plants. Minerals are bound together by an atom of one polarity seeking an atom of the opposite polarity. Positive seeks negative and vice versa. This is what is called magnetism. It can also be called love. Minerals, too, strive for orgasm. In every existing thing, a charging and tensing and a discharging and relaxation take place. This is the rhythm of life. This perpetual attraction or magnetism or sexuality makes it possible for physical and intellectual forms to exist at all."

"I've never heard anything like it!" says the professor. He looks on with distaste as Dr. Riege grows excited and gets charged with electricity or sexuality. An eerie tension has entered the laboratory. An alien force that makes the professor nervous and wary. He looks uneasily at the gesticulating doctor and is full of resistance and hostile polarity.

Dr. Riege talks on ecstatically. There is froth around his mouth again, and electric forces and currents seem to emanate from him. "Every body in nature constantly seeks another body of the opposite polarity!" he shrieks. "It seeks vibrational harmony. The conjunction between these atoms or bodies or people or other beings is orgasm. This is what we commonly call happiness. Slumbering or resting happiness in minerals. Semi-slumbering, unconscious happiness in plants. Conscious sexual satisfaction or conscious happiness in people. Everything in existence seeks to complete itself by a union. This is the purpose of life. The sole impetus of elementary life-energy is to seek the pleasure experience!"

"This is incredible!" says the professor. "Fantastic!"

And Dr. Riege talks on in a shrieking voice with spit around his mouth. "Thus, all matter is alive! We could also call it animated. Animated by what we call magnetism or sexuality or vitality or life. We can differentiate between the magnetic life-element and the vital-chemical one. The chemical life-element makes it possible for solid matter, which is created by electro-magnetism, to be built up into different forms, as we know from the case of so-called organic matter. This vital-chemical element thus has the capability of producing what you call growth. It can, so to speak, organize matter!"

"Good Lord!" says the professor.

"What I have been explaining is the same thing that you call evolution. All development and growth is a consequence of oscillations or vibrations. Atoms produce matter during constant vibratory motion."

"Mr. Riege! Are you serious?" says the professor. "Do you really intend to attempt to make a homunculus? A living human being complete with hat and walking-stick and wishes and desires? What had you thought of doing with it? Is this a joke? Or do you seriously intend to do this?" The professor has gotten up and stands facing Dr. Riege in a slightly threatening posture. He is holding the rabbit by its long ears, looking as if he would like to throw it in the doctor's face. But he controls himself and quietly puts it back in its wire cage, where it promptly starts munching on some carrots.

"Of course I'm serious!" shouts Dr. Riege. "I am absolutely convinced that I can make a living being. A person like you and me! And with the potential for development which I hope will far exceed what one can expect of a professor of biology! The purely technical procedures are my own invention. When I was in America, I saw with my own eyes how my teacher made organic matter out of inorganic objects. Why on earth shouldn't it be possible to produce the vibrations necessary to organize matter into the form of a genuine, individual being with feelings and intelligence? I can do it! I have the power to carry it out!"

"But good God, man! You don't seriously expect me to entrust a laboratory to you for such idiocy! I've sat here being nice and patient listening to you. By God, you can't demand any more than that!"

"Ho, ho! You're against me! You're persecuting me just the way your predecessors persecuted Paracelsus and Giordano Bruno!"

"I certainly haven't given any thought to persecuting you. But I can't put the university's and Mr. Rockefeller's rooms at the disposal of something I consider to be raving lunacy. Though it wouldn't surprise me if you could get other people to help you. Aren't you well-to-do yourself? Hasn't sex cosmology given you a pretty good livelihood? You have friends and followers, after all. I would imagine it might be possible for you to set up a laboratory in your own home."

"I can assure you that your opposition will not prevent me

from continuing my work," says Dr. Riege, his eyes shining. And he again points at the professor with his long index finger that resembles a pistol. "The scientific establishment will not succeed in standing in the way of progress this time either!"

"No, I quite agree with you. And you might just be able to get hold of this mysterious Danielsen, the one they've been writing so much about in the newspapers. I wonder whether this wouldn't be something for him?"

"Do you know who Danielsen is, Professor? Will you give me his address?"

"No, I'm afraid I don't have the pleasure of knowing Mr. Danielsen. But you can put an ad in the paper for him. That's what a lot of people are doing."

# *IDEALISTS*

# [ 11 ]

O UT IN THE Nørrebro section of Copenhagen, there is a street
called Stengade. It is a side street off Nørrebrogade. A drab little
street with no traffic and with no shops or bars.

Not much happens on Stengade. But in the spring of the same
year that the mysterious benefactor Danielsen appears on the
scene, and Kados and Dr. Riege are starting their experiments
to produce living beings, preparations are in fact being made on
Stengade for something that, in a strange way, is connected with
the activities of these three men.

A man by the name of Damascus owns a small print shop here
on Stengade. In an archway between the two buildings hangs an
enameled sign with a pointing hand and the words: DAMASCUS
PRINTING. And inside the courtyard behind the building,
where there are always some men wrestling with large crates,
there is also a sign with a hand that points diagonally up the side
of a wall. An exterior iron staircase leads up to a third sign,
where the hand indicates a door with dusty, dull windowpanes
in it.

You first enter a small office, which is also a stockroom with
large piles of printed materials. From here an open door leads
into a larger room, where the floor shakes to the din of a printing
press. One offset press is running, but a second offset press
stands idle. There are also a couple of so-called "flyswatters," or
hand-platen presses, and a large, slanted letter case.

The place smells of newsprint and kerosene. And the floor is
littered with paper. The offset press roars like the ocean surf,
making all conversation extremely difficult.

Nevertheless, a lot of conversations go on at Damascus's print
shop. Everything is discussed and explained, from mundane
matters to significant and intangible ones. The little print shop is

a meeting place and a club for many singular individuals who
like to talk about their ideas.

Damascus is never alone. People come and go all day long.
People who need to have something printed. And people who
just come in to be someplace and discuss something. Sometimes
people bring their lunches with them and sit eating their sand-
wiches in the little office with the three red overstuffed chairs.
People come with bills too. Unpleasant people who grumble and
make threats.

Everywhere there is a lot of dust. You wade through strips of
paper from the cutter, lost pieces of type, and scraps of metal.
Two thin rays of sunlight shine into the room from the window
and light up the dust.

In the middle of it all stands Damascus the printer. A small,
kindly man with gray hair and a beard. In a threadbare suit and
in his bare feet. He has friendly blue eyes and smiles at his little
print shop. He looks lovingly at his press, which is working for
the sake of humanity, reproducing good and useful thoughts.
White paper goes in one end, passes through rollers and presses,
and shoots out the other end of the machine filled with good
words.

Damascus has a man helping him. A tall, thin man with watery
eyes and an ironic smile. His name is Olsen. He is not a trained
typographer. He has been in the penitentiary and he is knowledgeable about many things. Damascus took him on out of kind-
ness upon the recommendation of old tailor Henningsen, whose
son is an employee of the prison system. Damascus knows that
Olsen is no criminal. He's just a weak man.

He didn't get angry when Olsen took the typewriter from the
office and pawned it. "But at least you could have given me the
pawn ticket. I might have had the money to get it out of hock
someday."

"I hocked the ticket too. To a man down on Dannebrogsgade.
Twenty-five øre to the krone."

"But you got a ticket there too, didn't you? You really could
have given it to me."

"I don't guess I could have, since I sold it. Eh?"

"Well then, I guess there's nothing to be done. But that
wasn't nice of you, Olsen. Just when I'd paid the final installment on that typewriter."

"Right. Otherwise I wouldn't have been able to hock it, would I?" says Olsen.

If one of the offset presses is standing idle, unable to print good and useful things, it's because Olsen has removed some of the machine's inner parts and sold them to a scrap-iron dealer. A printing press has so many parts, and even though they look unnecessary, each one is essential and cannot be spared.

"I know you're not a bad person," Damascus says. "You're just weak. But this business with the machine is a real annoyance to me. In the first place we won't be able to finish the things we promised. And in the second place there's a lien on that press, you know. And now if the lien officer sees that it's been ruined . . ."

"I don't guess it's ruined because there are a few chunks of iron missing. I guess it can be repaired."

"Of course it can. But it's annoying anyhow. You've put me in a difficult position, Olsen, even though it wasn't your intention to do me any harm."

"Well, then just report me to the police! Go ahead. Just give them a call. I've been there before. I know the routine."

"Why, you know very well I'd never do that," says Damascus.

"Oh yeah? Just do it! Just report me. Go ahead and run me in!"

"You mustn't talk like that. I'm not angry with you. I know you're a good person, Olsen. You're just weak."

"Yeah, but you squawk and chew me out," says Olsen. And Damascus is forced to apologize as Olsen begins justifying another form, silent and smiling bitterly.

Oh, that money. It poisons life for Olsen and Damascus. Damascus is a modest man. His life doesn't cost very much money. He has an apple and a couple of carrots and two slices of rye bread with radishes on them in a piece of newspaper. That's his lunch. He walks around in his bare feet. Not out of thrift but because it's healthy. He's an idealist. Shoes and socks are unnatural inventions that cause many illnesses. Damascus once suffered from a kidney ailment, but it disappeared after he started going barefoot. He wears galoshes on the street in order not to attract attention. And perhaps this is a weakness. But in the print shop and at home he walks around on his little bare feet. He doesn't spend much on shoe leather or on food.

He has a lot to print. But not all his customers are able to pay for what they have printed. They aren't wealthy, these people who want to speak Esperanto and eat raw vegetables and create good conditions in the world, without tobacco and alcohol and vivisection. But Damascus has a hard time turning down an idealist or dunning him for payment.

And while Olsen sits gloomily over his type cases, messengers come into the outer office with bills. Damascus has to walk out there on his little bare feet and speak words of reassurance to them and ask for patience. He'll pay them all right. He'll get the money all right. It'll all work out fine. But if only he knew this Danielsen fellow, whoever he is!

# [ 12 ]

Damascus's shop prints one publication that is against the consumption of alcohol. And another that is vigorously opposed to smoking. But Damascus also prints a magazine that comes out strongly in favor of an individual's personal freedom and maintains people's inalienable right to drink and smoke. Using concise arguments and statistics, it even goes so far as to prove that tobacco and alcohol are healthful and necessary for both individuals and commercial life.

Damascus is anything but one-sided. He prints propaganda for the Esperanto movement. But he also prints propaganda for that new artificial language, Novial, whose adherents bitterly attack the Esperantists. He does printing for Theosophists. And he does printing for their opponents, the Anthroposophists. He prints two entire magazines for the Anthroposophists, since these people are divided into two hostile camps, both of which recognize the superhumanness of Rudolf Steiner, of course, but who disagree on the question of whether this superhuman might someday be equaled by other mortals.

Damascus also prints *Spiritism Magazine*. He prints *Sex News*. He prints small flyers for the Jehovah's Witnesses. And he prints *Academic Intelligence Journal*, which is edited and published by Skodsborg, the young university student. He prints tracts for bird lovers and people who eat raw fruit and vegetables and anti-vivisectionists and those who go barefoot and sandal-wearers and the disciples of Krishnamurti and the GYP movement.

If all the items he printed were paid for, Damascus would be a wealthy man. He prints and prints. His machines keep running — that is, if Olsen doesn't pick out their vital parts and sell them as scrap iron.

Olsen is a weak man. But the fact that Olsen can't always get his weekly pay on time may serve as some excuse for him. Sometimes Damascus simply doesn't have any money on Friday. "You can wait a couple of days, can't you, Olsen?"

"Wait? And what am I supposed to live on while I wait?"

"Don't you have anything to live on at all?"

"No. Where the hell would I get it?"

"Do you mean that you are literally without food?"

"Damn right I do."

"Well then, wait a second, Olsen," says Damascus. He ducks down and looks for something under the desk where he keeps his galoshes, pulls out a large bundle wrapped in newspaper, and unpacks something.

"Take a look, Olsen! Here's a nice big kohlrabi. We were going to have it for supper at home, but you need it more than I do. Just take it, Olsen! It's something healthy. But it's best to boil it in two changes of water. Otherwise it has a way of tasting a little rank."

"Go to hell!" says Olsen. "And eat your damn turnips yourself!"

It's probably not completely true that Olsen is literally starving. He has his irons in the fire. He has a lot of little schemes and projects going on. He has tried a lot and learned a lot and has been in the penitentiary a couple of times. He knows life and knows how to act respectable and fastidious. He was once a servant in the home of a squire in southern Sjælland. He has watery eyes and an ironic smile. Maybe it gives a man backbone to smile slightly in situations where he can't talk back. It's not a good thing for a servant to argue with his superiors. And it's not a good thing for an inmate to contradict a prison guard. But it helps to smile slightly to oneself. There are people who think

that Olsen is a supercilious person who smiles ironically because he knows something he's not telling.

There is a wash basin in the small office where Olsen can wash off the printer's ink. He lays his coveralls on one of the red upholstered chairs and takes his good clothes out from behind a curtain. A light-colored summer suit with padding in the shoulders. And a striped tie and a silk handkerchief flowing out of his breast pocket. Damascus shuffles around in his bare feet puttering in his print shop, straightening things up a little and putting things away. He is thinking about the bills that will arrive tomorrow, and about an I.O.U. But fortunately tomorrow is Saturday, and the banks will be closing early, so nothing can happen before Monday, that is to say Tuesday. He has time until Tuesday at one o'clock. A lot can happen before then.

After Olsen has finished washing, Damascus takes his turn and rubs water on his face and snorts and shakes himself. And he peers at Olsen, who is silent and offended and smiling bitterly. Damascus knows that when he gets home to Kapelvej, his

wife will be offended and silent too. Damascus loves people. But
they are offended and silent with him. He looks around at things
with friendly, kindly blue eyes. But people smile bitterly and
ironically.

He sticks his little bare feet into his galoshes and tucks the
newspaper-wrapped bundle with that good kohlrabi in it under-
neath his arm. He tries out a conciliatory smile on Olsen, but
there is no response. Olsen stands there cold and reserved in his
light-colored summer suit with its shoulder pads and creases and
silk pocket handkerchief.

They walk down the iron staircase together in silence. "Goodbye, Olsen," Damascus says when they are out on the street.
But Olsen doesn't answer him. And they go their separate ways.
Damascus walks in the direction of Kapelvej. Olsen walks in
toward the lakes in the center of town. He has his own shadowy
pathways in the inner city. He has irons in the fire that have to
be looked after.

Olsen is a weak person. But he can still be the cause of many
things.

# [ 13 ]

T HE PRESS IS RUNNING. Sheet after sheet is being filled with
idealism and stacked in piles.

Damascus is standing at the letter case. Short and gray, with
bare feet and friendly blue eyes. And as he sets type from a
manuscript, he nods approvingly because these are good and
appealing thoughts that are going to be reproduced.

There aren't as many letters in the small compartments of the
type case as there ought to be. *E*'s are particularly hard to find.
The used galleys have to be broken up quickly so there will be
enough letters for the new material to be typeset. Letters disappear from the case from one day to the next. He doesn't want to
suspect Olsen without proof. But you can get a good price for
lead, and the world is full of temptations.

Olsen is sullen and uncommunicative. Damascus can smell that he has been drinking a lot of beer. And yesterday he didn't have any money at all. So somebody must have spent money on him and lured him into drinking. Bad friends and acquaintances. There's nothing bad about Olsen. But he is weak.

The first messengers have been there with their bills. They'll be paid all right, says Damascus. Within the week. Maybe as early as Monday. And there's a messenger from the paper supplier who says that if the bill isn't paid that day, there won't be any more paper. The paper supplier sends his regards.

"Oh, but that's the paper for *Sex News*," says Damascus. "That's the only one of the journals that pays. If you won't give us paper, the whole thing will go down the drain."

"Well, that was the message I was supposed to give you," says the messenger.

Once in a while the telephone rings. "Be a good fellow and get that, Olsen, and say I'm not here if it's somebody who wants money."

"Yeah, a person can learn how to tell lies here," says Olsen.

But the call is only from the Equine Protection League. "How is everything going with those pamphlets that were supposed to be finished yesterday? Won't they be ready soon? It's urgent!"

"Oh yes, they're finished," says Damascus. "They've been sent to the bindery to be stitched. As soon as they're back from the bindery, we'll deliver them. Maybe as early as this afternoon. It won't take too long."

Telephones are a bother. They should never have been invented. The ink supplier calls up and tells him that they've just about had it. Didn't Damascus specifically promise that the money would be paid last Saturday? So where is it? Did it ever get here? Can't you depend on anyone at all anymore?

The *Cat Lover* calls up and tells him that the article he just set will have to be reset. The author has had a new idea, and it will have to be included. The article simply must not be printed in its present form. And *Star in the East* demands a second proof. In the last issue, there were serious misprints that completely changed the meaning. "On page 3, column 2, for example, it said: 'the six-fold Dyanis, which are the givers of the five bodies, which to be God's equal shall be a trinity together with a pentad functioning through a heptad.' But of course it should have said: 'A trinity together with a heptad functioning through a duodecad.' Anybody can see that this sort of mistake just won't do. In the future the proofs will have to be read twice!"

Telephones are a nuisance that ought to be banned. On top of everything else, he has received a letter informing him that his telephone will be disconnected if the bill, plus fees and interest, isn't paid within three days.

"Oh, that miserable money. I despise it. But I still can't do without it," says Damascus.

"You can very easily do without money!" says Mr. Sivertsen, B.A. "Money is the most superfluous and foolish thing that this world has ever come up with."

Mr. Sivertsen, B.A., is a well-read and versatile man who has been to America and is well informed about things. He is no longer young. But he has never found a profession that fits his abilities. He has sacrificed himself for idealistic objectives and not used his energies on ordinary work. He has inherited a small fortune and just manages to live on the interest. He is an irascible man with white hair and black eyebrows and a black mustache. "An idealist," says Damascus. "And a good person, even though he is hot-tempered."

Regarding money, Sivertsen has devised an entire system for society so that it can function and remain solvent without the aid of the medium of exchange that we call money. All right, maybe he didn't exactly invent the system himself, maybe he simply heard of it or read about it. He spends all his time and energy campaigning for his ideas. This campaign takes place via a small journal with the peculiar name of GYP, which is an acronym for the words Geography, Yield, Purchase.

A group of people has rallied around the journal, and someday they will form a political party. A party beyond parties. A nonpolitical league. A movement. Three letters that will be a philosophy of life and a gospel.

Every day Mr. Sivertsen, B.A., puts in an appearance at Damascus's print shop to supervise the printing of GYP. Granted, it is still only a monthly magazine, but it is edited with extreme care. The proofs are scrutinized and revised. Changes are constantly being made. Things are constantly being added to

Sivertsen's proclamations when new ideas intrude after GYP has gone to press. Its form must continually be perfected.

"Of course people can do without money!" says Mr. Sivertsen, B.A. It's a sad thing to hear a gifted man like Damascus assert the contrary. "That's the type of thoughtless remark that can do more harm than we realize. And a harmful sentence, once it has been spoken and sent out into the world, will roll on through all eternity and bring about misconceptions and cause trouble."

"But how would *you* actually manage without money?" says Skodsborg, the young student who edits *Academic Intelligence Journal*. "How in the hell would you support your GYP without money for the printer or postage or supper?"

"I'll tell you how, young man," Sivertsen replies. "This can be arranged in a very simple way: the state will prohibit the existence and use of money. Instead, all wages for services rendered will be disbursed in scrip. And all goods and all consumption will be paid for by this state-issued scrip."

"Isn't it kind of irrelevant whether we call it money or scrip or something else entirely?"

"If you will stop interrupting me, young man! It is not irrelevant at all. Because, you see, scrip is not money. It doesn't have the exchange value of money; rather it's a kind of voucher which is disbursed as compensation for work performed or goods delivered."

"That is, exactly the same thing as paper money!" says the student, who is studying economics and is knowledgeable about questions concerning the economy.

"If you will let me finish speaking! Scrip is not money. Scrip is organized in such a way that it only has its full exchange value on the day on which it is disbursed. The very next day it depreciates in value. And on the next day after that, there's an even greater depreciation, and so on until the end of the week and the next payday, when scrip has become worthless. Successive inflation, if you will. Since scrip is worthless at the end of the week, the result will be that people will be forced to spend their money — that is, their scrip — as quickly as possible. They would do best to buy things with it on payday itself to get their full exchange value in merchandise. Can you possibly imagine the kind of turnover that would create? No superfluous inventories! No idle factories! No unemployment! Scrip is out circulating constantly, creating work and employment. Nobody will be able to hoard money. Capitalism and exploitation will be impossible."

"But what if you're supposed to get your weekly pay on Friday but you have to wait until Monday because your employer doesn't have any money? Then what?" Olsen suddenly says, breaking into the conversation. "Then you'd be losing money, that's what! And if you're supposed to buy everything on Friday and you want to eat fish on Tuesday, the fish'll get pretty damn old and rotten!"

"Yes, Olsen is absolutely right," says student Skodsborg. "This is utter nonsense, of course. For instance, people would have to buy their food for a whole week at a time. They'd be eating rotten meat every Thursday!"

"Oh no, my young friend, they wouldn't! You see, people shouldn't be eating meat at all. People are not predatory beasts. To a vegetarian, your objections to our system don't amount to a thing."

"I've certainly got to agree with Sivertsen there," says Damascus. "It isn't human nature to eat carrion. A lot of things would be different in this world if most people hadn't poisoned their bodies with toxins from corpses and destroyed their spiritual being by turning themselves into predatory beasts and regressing millions of years in their evolution."

"But that baloney has nothing to do with Sivertsen's GYP!" the student shouts.

"Oh yes, it certainly does," says Sivertsen. "The vegetarian way of life is the ethical foundation for all social evolution. I made that statement in the very first issue of GYP."

"Oh, go to hell!" the student says. "It's utter nonsense! You're living off your inherited money yourself. You're a coupon clipper and an annuitant! You're quite a Danielsen!"

"And you're a bigmouth!" Sivertsen shrieks. "A real lout. It would serve you right if I gave you a thrashing on the spot!"

"No, no!" says Damascus. "Don't do that. We mustn't settle

this with violence. Now you were the one who got carried away first, Skodsborg. I think you should apologize to Mr. Sivertsen, Skodsborg."

"Damned if I will!" the student says, and walks indignantly out to the small office and sits down in one of the red chairs and bites his fingernails.

"What an impertinent rascal!" says Sivertsen. "You take the trouble to explain to him . . ."

"We shouldn't take these young people too seriously," says Damascus. "There's a lot of good in Skodsborg. He's an idealist. His language may be a little coarse, but he doesn't mean anything bad by it."

Damascus dissipates the anger and smooths things over and makes peace in his little print shop, where so many singular individuals meet, and where opinions and ideas clash.

# [ 14 ]

OUT IN THE COURTYARD men in overalls are working and sweating, lifting heavy crates. Up in the annex men in smocks are stacking cartons and sorting sacks and writing numbers on slips of paper. In another annex girls stand wrapping caramels all day long.

The world is full of ordinary, normal people. People live behind all the little windows on Stengade. They have hung up curtains and put potted plants and knickknacks in their windows and are trying to make things around them nice and pleasant.

People are walking along the street. And bicycles and trucks and delivery vans are driving by. Everybody has things to do and places to go. They have their wishes and sorrows and pleasures and children and bicycles and rented garden plots. They pay their union dues and their health insurance premiums and don't consider themselves idealists because of it. They wouldn't mind getting a little more for their work and having a little nicer place to live, and if they stick together, they'll probably succeed.

"If only people would simply learn to go barefoot or at the very least wear sandals!" says Damascus. "Then this world would be a happier place. Then disease and dissatisfaction would disappear. Class struggle and wars and revolutions wouldn't exist."

"Sandals aren't enough," says Mr. Sivertsen, B.A. "GYP's system of scrip must be introduced. And people must live on vegetarian fare and not on other living creatures."

"Yes, of course. The vegetarian way of life is a precondition for a better world. That goes without saying," says Damascus. "But it would certainly be of the utmost significance for humanity if we could abolish footwear too. As long as we slaughter animals and flay them and make leather out of their hides, the vegetarian way of life won't work. I don't understand why you want to walk around in tight leather boots, Sivertsen. Throw them away! Just walk naturally on the ground!"

"I've tried going barefoot. But it's very difficult for me. I have bunions, and it hurts."

"It will pass if you keep at it. Your bunions will disappear. Just try it, Sivertsen. Just stick with it!"

"I really can't. It's not that I lack persistence. But I can't. And I catch cold when I go barefoot."

"That's only until you get hardened. I haven't had a single cold since I started. I had kidney trouble. But it went away completely after I had been going barefoot for a while."

"But you do wear galoshes on the street."

"I do, yes. And that's probably a mistake. I do it so I won't attract a crowd. But you must remember, galoshes are made of rubber. That's a vegetarian product. We don't need to kill animals to produce galoshes."

"I'll think over the business about the galoshes," says Sivertsen. "But it's difficult when you have bunions."

"I know that you're an idealist and that you'll make this sacrifice too," says Damascus.

People need so little to be happy. It shouldn't be necessary to struggle and fight in order to earn a few more øre an hour, say the Anthroposophists, who also have their journals printed by Damascus. "After all, it's the inner life that matters, not the outer life. People should learn to relax and become immersed in their own selves. Drift off into passive meditation. Pick up a beautiful stone and keep on gazing at it. Keep on until there's a blue ring radiating around the stone! Keep on until the stone's aura becomes visible to the naked eye! What do wages and money and outward prosperity really matter compared to the profound feeling of inner happiness that meditation and relaxation provide?"

Dr. Riege and his disciples also prescribe relaxation and passive submission as a means to humanity's release. "We must relax. We must learn to recognize the things that make us tense and alleviate them," writes *Sex News*.

The "Jazz-Pol" party also sings the gospel of relaxation. People's stomach muscles have become too taut. The abdomen has been neglected in favor of the head. "Relax those stomach muscles! Make your abdomens soft and pliant! This will bring true happiness and equilibrium!" And the party sings:

> C'mon, we gotta relax,
> C'mon, we gotta relax,
> Why do we gotta?
> Well, 'cause we oughta.

So little is necessary. "Just look at Gandhi," says Damascus. "His clothing is a simple piece of cloth. A little fruit and goat's milk are his food. It's not material goods we should be striving for. It's the inner life that should be cultivated. Why doesn't everybody in Denmark have a goat? This gentle, frugal animal that can give three liters of nourishing milk a day and costs so little to keep. If Gandhi can take his goat along with him on long trips, it really ought to be possible for every Danish worker to keep a goat too."

"Ah yes, humanity!" says the poetess, Sylvia Drusse. "We struggle for it, we idealists. But is it worth the struggle?"

"Yes, Mrs. Drusse, it is. Humanity deserves to be happy!" says Damascus, looking at her kindly. "And so little is necessary. A simple, frugal vegetarian way of life. Bare feet or sandals, instead of footwear that pinches and disturbs, produced from the hides of dead animals. Thoughts directed toward the inner life. Meditation."

"But that's not enough," says Mrs. Drusse. "As long as

humanity continues to observe Monday on the day that in reality is Sunday, there is no possibility for a life of true harmony."

"How do you mean, Mrs. Drusse?"

"Sunday and Monday have been switched around! And it's our duty to enlighten humanity about this fateful mistake. You know just as well as I do, Damascus, that there is an interdependence among the seven days of the week and the seven planets and the seven colors and the seven musical tones. The sequence of days and musical keys runs parallel.

"But over the course of time, an error was made because exoteric astrological knowledge was predominant, whereas the esoteric—the inner school—was kept secret for centuries. It was kept secret that the earth itself is one of the seven planets. And that is why Sunday and Monday have been switched around in the enumeration. The sun—Vulcan—is the primary and leading element in the system and rules the day that is now erroneously called Monday. Monday is thus 'the day of the sun,' or Sunday. This day's first quarter is ruled by the sun and by the musical note C and by the color indigo."

"Well then, what about the day that we call Sunday?" asks Damascus.

"Ah, Sunday! The day we now call Sunday, but which in reality is Monday, begins its first quarter with the earth. Monday means 'Moon-day,' of course, 'Luna's day.' *Lundi*. It should therefore show up with its name in the sequence after Saturday. The first quarter of the day thus has earth's yellow color. And earth's musical note F, which in continuation of a gradual progression between musical keys is F sharp. So can't you see, Damascus, that it's insanity to want to call this day Sunday, or 'the day of the sun'?"

"That sounds very significant, Mrs. Drusse. Why haven't you ever told me this before? Have you spoken with Kados about it?"

"Yes. Kados knows. And he has always known. But he has kept it a secret because he didn't feel that humanity was ready for this knowledge yet. But I believe in people. And I feel that the truth must come out!"

"You're right, Mrs. Drusse. People have a right to know the whole truth. I think that Kados has done the wrong thing by keeping his knowledge secret."

"That's what I've told him a number of times. But Kados has contempt for all of us. I don't like Kados. He's in league with Lucifer. I'm frightened of that man. He's a demon. But I don't dare oppose him. He has greater power than I do."

"I think you're doing Kados an injustice. He's an idealist. For him Lucifer isn't Satan, or the principle of evil. But the overthrown bringer of light. Prometheus. Loki. The friend of earth and humanity, overthrown by Jehovah, who is only a demigod, a demiurge, for Kados. Kados has made common cause with Lucifer. He wants to depose Jehovah and reinstate the overthrown bringer of light in his stead. It is a great task he has taken upon himself, Mrs. Drusse."

"Yes, it is a great task. If only it isn't too great for him. And if only he doesn't go too far. I am frightened of this Kados!"

"Do *not* call him Kados! Call him the Beast of Østre Farimagsgade!" says Sjögren the astrologer.

"You mustn't say things like that about Kados," says Damascus. "Kados is an idealist."

# [ 15 ]

Mrs. Drusse is a clairvoyant. She has been known to perceive and fathom things that were hidden from other people. She is not a quiet scholar and brooder like Kados. She has not acquired the ancient, occult sciences. Ideas come to her from outside herself as sudden impulses. Like flashes of light and lightning.

Her hand writes words that she doesn't understand herself. She writes with her eyes closed, her hand racing across the paper pushing the pencil without the guidance of her own will. When she reads her manuscript afterwards, she is often amazed at what she has written.

She can remember being an Inca princess in a previous life. And she can recall that she voluntarily went to her death for her people in order to placate the gods. She was an idealist back then

too. She was sacrificed at the temple of the Moon God after the high priest had ravished and consecrated her. "I can remember it as if it were yesterday!" she says. And she has written a novel about the event.

She has also written a poetry cycle, *A Mother's Heart*, which is dedicated to her son. Her son went to America a long time ago and is working someplace over there with no idea of the way a mother's heart can suffer and bleed.

"They fly from the nest, our young birds!" Mrs. Drusse says. "Their wings unfurl. Something calls them. Something draws and attracts them, and they have to fly off." And when she talks about flying away, she spreads out her arms, which actually do look like wings because she has long fringes on her sleeves. She wears large earrings with green stones, and garishly colored shawls and scarves, and silver brooches and tassles and fringes. Her face is enigmatic and inscrutable when she leans her head back and closes her eyes halfway.

Once she was a spiritualist and spoke intimately with the spirits of the deceased. But she has abandoned spiritualism because the séances had a harrowing effect on her and threatened to destroy her physical sensibility. She still starts to shake sometimes when she thinks of the dreadful séance when her two deceased husbands wanted to speak at the same time through the same medium, pulling and tearing at the medium so that he nearly lost his life. If Damascus hadn't intervened, things would have ended in a catastrophe.

She could have been an excellent medium herself. But she doesn't dare use her mysterious powers, like the organist who doesn't dare play the organ full blast so that he won't make the church collapse into rubble. But she does draw on the well of her subconscious and on the rich fabric of her memories from previous incarnations, especially from the age of the Incas. And she lets intuition come to her from outside, from mystical intelligences and powers which use her as the intermediary for their thoughts.

She often sits in the dark, quiet and half-conscious, with her eyes closed while her hand writes and writes. This is how her poetry comes into being, and that's why she can smile at the opinions of critics and readers about it. "I wasn't even the one who wrote it anyway," she says. In addition to her poetry, she writes recipes for a weekly magazine and endeavors to inject something more elevated into cooking by presenting idealistic dishes.

Mrs. Drusse lives on Fiolstræde. In the old Latin Quarter with its distinctive atmosphere. She has furnished her little apartment with dark curtains and draperies, copperware, a spinning wheel, weavings, and a profusion of candlesticks with wax candles sticking out of them. And she even has Buddha figures, rosaries, an incense pot, and an enigmatic crystal ball. "This is my artist's garret," she says. "Simple and poor, but good enough for me."

"You have a very nice place, Mrs. Drusse," says Damascus with a sigh, thinking of his own gloomy apartment on Kapelvej where his ideas are met with coldness and hostility. Occasionally the poetess invites him in for tea in the evening, and he is happy to be able to escape the discord and money worries in his own home for a little while, and relax and discuss idealism in all innocence with Mrs. Drusse.

"Your tea tastes wonderful. At home we usually make only herbal tea. That's the healthiest kind. I honestly don't know whether it's proper for me to be drinking Indian tea, which, after all, contains stimulants and narcotics that might have a bad influence."

"Tea is a sacred drink, Damascus. I have drunk a lot of tea and I think I can say with certainty that it has never had a harmful effect on my spiritual faculties. On the contrary. Nicotine destroys the astral body little by little and dulls and debilitates the psychic forces. But tea invigorates."

"Yes, maybe you're right. I don't know, though, if I'd dare drink tea every day. But I guess one time won't hurt."

"Just come to my home and drink tea as often as you like," Mrs. Drusse says, patting the little printer.

He feels a quiet, spiritual peace, and Kapelvej and its worries disappear. "It's so peaceful here in your home," he sighs.

"I'm never lonely here. The walls in this room have drunk up memories. The dead are present here. They live in everything they have touched. These pictures, these things are not lifeless. They are living witnesses that I speak to in the dusk."

There are photographs of the late Mr. Drusse, who was an actor and a temperamental and cantankerous man. And there is a self-portrait of the young painter Hakon Brand, who was Mrs. Drusse's friend. "You didn't know Hakon Brand?"

"No, only from séances."

"He died. In Paris. In a dreadful manner. Pursued by powers that he didn't recognize himself. He was a person in despair. But a marvelous artist. Take a good look at his picture!"

"He had a red beard," says Damascus.

"Yes, it was red. Red like the planet Mars. His life was restless here on the earthly plane. And I fear that he hasn't settled down on the other plane either. Life is so multifarious and strange."

"Yes, it is," says Damascus.

"Can you hear the silence in this room?" asks Mrs. Drusse. "After I've finished writing the week's recipes, I sit here and listen to the silence. I hear it singing in the key of B-natural. And I'm filled with the purple color that the Tatwa-stream brings down to us from the hierarchies of Aquarius and Capricorn."

"So you're a Saturn person, Mrs. Drusse? Born in December?"

"Yes, I'm a Saturn person. I was born under the sign of Capricorn, and my musical tone is B-natural, and my color is purple. We are old, we Saturn people. We are born old. I remember the empire of the Incas. And I remember Egypt and Atlantis. Ah, Atlantis! Look, this scarab in my ring here. I have always owned it. In my previous incarnations too. It comes to me in every new life. Isn't that strange?"

"And what sort of a glass ball is that you have? Where does it come from?"

"It's from China. It's ancient. I owned it in previous lives too. Everything returns."

And Mrs. Drusse picks up the heavy crystal ball and places it in her lap. The wax candles are reflected in it, and she gazes at the shiny ball as if hypnotized.

"What do you see?" Damascus asks quietly.

"I see. I see humanity. I see suffering and struggling humanity. Ah, humanity! And what more do I see? Ah yes, I see a person. A man. Beware of him, Damascus!"

"Who is it?"

"I see a tall man. He is standing beside a machine. What kind

of a machine is it? Ah yes, I think it is a printing press. The man has shiny, watery eyes."

"Why, that couldn't be Olsen, could it?"

"I see a tall, thin man with shiny eyes beside a printing press. And I see a building. A large building with very small windows. It must be a prison. The man has come from the building and he will return to it."

"Oh my goodness gracious! Is Olsen going to be locked up again? That would be a shame. Olsen isn't really bad. He's not bad by nature. He's just weak."

"And what more do I see? Oh, I see something red. It's blood. I see red blood. And something shiny. A knife. A dagger. And the man's hands are red. Red with blood."

"You mustn't say that, Mrs. Drusse. Olsen could never do anything like that. He might take it into his head to filch a few things, but he would never harm anybody on purpose."

"I see blood flowing. And I look into the eyes of the dying victim. 'He has murdered me,' the eyes are saying. And I see gold. Red gold. Blood and gold. I see fingers curling around the gold. Red, bloody fingers."

"No, you mustn't say any more, Mrs. Drusse! I don't want to believe anything bad about Olsen. Olsen is a good person. He's just weak."

"Beware! Beware of the man with the shiny eyes and the red hands! Beware!"

"Oh, please do stop, Mrs. Drusse! Please put that ball away! It's not for us to see things that are supposed to be hidden from us. I don't want to believe it!"

And Mrs. Drusse puts the ball away.

"How can you *think* such things about Olsen?"

"Olsen? What Olsen? I don't know any Olsen!"

"You do too know Olsen. He helps me in the print shop."

"Oh yes, well what about him?"

"But you were talking about a man beside a printing press. A tall, thin man with watery eyes."

"I was?"

"And you were talking about blood and gold and a knife. And about the prison and a man who was being murdered."

"I was talking about that? When?"

"Just now. When you were looking into the ball."

"I can't remember that. Did I say anything?"

"But Mrs. Drusse, you make me feel so weird. Can't you remember what you said just now?"

"No, I remember nothing. Did I really say something?"

"Then it must have been someone else speaking through you. It's quite eerie."

"It happens to me so often. I'm not always myself. Who are we? Do we have any identity? Maybe I died a long time ago."

"You have peculiar abilities, Mrs. Drusse."

"We artists aren't like other people. Was I really talking? Was I looking at the ball?"

"Yes, just a moment ago you were sitting with the ball in your lap. And you saw something and you were telling me about what you saw."

"It's a very old ball. It has mirrored many lives. It has absorbed much that has happened and will happen. What is the past and what is the future? Aren't they the same thing? Perhaps everything has happened before."

"I don't like that. I want to improve people. I want them to advance. I don't want everything to have happened before. I want to believe in the future."

"You're an idealist, Damascus. May luck be with you! You have such good, kind eyes. You will do good things in this world. You will help suffering humanity. Unobtrusively and unpretentiously you will soothe and help people. You're a good man, Damascus."

"I only hope you're right, Mrs. Drusse. But now I have to go. I have to get up early tomorrow. There's a lot to do. I'll have to have a serious talk with Olsen. And there's an I.O.U. that's coming due. Ah, money! Thank you for a nice evening, Mrs. Drusse. Goodbye."

"Goodbye," says Mrs. Drusse. And she spreads her arms out so that they look like black wings with ruffled feathers. "Goodbye, Damascus. And come back whenever you feel like it."

And after Damascus has left, she picks up the ball again. And she sits quietly staring at its shiny surface, seeing peculiar and hidden things. A little man with good, kind eyes who walks around in an old fur coat distributing bundles of money to charitable institutions.

"Could he be the one, I wonder?" she whispers.

# [ 16 ]

THE TREES ON KAPELVEJ have turned green. It's the month of May and the sun has entered the constellation of Taurus, which is now ruled by the planet Venus, whose color is green.

The projects that were supposed to have begun under Mars during the period from March 21st to April 21st are already in progress. Kados, who wanted one of the university's rooms for his fire salamanders, has set up his own little furnace of fire that burns night and day and radiates heat all through his apartment on Østre Farimagsgade. And Dr. Riege, who wanted the Rockefeller Institute's help for his experiments on organizing living cells into a living being, has set up a nice laboratory in conjunction with his apartment and clinic. He has loyal disciples who aren't afraid to pay what it costs. He boils things in flasks and mixes ingredients, and at some future time it is to be expected that life will manifest itself in a large glass bottle containing a milky fluid.

Both Kados and Dr. Riege got started at the right time, under the right aspects, while the earth was exposed to irradiation and vibrations from the red planet Mars under the sign of Aries.

Children are drawing hopscotch games and hopping along the flagstone sidewalks on Kapelvej. And Assistens Cemetery is lush and green like the Garden of Eden. Weeping willows and drooping birches are full of sap and life. The birds are chirping and making noise and mating in the cemetery, and they wake up Damascus every morning.

The many flower shops on Kapelvej have potted plants and wreaths out on the sidewalk, so the street looks like a garden. Damascus is transported by happiness and delight with the colors and with springtime as he walks to his little print shop on Stengade.

Damascus is a man of peace who loves and respects every living thing. But there is no peace around him. There is sulking and surliness in his home. And in the print shop, Olsen stands looking aggrieved and full of reproach.

"Why aren't you happy, Olsen? Nature is so beautiful today. Can't you feel what a blessing spring is for body and soul? You know what you ought to do, Olsen? You ought to go take a walk in Assistens Cemetery and see how everything is turning green and blossoming. It's so lush and beautiful in there. Just go in and see the way life and spring are unfolding. It'll cheer you up if you're in a bad mood, Olsen."

"I won't be cheered up by walking in a cemetery and looking at the crosses on the graves," says Olsen.

"Has something got you down, Olsen? Tell me what's wrong. Please have confidence in me."

"It would be nice if a person could be left in peace. You gape at me all day like you're afraid I'm going to steal the print shop. I know that I've been in prison. But that's no reason for you to keep referring to it all the time!"

"But I'm not referring to anything."

"Oh yes, you are. You gape at me. And you ask me if anything's wrong, if something's got me down, and if maybe I wouldn't like to unburden my conscience. You're just like the cops down at police headquarters. They were real interested in my conscience and my peace of mind too."

"Oh, you really misunderstand me," says Damascus. "I only want what's best for you."

"That's what the judge said too, when he gave me three years. 'This will be for your own good,' he said, 'if you understand how to use your time properly and improve yourself and think things over.' "

"But I've never said anything like that. I don't think people get any better by being put away."

"You'd like to have me put away again, though. You're just going around watching and waiting for a chance to turn me in."

"Now why should I turn you in? You certainly haven't done anything to me."

"Oh yes, you're always thinking about that typewriter that I happened to hock."

"I've forgotten the typewriter," says Damascus.

"And the scrap iron I sold."

"No, Olsen, I'm not thinking about the parts you took out of the machine anymore."

"But you keep referring to them!"

"If only you'd understand me, Olsen!"

"If only you'd leave me in peace!"

With his kindly blue eyes Damascus looks worriedly at Olsen, anxious about how things will go for him.

Messengers come with bills. And the telephone rings. "The *Buddhist Emissary* was supposed to be finished today, but it hasn't arrived! What's going on?"

"You'll get it on Wednesday," says Damascus.

"Where are the proofs for *Spiritism Magazine*?"

"They're on their way. — Say, Olsen, couldn't you just ride your bicycle out to the spiritualists with those proofs?"

Discord and unrest surround Damascus. Mrs. Mannia of *Cat Lover* and editor Christensen of *Star in the East* are discussing the purpose of shoulder blades and the question of whether shoulder blades might be the vestiges of wings from a bygone Golden Age or whether, on the contrary, they are the beginnings of angels' wings that won't develop until some time in the future. The discussion turns into an argument and starts getting personal, so Damascus has to mediate and make peace, receiving angry words and ill-will from both sides of the dispute.

And student Skodsborg and Mr. Sivertsen, B.A., are arguing about the GYP movement. Skodsborg is disrespectful and teases Sivertsen. And Sivertsen loses his temper and gets red in the face. Then an Esperantist gets into a fight with an advocate of the new artificial language, Novial. And they get so excited that they both switch into their own artificial languages so that it's impossible to understand the insults they're shouting at each other, and nobody can make peace.

They are all idealists. And they all want to help humanity. But they don't agree on the ways or the means.

The people who eat raw fruit and vegetables criticize the vegetarians for leading unnatural lives and destroying nature by scorching and boiling vegetables. The people who wear sandals are angry and filled with hatred toward people who wear shoes.

Damascus likes them all. He loves their idealism regardless of what it's based on. He himself goes barefoot and lives modestly on vegetarian fare. And if he is able to afford it, someday he might make the switch to nothing but raw fruit and vegetables.

But his finances still don't allow him to give up baked rye bread completely and eat raw fig bread instead. He's no fanatic. He's a member of several different leagues and movements, but above all he is an altruist. His life and his aspirations are dedicated to the benefit and happiness of others.

He is a member of the board of directors of the Danish Altruist League, which is a subdivision of the International Altruist League with headquarters and main offices at 114 West Franklin Street, Baltimore, Maryland, U.S.A. and whose motto is: "We will plant flowers in Eden."

It is a league with no dogmas and it can accommodate people of any religion and philosophy of life, and it was founded on the thoughts of Neophit and the monadism of Giordano Bruno. Damascus prints the League's publications free of charge. They have to be printed on light green paper because light green is the color of altruism and of spring. Someday, when the League grows strong, their idea is to establish a colony where the League's members can live together side by side in unselfish work for the welfare of humanity. An earthly paradise, which will grow with time so that other paradises can be set up around the country, until every single region has its own Eden.

Concord, tolerance, selflessness. These are the ideals of Damascus. But it's hard to get idealists to agree. Here comes Mrs. Drusse, for instance, breezily asserting that it is the moon which produces the etheric double and that Jupiter produces the Adi-Tatwa.

"That's insane!" says editor Christensen of *Star in the East*. "The moon isn't a planet at all, you know, merely the consort of the earth which guides certain solar streams toward this globe."

"Yes, but the moon is the representative of a planet that is being kept secret," says Mrs. Drusse.

"That's correct," says editor Christensen. "But the planet that is being kept secret is simply the earth in its attachment to Saturn. You're confusing Jupiter with the sun in your enumeration of the Tatwas, Mrs. Drusse, because the Occultists called Jupiter 'the old sun.' Blavatsky herself says that the moon is *kama-manasic* in its effects. The astral form is only the interim emanation of the auric egg. To claim otherwise is insane!"

"You're a pedantic bookworm. You're a quote-dropper. You

latch onto the written word. You cling to Madame Blavatsky. You lack feelings and intuition, sir!" Mrs. Drusse says indignantly.

"And you're simply ignorant, madame! You blurt out frivolous babble because you lack serious insight. You cause disarray and do irreparable harm by spreading gossip and mixing up concepts in a superficial and irresponsible manner. It's because of people like you that the ancients thought it advisable to keep occult knowledge secret."

"Ah, you are a Nureddin, my good man. I am an Aladdin-nature. I am spontaneous and let ideas stream into me from without. I can sense what is right. I can take it into myself while my physical consciousness is slumbering. You stand at a lower stage of evolution. You're dependent on coarse physical sensibility. I have lived longer than you and have ascended and become purified through my many lives. I stand closer to the Buddhist plane than you who are still stuck in the mire of the physical plane. I no longer wish to speak with you about these matters. Come back in 10,000 years, then we can discuss things!"

Mrs. Drusse angrily leaves the print shop.

"You've insulted her," says Damascus. "That wasn't right."

"But that female is running around talking nonsense and destroying the whole system!" shouts editor Christensen.

"You mustn't talk about Mrs. Drusse like that. She's a great poetess. And she's an idealist!" says Damascus.

# [ 17 ]

ECCENTRIC PEOPLE WALK in and out of the archway on Stengade. It's a good thing to be an eccentric person and not resemble other people.

There's a man who doesn't know how to ride a bicycle. This makes him an interesting and distinctive individual. He says, "Can you imagine, I don't know how to ride a bicycle!"

And people look at him and say, "Now that's odd! How can that be? Did you ever try?"

"No," says the man. "I never tried." So he's an odd and distinctive individual who stands out from other people because he's never tried to ride a bicycle.

And there's a man who doesn't like to eat meat but prefers vegetables because he thinks they're healthier for the stomach. And because he doesn't eat meat, he is an idealist who is identified with a cause. "I'm an idealist," he says. "I don't eat meat."

A newspaper publishes an interview with the owner of a shoe store who has turned 60. He has sold more shoes than any other shoe dealer. For twenty years he has devoted himself entirely to his business and hasn't allowed himself time for anything else. "He is an idealist," the newspaper writes.

"What do you do in your spare time?" the interviewer asks.

"Spare time? I don't know what spare time is! I've never taken any time off. I haven't read a book in 30 years. When my staff takes time off, I sit doing the accounts and making calculations."

"You've earned a lot of money selling footwear, haven't you?"

"Yes, and everything I've earned, I've put into the business. I've expanded and expanded. I've used the profit to expand even more and buy even more footwear so I could sell even more."

"And what are your wishes for the future on your birthday?"

"My wish is for the business to make an even bigger profit so I can buy even more shoes and sell even more. I don't spend anything on myself. Everything is put into shoes. I devote myself entirely to my business. I'm an idealist!"

There are people who have taught themselves to breathe in a particular way and to fill their lungs completely with air. And they feel that their unique way of breathing is especially healthful and beneficial. Breathing and respiration have become a cause that they fight for and devote themselves to, and it is very important for them to persuade everybody else to breathe in this special way. They have large posters printed at Damascus's shop: LEARN TO BREATHE PROPERLY! And they publish pamphlets and little textbooks and hold classes and study groups. Breathing the right way becomes a religion, a gospel. Society's problems can only be solved by breathing.

But there are other people who feel that only uninhibited sexual expression can liberate humanity and create beneficial conditions in the world. Sexual liberation is the prerequisite for economic liberation. "Get rid of your sexual inhibitions! Then exploitation and oppression will disappear by themselves," they write in *Sex News*. "The struggle for a liberated sex life renders the class struggle superfluous!"

"On the contrary," writes the *Buddhist Emissary*. "Control your urges! Combat desire! Only abstinence and asceticism can liberate people. When we have vanquished our life-will and renounced all earthly pleasures, we bring ourselves into a state of bliss beyond desire and aversion. When we no longer crave something, we no longer miss it, either. It is folly to struggle for higher wages and better housing. When we have obtained these things, we will only want more. Are people happier on suburban Strandvej than in a west-side slum on Saxogade? No. Get to the point where you want nothing! Vanquish desire! Then you will have attained perfect freedom."

"But it is cubism above all else that must blaze the trail for freedom," one man says. And in his writings and speeches he fights for his ideal with great ingenuity. "Cubism has shown us the beauty of little things, of the inexpensive and the simple. A piece of tin and a scrap of newsprint. Everyday pleasures that cost nothing. Cubism has revised our values. It has shown us that a raindrop is just as beautiful as an expensive diamond. It has revolutionized our concepts and made the inexpensive and the despised valuable. Cubism has done away with class distinctions and points ahead to true democracy."

"Don't listen to this petit-bourgeois, reactionary talk!" say the surrealists. "No. Enter the cosmic night with us and forget the worries of this world! We will open up to you the mystical world of dreams and the unconscious. Sail out among aquatic plants and arabesques and float into the ocean of stellar nebulae, where true reality lies, beyond apparent reality. Leave this pseudo-world where people struggle and wear themselves out, and swim out into the transcendental world of dreams!"

"It's 'hot,' it's 'hot,' it's 'hot' that's going to overthrow the old world!" the Jazz-Pol party sings. "Jazz represents a shattering protest against an unjust society. Jazz and dancing will liberate people. Relax those hips! Make them loose and limber! Make your abdomen lithe and supple the way primitive peoples do! That's where you'll find release and deliverance!"

"Esperanto will bring world peace! Esperanto will bring about understanding among peoples. Esperanto is the way to unity and brotherhood and harmony. Esperanto means happiness and peace and prosperity!" say the people who have mastered this language.

"No, no, no, no!" other people shout. "Not Esperanto! Novial! The new, perfect, artificial language that's a thousand times better than Esperanto. Esperantists are frauds! Be a Novialist!"

They have all found their own way to the millennial kingdom starting from their own special interests. They are unselfish and they mean well. Why class struggle? Why economic warfare and wage disputes when salvation can be achieved by contemplating one's own soul? Or by eating raw fruit and vegetables and wearing sandals or speaking Esperanto or painting cubist pictures or dancing to swing music or cultivating an uninhibited sex life? Why all this talk about wages and rent? Economic matters aren't everything, after all. The world can be saved in many different ways. Every single one of these people has his own little special interest that makes class struggle and political activity superfluous.

They are all idealists.

And Damascus prints their idealistic publications so they can be disseminated in the world and be effective and do good.

He likes all of them and appreciates their idealism and their good intentions. Only with student Skodsborg's *Academic Intelligence Journal* is it somewhat difficult for him to make out what the intention is. But it must have a purpose too, because otherwise student Skodsborg's father wouldn't pay to have it printed. And old Consul Skodsborg is an esteemed and well-to-do man who must know what he's doing.

"I've just about had it with that Stalin character," says student Skodsborg. And in his *Academic Intelligence Journal* he puts Stalin in his place; he loses patience with him and points out a number of errors. Student Skodsborg is unrelenting and doesn't know the meaning of forbearance when international politics are involved. He is far to the left of the reddest of the red. He is, in a manner of speaking, ultra-red. Completely beyond the spectrum. And with his "academic intelligence" he adroitly and expeditiously solves the problems that uneducated workers are fumbling helplessly with in their vast country.

He understands how to recruit brilliant associates for his journal, which despite its modest circulation seems to enjoy international esteem. Several professors from Germany write for the journal and make razor-sharp analyses and point out deviations and aberrations from the true doctrine. Even Leon Trotsky over in Mexico is a frequent contributor to student Skodsborg's *Academic Intelligence Journal*.

There is discord and dissension among the idealists. But it is Damascus's conviction that it ought to be possible to gather them all into an altruistic colony. Here they would walk around in idealistic garb and eat simple vegetarian meals together, with mutual esteem and respect for each other's opinions. This is his grand idea, one that he putters with and fantasizes about. He has sketched plans for the colony and has furnished the simple houses and the many small gardens with herbs and flowers. Nothing is standardized or uniform; everything is varied and individual out of consideration for the wishes and tastes of each person. Houses with thatched roofs and houses with flat roofs. Houses in the style of temples and ordinary houses and tents and palatial mansions. Houses constructed in the perfect form of the sphere. Areas for nudists and garden plots for those who eat raw fruit and vegetables. A grandiose and magnificent plan with many small ingenious details. It is his plaything and his diversion. And if someday the money can be found, his plan will become a reality.

If only Danielsen were interested in it.

# [ 18 ]

"I DON'T SUPPOSE you'd know that Danielsen fellow?" says Mr. Sivertsen, B.A., looking fixedly at Damascus.

"Now where would I know him from?"

"You're answering me with another question, Damascus. But God forbid, I don't want to pry."

"You're welcome to ask me about anything you want."

"I see. I am, am I? Uh-huh. Then perhaps I might also ask whether you own a fur coat?"

"A fur coat? No. I don't go around wearing a fur coat. It's much too hot now anyway."

"But do you own a fur coat? A person can certainly own a fur coat even though he isn't wearing it."

"What would I do with a fur coat? I couldn't imagine myself dressing in the skin of another living being. I wouldn't be a party to having an animal flayed so I could keep warm."

"You never give a direct answer to my questions. You're avoiding me and evading the issue!"

"I don't understand what you mean."

"Why, exactly, do you call yourself Damascus?" says Mr. Sivertsen, B.A., giving the little printer a piercing look.

"Why, I do it because it's what I'm called. Damascus is my name, after all."

"Don't you have some other name?"

"No, no other last name."

"And you aren't fond of using a pseudonym on certain occasions?"

"Now why should I do that?"

"It is a remarkable and noteworthy fact that the name 'Damascus' begins with a 'D'!"

"Well, what on earth should it begin with? You can't spell it any other way. I can't imagine why you'd criticize me for that."

" 'D' is actually a very interesting letter," says editor Christensen of *Star in the East*. "In the Hebraic alphabet the sign called *daleth* corresponds to the Latin 'D.' It is the seventh letter

81

in that alphabet. And *daleth* represents the third of the seven spirits of God, whereas the first four letters represent the four elements, or the unmanifest Divine Father, the manifest Father, the Mother, and the Son. The Son is *aleph*—which corresponds to the second letter in *Damascus* and the first letter in the Latin alphabet, but the fourth letter in the Hebraic."

"Oh, is that the way it is?" Sivertsen sneers. "You have a unique ability, Mr. Christensen, of talking about something else and spreading fog when people want clear and unambiguous information. I won't let myself be duped by the tricks you gentlemen employ."

"Why are you being so testy, Mr. Sivertsen?" says Damascus. "Certainly no one has insulted you. You're not at all yourself. What on earth is wrong with you?"

"I don't think I'm the one there's something wrong with, ha ha! I can see that there are things going on here that I'm supposed to be kept in the dark about!" Sivertsen shrieks. "There's some chicanery and mystery here. I think you'd just as soon be rid of me. And you won't give my questions a direct answer. Well, all right! I know how to take precautionary measures!"

"But I don't understand a bit of this," says editor Christensen. "When I say that the Latin 'D' corresponds to *daleth* and that it's the seventh letter in the Hebraic alphabet, there can't be anything insulting or objectionable about that. And if you'd like to know—"

"I *wouldn't* like to know!" Sivertsen shouts, foaming. "Stop spewing out words! I'm not going to annoy you gentlemen with my presence. I'll go elsewhere, where people have more confidence in me and aren't in collusion."

"No," says Damascus, "stay here. And explain what you mean and what you're mad about. I don't understand a word of any of this. What is it you want to know?"

"Will you answer two questions for me? Directly and without beating around the bush?"

"Yes, of course. If I can."

"You can!"

"Well, what is it?"

"Answer me honestly, Damascus, or whatever your name is. Are you interested in the fight against the disease called cancer?"

"Yes, I truly am. I'm very interested in the fight against cancer, or rather in its prevention. Because it's a disease that can be prevented if one follows a vegetarian diet—"

"Say no more! Thank you, that's fine. Now here's the second question: Are you interested in the fight against tuberculosis?"

"Of course I am. It's the same with tuberculosis as with cancer. Food means everything. A low-salt, vegetarian diet—"

"Thank you, thank you, that's enough! Will you permit me to ask you one more question? Are you so interested in the fight against these two diseases, or their prevention, that you would sacrifice something for it? Would you, for instance, give your fortune for these causes? Yes or no?"

"But I don't *have* a fortune."

"Answer me yes or no! Would you, if you had a fortune—or if you had had a fortune, which you possibly no longer have because you have already donated it to what we are talking about—would you give it to—"

"I don't understand what you mean."

"Answer yes or no! Would you, in this instance, bequeath it to these purposes?"

"Yes, I certainly would. I would gladly give money for the fight against cancer and tuberculosis if I had the money. But why are you asking me about this?"

"Thank you! You did indeed answer with a clear 'yes'! Fine. I wonder if anyone among those present can now tell me who this mysterious, so-called Danielsen is?"

"I can't tell you," says Damascus.

"You don't want to tell me! But I wonder if other people might not be able to guess?"

"I know who Danielsen is," says Olsen.

"Do you know, Olsen?" says Damascus.

"Yes, of course Olsen knows," says Sivertsen.

"Well, who is it then, Olsen?" says Damascus.

"Yes, Olsen. You tell us, since Damascus doesn't want to!" Sivertsen shouts.

"He's a big fake," says Olsen. "But I think I'll keep my mouth shut until the time is right. You're a pretty smart man, Mr. Sivertsen, B.A. But that doesn't necessarily mean you know everything."

# [ 19 ]

Mrs. Drusse, the poetess, has been staring into a Chinese crystal ball and has seen some strange things. For example, she has seen a little man with friendly blue eyes going around giving away large bundles of banknotes. She thinks she knows the man. She doesn't keep her suspicions to herself but tells them to everybody who is interested.

The mood is somber in the little print shop on Stengade. Damascus feels that he is surrounded by coldness and mistrust. And Olsen is walking around smiling quietly to himself. He knows something.

Letters are disappearing from the type case, and Damascus is having a hard time finding enough letters to go around. *Buddhist Emissary* is being typeset. The next issue of *Nudist News* is waiting impatiently. Sivertsen is proofreading GYP, which stands for Geography, Yield, and Purchase, and which will one day be a significant factor in public life. *Sex News* is already on the press and will be sent to the bindery tomorrow, and after that on to the people who will be freed from their inhibitions and complexes. In spite of its missing letters, the little print shop is working and sending its messages out into the world.

People come and go on Stengade. With bills and new manuscripts and new ideas. An old tailor comes by bicycle all the way from Præstø to have some tracts printed because Damascus is cheaper than the local printer. The tailor's name is Henningsen, and he is also a religious fundamentalist and idealist who has done great and selfless work for the Salvation Army and the Prisoners' Aid Society.

He gives Olsen a friendly hello and asks him how things are going, and whether he's making sure to live a respectable life now and is giving his heart to Jesus.

"I am," says Olsen.

Old Henningsen has twice gotten Olsen a job and another chance in life. The first time was as a servant on an estate in the vicinity of Præstø. The second was in Damascus's print shop. "Now I hope you won't disappoint me, Olsen!"

Henningsen was able to save Olsen because Henningsen's son is an assistant warden at the penitentiary and recommended Olsen to old Henningsen's care.

Sometimes Olsen has dreams at night about Assistant Warden Henningsen. A flabby little man who felt inferior because of his small stature and who was afraid of the prisoners and was therefore brutal and vindictive. Olsen knew how to handle him. He had the ability to adapt and take care of himself. He possessed what Henningsen called "prison etiquette." But other prisoners, who didn't have Olsen's talents, weren't so well off. Little Henningsen was good at giving them disciplinary punishments and additional penalties, and he knew how to make their lives miserable if they lacked prison etiquette.

"It's marvelous to see that Olsen is on the straight and narrow," old Henningsen the tailor says to Damascus.

"Olsen is all right. He's not bad by nature. He's just a little weak," says Damascus.

"But Jesus will give him strength!" says old Henningsen. He is sitting in one of the red chairs. It's a long way to bicycle from Præstø to Copenhagen, and he is tired.

"Is it really worth it to ride your bicycle so far?" asks Damascus. "Don't you have more wear and tear on your bicycle than the train ticket would cost?"

"I've always been accustomed to saving money," the old tailor replies. "I scrimped and saved so I could keep my boy at his studies. I've gotten it in my blood. I suppose I could have bought a ticket for the railroad, but it irks me to spend money that can be saved for something better."

"But you can't ride back today. You'll have to spend the night in the city, won't you?"

"Yes. I'll spend the night at a little temperance-league hotel. It costs money, but it's still a lot less than a round-trip train ticket would cost."

"Couldn't you stay with your son? It's not that far down to where he lives, is it?"

"He has an official residence down there at the penitentiary.

But I really don't want to bother him there. My clothes aren't very nice, you know, and besides my son doesn't like me to visit him. Sometimes I meet him in Copenhagen, and we go to a milk bar together. And of course he does come to Præstø on his vacations to visit his old father. But he doesn't really want me visiting down where he lives. He has to take so many things into consideration and think of his position and his career and everything. It's not as if he was ashamed of his father, though. But he does have to consider what other people think."

"Yes, I see," says Damascus, being considerate and not wanting to offend the old man by criticizing his son.

"I suppose it's all right for me to eat my sandwich here?" asks Henningsen, taking out a small package. He says a short blessing over his lunch and eats it with a hearty appetite. Salami and liverwurst, which are made out of dead animals and are an abomination to Damascus.

"I don't understand why you want to eat animals that have been killed," Damascus says. "Now why aren't you a vegetarian, Henningsen? You're usually such an idealist."

"Oh fiddle-faddle and folderol! Of course the good Lord created animals for us to eat. I don't like vegetables at all. My system can't take them. I'm over 70 now, and I'm fit and healthy on the diet that I eat. You wouldn't have a glass of water, would you, Damascus?"

"Of course," says Damascus, getting out a glass. "Just drink water. It's a healthy drink."

"Yes, it's marvelously refreshing. Did you know that Squire Skjern-Svendsen of Frydenholm down where I live, who is a very wealthy man, never drinks anything but water with his meals? And he certainly could afford to stock a wine cellar."

"That's very sensible of him. Could he be an idealist?"

"Yes, he certainly is an idealist. I know him very well. As a matter of fact, I visit him at his castle, and he says, 'Please sit down, Henningsen,' and talks to me as one friend to another. He's a magnificent man. And he's been good to the evangelical cause."

"I don't think he was very good to Olsen when he was a servant down there. There was some trouble about his pay."

"The squire is a strict man. And he's a thrifty man who

doesn't let anything go to waste. Olsen is a weak person. You even say that yourself. And I can tell you in confidence that there was something about a silver spoon that the squire found in Olsen's pocket. For my sake, he didn't want to press charges, and he even let Olsen keep his job. But Olsen himself wanted to leave. Unfortunately, he took off prematurely."

"I don't think the squire treated Olsen right."

"Oh yes he did, you can be sure of that. The squire was patient and forbearing. And the reason I didn't leave Olsen to his own devices when he took off was because my son asked me to look after Olsen. He really liked him when he was in the penitentiary. Olsen told him what the other prisoners were saying and things like that. And in return my son got Olsen special treatment. He asked me to look after Olsen and help him onto the straight and narrow."

"I'm very sorry to hear that. I wouldn't have thought that of Olsen, that he would have been some kind of spy toward his fellow prisoners. Yes, Olsen is truly very weak. But it was also wrong of your son to use him like that."

"You don't know life in prison, Damascus. You don't know what the people are like that my son has to take care of. If he isn't on his guard, he could risk being murdered at any moment. He has to deal with depraved and vicious people. Strict discipline is needed to keep their respect."

"Well, I think all people are good at heart," says Damascus.

"If that's the way things are, why do you think God created hell, where there will be weeping and gnashing of teeth through all eternity?"

"I don't believe in hell," says Damascus.

"No, I know you don't. You don't have the faith, Damascus. You have thoughts and ideas, but you lack the faith, which is the only thing necessary. It will be hardest on you if you continue on in your obstinacy. Not even you will be able to avoid perdition and eternal torment!"

"That's not kind and humane talk," says Damascus. "And those words aren't like the words of Christ. But I don't wish to offend your faith. And I don't wish to discuss these questions. I know you're a good person. And an idealist."

# [ 20 ]

PEOPLE ARE WHISPERING about Damascus. And he's the object of conjecture and speculation.

For instance, there's the brother they know Damascus has in America. Actually, there's nothing to prevent a brother like that from dying and leaving Damascus a lot of money.

They know that Damascus hasn't had any contact with his brother. And Mr. Sivertsen, B.A., who has been to America and knows the way things are over there, explains that the reason for the bad relationship between the brothers is the simple fact that Damascus's brother is a butcher. In a way he's actually something even worse than that. He's the director of a firm that makes meat extracts and bouillon cubes. He is, in a manner of speaking, a mass butcher and the direct cause of the deaths of thousands of innocent cattle, and he has poisoned vast areas of the world by exporting his extract and cubes, which are the concentrated products of the corpses of all those dead animals. That's what Damascus's brother is like. It's understandable and commendable that Damascus doesn't want to correspond with him.

Now if this brother were to die over in America and didn't leave any heirs, there would be nothing to prevent Damascus from inheriting his fortune. And since it would naturally be impossible for an idealistic person to use that kind of blood money, it would be understandable if he gave it to a good and idealistic cause, in order to atone somewhat for the sins of the money's previous owner.

But why give the money to institutions that just support the scientific establishment? Why not support some of the movements that operate in spite of the prejudices of science? Who will guarantee that the money given to the Cancer Foundation won't be used for vivisection and thus result in even greater crimes than those the ill-starred extract manufacturer from America was guilty of?

But why act on the sly? Why hide the truth from your friends and sympathizers? Why this masquerade with the name Danielsen? Such lack of candor and openness comes close to being outright skulduggery.

Damascus feels the coldness and the hostility around him. This is a difficult time for him. He had wanted to borrow 100 kroner from Sivertsen. He's done it before and repaid it punctually too. But under these circumstances, Sivertsen doesn't want to lend out any money. "Wouldn't you rather lend *me* a couple of thousand kroner?" he says bitterly, glowering at Damascus.

"I'd like to very much, if I could," Damascus says.

"Ha, ha!" says Sivertsen maliciously.

And Olsen walks around smiling. He knows something. But he keeps quiet.

"Do you really know who this Danielsen is?" Damascus asks.

"Of course I know," says Olsen, "But I don't think I'll be telling anyone. I'm going to be watching to make sure that nobody pulls any tricks."

Olsen is up to something himself. Damascus looks at him with apprehension. This constant smiling isn't a good sign. And when Olsen asks if he can have a few days off, because there's something he has to do in the provinces, Damascus doesn't like it at all. "We're actually pretty busy right now. Can't you wait until next week, Olsen?"

Olsen wouldn't mind a small advance on his salary either. Just 20 kroner or so. But Damascus doesn't have it. "Well, maybe you could at least spare me 10 øre for a stamp?" says Olsen.

Damascus doesn't have 10 øre. But he's sure he has a 10-øre stamp. He remembers that there was one in his desk drawer. And if somebody hasn't taken it, it must still be there.

"I don't steal your stamps," says Olsen.

"Nobody's saying you do either, Olsen."

"No, but you insinuate and imply that I do."

Damascus finds the stamp. And Olsen writes a letter. He is secretive, holding his hand over it so nobody can see what he's writing. The letter is addressed to a well-known man who once helped Olsen when things looked pretty bad. That was when he was homeless and sleeping in railroad cars and empty piano cases.

The day is long and difficult, with none of the cheerful conversations and exchanges of ideas that Damascus is so fond of. He looks at people with his friendly blue eyes, but they avoid his gaze, and their faces are hard, and they whisper in the corners. And when they do talk, their words are full of dark innuendoes and accusations. This is an intolerable situation.

The little print shop is no longer a club and a sanctuary and a forum. It is just as dismal as his home on Kapelvej. And if Mrs. Drusse hadn't seen something in her crystal ball, and if "Damascus" hadn't started with the same letter as "Danielsen," and if he weren't a short man with kindly blue eyes and gray hair, things wouldn't have developed the way they did. One thing is intertwined with another, and everything is mysteriously interconnected.

Damascus putters about in his print shop cleaning things up and putting things away, while Olsen tidies up at the wash basin and puts on his nice summer suit. Damascus washes the printer's ink off his hands and sticks his little bare feet in his galoshes. He walks down the iron staircase with Olsen. "Now do be careful, Olsen," he says. "Don't get mixed up in anything risky. I'll certainly try to get the money for you tomorrow or the day after. Just don't do anything foolish, Olsen."

"If I can't get the money from you, I'll have to try to get it from somebody else," Olsen says, looking somber and ominous. "This is money I have to have. It will multiply and come back many times over. You can be sure of that."

"I'll get it for you, Olsen. But just don't do anything rash. I beg you!"

"I won't guarantee a thing," Olsen says darkly. "And if anything should go wrong, it's your fault because you wouldn't lend me the lousy 20 kroner!"

"You'll get it tomorrow. I promise you, Olsen."

"It'll probably be too late by then," says Olsen.

Damascus walks home along Kapelvej, where everything is green and pleasant. Things are happening around him that he doesn't understand. He is full of worry and anxiety. And up in his apartment his wife and daughter are waiting for him with new recriminations.

The blackbirds are singing so beautifully in Assistens Cemetery, which looks like the Garden of Eden with its blossoming trees and pale-green weeping willows and drooping birches and dark green cypresses. The smell of the lilacs drifts all the way out to the street. Maybe he should walk through there and breathe a little fresh air and gather a little strength and peace of mind before facing the reproaches and sullenness at home.

Damascus goes into the cemetery. And Olsen heads for the inner city, where he has his hangouts and can meet his cronies. There are certain plans he has to get ready. He has a letter that he drops in the mailbox. And if he can just get hold of 20 kroner, he'll be able to accomplish something important.

# THE VILLAGE

## [ 21 ]

THE YELLOW BUS drives through the village. Between small whitewashed houses, picket fences, and gardens. It stops at garden gates and picks up passengers. Down at the inn it turns around and drives back.

The driver knows the names of everybody along his route. Once in a while he stops to toss a package off in front of a picket fence. One cardboard box is making peeping sounds; these are day-old chicks for Panty Marius, and they have to be delivered with care. It takes a little while before Marius manages to find the money, because he's dull and slow and has to keep wiping the snot from his nose all the time.

There's a storage battery for Martin Olsen's radio that has been in for recharging. It's expensive to listen to the radio when you don't have electricity in your house and have to keep changing wet- and dry-cell batteries. Martin's house is located beside the reservoir. The bus driver sets the heavy storage battery in the grass, beeps the horn, and drives on.

The bus stops at the crossroads and picks up schoolchildren. They have a long way to go to the grammar school, and they have heavy schoolbags full of books, notebooks, and learning. They have already taken a number of exams and still have many left to take, because it's impossible to be anything without taking exams. They study their lessons in the bus and practice their word lists and vocabulary exercises. "They're getting so damned smart," the bus driver says.

They ride along close to the little houses, peeking into living rooms and talking about this and that and what's going on in the world. Baker Andersen's house is just about finished now. It must be one of these modernistic houses, with a porch and a flat roof and picture windows. It's got to be elegant and modern, of course, if Andersen is building it. But Mrs. Andersen is really the one who wants it elegant. She's, well, a little unusual and a little better than other people. And they're probably going to put in a real toilet with a flushing mechanism and a septic tank and the works. It is almost sacrilegious, though, to let all that expensive fertilizer disappear down a hole. A chamber pot is a darn good thing for a garden. Especially when you apply it properly and use it sparingly. Old Emma had leeks *this big around* in her garden! And she never used anything but the little bit she got from her own chamber pot. No sir, it's just a matter of proper application.

It looks as if an entire housing development is going to go up out here near baker Andersen's house. Rasmus Larsen's house has been finished for some time now. And it sure is a nice home Rasmus has got. A red-brick house with an outside staircase and a terrace and a rock garden and a flagpole in the middle of the lawn. It's quite luxurious. Who would have thought that Rasmus used to be a red socialist and a real dangerous character to have walking around town? Now he's chairman of the trade union and has a desk and a telephone and official rubber stamps, and the unemployed have to come to his house to register. Some of them gripe that they have to stand outside and wait in the wind and rain. But you really can't blame Mrs. Larsen for not wanting to have them all in her living room messing up her new floor.

Things are going on in the world that people are bound to discuss. For instance, it so happens that Panty Marius has gotten himself a new housekeeper. She's actually not too bad looking. Still, it must be weird to live in the house of somebody like that. He's probably harmless enough. But still it's spooky and strange when he roams around at night that way with his lurid inclinations. That new housekeeper had better be real careful with her own panties. She'd probably better lock her chest of drawers, hee hee hee!—And she won't dare hang her clothes out to dry near the house. She'll probably have to send them to the steam laundry in Præstø. There are a lot of weird things going on. It's not because Marius isn't a pretty decent fellow otherwise. He doesn't swear or anything. And he's religious too, and goes to the evangelical meeting house and that sort of thing.

It was after the new pastor came that Panty Marius became religious. Because that pastor is sure energetic. Now take the way he got the young people to go along with him! All the young girls have to be in this YD thing now. And that certainly can't hurt. It's a real pleasure to see them bicycling off in their uniforms. So straight-backed and cheerful. And how they can sing! It keeps their minds off other things. Because young people really do have so many ideas in their heads these days, and all they think about is dancing and sex. It's good for them to have a few diversions.

He sure is good at it, that Pastor Nørregaard-Olsen. And just as down-to-earth as a regular person. And the parsonage is in the process of being remodeled now too. It *is* an old building, and it probably does need to be modernized. They say it's going to cost 40,000 kroner. That *is* a lot of money. But the pastor is going to pay for the porch out of his own pocket. And a lot of other things are going to be installed. An electric kitchen and an electric pump and all that. There'll be rooms on the second floor too. And some of the rooms on the first floor are going to be combined so they'll be like ballrooms. And a new driveway with a stone curb and a sidewalk. And a garage that will be dug out of the hillside so it'll look like an ancient burial mound.

But things do have to look elegant now, since the squire visits the parsonage. And by the way, the squire is building an ancient burial mound up in the cemetery too. Something like that really costs money! It's supposed to be so gorgeous inside. With bronze and marble and artwork. Of course it's good to have something like that built, so people will have something to dig up in a thousand years to show tourists how people lived in our time.

Something like that prehistoric burial mound probably costs quite a bit of money, with its granite and grillework and tiles and ceramics. But he's got plenty of money for it. It's almost as if everything the man touches turns to money. He's a squire, but he's a lot of other things too. He's a nationally known man. It's a blessing to have a man like that in the community.

People talk about him on the bus. And they talk about him in the small houses along the road. The village ends at the castle. It looks as if the road doesn't go any farther than the wrought-iron gate. There are ramparts and moats all around the red castle. And an enormous park that merges into the woods behind it.

At one time, the lord of the manor probably owned the whole village and surrounding area with its houses and farms and animals and people.

Things aren't like that anymore. People have been set free and aren't owned by anyone. The practices of compulsory servitude and serfdom and villeinage are things of the past. People own their own houses, as long as they pay their mortgage installments, interest, and service fees. They are protected by the Constitution and safeguarded by social legislation. They have the right to vote and can elect anyone they want to the government. Their residences are inviolable and their persons are unassailable.

But the castle is still there. Red, massive, and dominant. People don't have to pay their tributes to the lord of the manor, but the squire is the director of the savings and loan association, and everybody owes him money anyway. He is a factory owner and an employer. Several hundred families are dependent on him. Compulsory servitude and villeinage are things of the past, but when the workers at the Præstø clothing factory were discontented and laid down their tools, a law was passed decreeing that they had to continue working and be content.

Power still radiates from the old castle, which has been restored and repaired and brought back to its original form. It sits there dark, massive, and dominant at the end of the road. The other buildings are low and insignificant beside it, even though the doctor's villa and baker Andersen's new house rise above the average.

The village is one long street. From the crooked clay-walled building that the county has leased from the squire for use as a poorhouse, to the historic inn and the parsonage. There are two electric lamps for street lighting, and in front of the new houses there is a little sidewalk with gravel and curbing.

A feeble-minded girl is walking down the street. She has a blue hospital dress on and bare, thin, crooked arms. She has a whole bunch of barrettes in her straight yellow hair. She is talking to herself and laughing, and her nose is running.

# [ 22 ]

"WHERE ARE YOU GOING, Jenny?" somebody asks.

"Hee hee!" Jenny answers.

"You're not supposed to be running around loose like this, you know. Didn't they tell you that over at the institution?"

"Ooh, yeah."

"What was it they told you at the institution?"

"They told me I shouldn't be with men, hee hee."

"And what'll happen if you get together with men?"

"Then I won't go to heaven."

"Blow your nose, Jenny. It's running." And Jenny wipes her wet nose with the back of her hand.

"What's that you have in your hand?"

"Hee hee, it's mine!" And she holds up a 2-øre piece.

"Who'd you get that from?"

"Hee, it's mine."

"May I have it?"

"No! No!" She hides her hand behind her back.

She's bent over like an old woman, and she sticks out her arms like an insect. And when she walks past Niels Madsen's farm, she slinks cautiously over to the other side of the road, holding her hands in front of her face, and runs by quickly. People have a lot of fun watching her sneak past Niels Madsen's farm.

She was once contracted out by the county, and Niels Madsen was willing to take her on for 50 kroner a month back then. That really wasn't too much money, because a feeble-minded person like her can eat an awful lot. But of course the idea was for her to help out on the farm a little and do some chores for her food. Then Niels Madsen could save money on a farm hand. But Jenny got a crooked back because maybe she went at things too hard. And maybe she didn't get enough of those vitamins either. Then one day she ran away and hid in the woods. That was when she was sent to the institution.

It says "H x" on the blue dress that was issued to her at the institution. Those are the letters for a quiet, well-behaved section. But there was also a bad section where the inmates had to stay in bed and had gloves put on them and were given shots when they were disobedient. Jenny was always obedient and she was in the well-behaved "H x" section. And she was allowed to come home for visits and vacations. Now she's come home for good and has been given permission to stay. As long as she doesn't walk along the roads alone and as long as she stays away from men. She'll make sure to stay away from men because otherwise she won't go to heaven. But she can certainly walk along the roads alone. She's obedient and peaceful. And her mother can't watch her all the time. She has enough to do and she's old. She's had twelve children, and four of them are feebleminded. That's probably because her husband drank.

They've been an expensive family for the county. But of course that's the way it is these days; all the trash has to be kept alive, but they won't do any work and aren't good for anything. "It's the system!" says Niels Madsen. "It's almost getting so that other people can't get by!"

These are lean times for agriculture. Niels Madsen owns 80 acres of land, but he can show that his property can't pay for itself, that he's losing money and pouring more into it every single year. Those smart people in their offices up in Copenhagen seem to think that things can keep on like this. But they've got to have their tax payments right down to the last øre. You pay and pay, and your money goes to welfare.

Those smart people talk about idleness and unemployment and so on and so forth, but have they tried hiring a farm hand? Farm hands show up with their wage scales and their trade unions and make all sorts of claims and demands. And there's a farm workers' law that stipulates that there has to be wallpaper in the farm hands' rooms and there have to be windows and wood floors. Then when you do pay what they demand, the farm hand runs out on you at a bad time because he doesn't like the food and would rather lie in bed snoring than do any work. And he can get just as much on welfare as he can earn by working. That's the way the system is. Just wait, though! The system can't keep on like that. There are other countries where they've taught people to work! And if we can't straighten out our own "system people" here at home, maybe they'll come and help us put our affairs in order. Niels Madsen looks south and sniffs at the wind blowing from that direction.

Since it was impossible to hire a farm hand, Niels Madsen had girls as helpers. He's had both feeble-minded girls and fallen women from the asylums and shelters. He didn't really get an awful lot for it. But he did save money on farm hands and was able to operate his farm with a fallen woman as the foreman and a feeble-minded one as the feed master and a couple of girls as farm hands. And of course they got enough to eat and learned how to do some work and were allowed to sit in the living room when the inspection team came by. Besides, nobody really takes as gospel the stories that a feeble-minded girl thinks up.

But then Jenny happened to run off and hide in the woods. Over at the institution they discovered that she was under-nourished and had been neglected. But then you can't look fat and well-cared-for when you've been living in the woods like a latter-day Svend Gjønge either. It came close to being a scandal and a newspaper story. But Niels Madsen was known as a God-fearing and upright man, and the pastor and the parish council and the inspection team could vouch for him.

But in the future he didn't want to have anything to do with taking on these wayward girls. He had done it inexpensively enough, but he got aggravation and ingratitude in return. Then too, his wife didn't like having all those girls in the house. Since they were loose girls and all that.

Now he runs his farm with boys from the reformatory. He gets 3 kroner a day for each boy who learns agriculture from him. On the other hand, the boys are supposed to get 50 øre a week in wages from him in addition to their meals.

Things go much better with the boys than with the girls. They're big and strong and can do more work. And he can get his 50 øre back when he imposes small fines on them for the misdemeanors they commit. After all, you have to keep in mind that these boys are criminal degenerates who have to be dealt with firmly.

Niels Madsen is a member of the church council and the school board. His wife is a member of the ladies' sewing circle and is a regular visitor at the parsonage. They are esteemed and respected people. And Jenny is the only one who is afraid of them and holds her hands up in front of her face when she slinks past their farm.

# [ 23 ]

THESE SMALL HOUSES with their low hedges and little picket fences are set close to each other. And the people who live in them know a lot about one another and can keep an eye on what everybody else is doing, so they're never completely alone.

Still, they're all lonely individuals. Panty Marius has a house-keeper now, and people wonder what he can possibly find to say to her and what it must be like for a woman to be a live-in servant for Panty Marius. But Marius doesn't say a word to her. They sit at the table across from each other eating, and Marius makes sure he doesn't inadvertently look at her.

"Would you like some more?" she asks.

"Oh yes, please," says Marius. Then he looks down into his porridge dish and eats and doesn't say a thing. And in the evening she says good night and goes into her room and goes to sleep. And Marius sits quietly on a chair eating hard candy, and nothing happens. But people look in the direction of their small windows and speculate about the juicy things that might be going on inside and about just what kind of a person this new housekeeper is.

And there's Niels Madsen, who owns a good farm and is fat and well-to-do; he has workers and manpower enough and gets paid for it to boot. Every Sunday he sits in church with his wife, who looks nice and elegant with her fur collar and handbag and black hat with feathers on it. Afterwards Pastor Nørregaard-Olsen says hello to them in the churchyard, shaking their hands and saying "Ma'am" to Niels's wife. And people see Niels Madsen and his wife walk home with each other arm in arm. But at night they lie down in their double bed with their backs turned to each other and don't say good night. They take no joy or pleasure in anything and have to swallow pills to get to sleep. They've been married for twenty years and they don't have any children. Maybe they never really did anything to have any either. They have boys from the children's home in their house, and the boys eat at the table as if they were the family's own children. Niels's wife dishes up potatoes and starchy gravy to them, and her husband watches to make sure that they're not getting any of the smoked pork. There's not enough money for pork too, out of the 3 kroner a day they get for one of these boys. And besides they say on the radio that meat really isn't good for you. Especially not for children. Niels Madsen says grace and blesses the potatoes and the white starchy sauce and gives thanks for their gifts. Other than that there's no talking at the table. Order and respect prevail.

Niels Madsen is a lonely man in the midst of it all. His nerves are bad, and his face twitches. And as he walks along, he might just turn around suddenly to see whether one of the boys is sticking his tongue out at him. He has money in the bank and supplies and hams and brine tubs of preserved meat. His cows have shiny coats and are tuberculosis-free and give milk with a high fat content. But he has his annoyances and worries too. Impertinent people have gotten involved in his private affairs, and if it weren't for the fact that Pastor Nørregaard-Olsen was the chairman of the Child Welfare Agency, they might have taken the boys from the children's home away from him.

Niels Madsen's farm is well maintained and freshly white-washed with tarred half-timbering and footing. His hedge is attractively trimmed, and his yard is weeded and raked all the way out to the blacktop on the highway. There are pretty curtains in his windows and red geraniums in decorative flower pots. It looks so friendly from the road. A genuinely homey Danish farm. "The boys who go to a place like that are fortunate!" they say at the Child Welfare Agency.

Next door is Jens Olsen's farm, which is also neat and well maintained. Jens Olsen always has such good luck with his pigs. He's good to his animals and will stand and caress a sow for a long time, fondling her teats and saying "old girl" to her.

Beside Jens Olsen's farm is the fire reservoir, with green duckweed and frogs and fat white ducks in it. On the other side

of the pond, Jens Olsen owns a clay-walled house that he has rented out to a man whose name is also Olsen. His first name is Martin, and he's not related to Jens Olsen. Martin is really a decent and capable person even though his opinions might be a little drastic. But that will probably change. Rasmus Larsen was wild and went to extremes once too, and they called him Red Ras, but now he's a chairman, level-headed and calm; someday he'll probably even get into the parish council. It helps to get older. Martin is only 25. But he does have a wife and four children, and he has to slave hard to keep everything afloat. It's lucky for him that he has such low rent and that Jens Olsen is a good-natured landlord, who occasionally comes over and says "Kitchy-kitchy" to the baby in the buggy.

Farther on down the road is the "villa section" with the doctor's large white villa and baker Andersen's new modernistic house that's so new-fangled and peculiar that only a lady like Mrs. Andersen could think it up. And Rasmus Larsen's house with its flagpole where he raises the Danish flag on national holidays.

Then there's the grocery store and the dairy shop, where they've got a new dairyman named Oscar from Copenhagen. And there's the gardener's little shop with flowers and vegetables from the squire's garden. The gardener is a pious man who thinks of the Kingdom of God and goes to Bible study and the coffee fellowship hour at the evangelical meeting house. He is a serious, silent, and withdrawn man.

The little houses are set close together. Only the castle lies completely apart, with ramparts and moats and old linden trees surrounding it. And Squire Skjern-Svendsen is probably lonelier than anyone else, too.

People know so little about him. They see him riding by in his car and turn around to watch the car and say, "Yep, there he goes."

Small and lonely, he sits in the back seat of his car and doesn't talk to his chauffeur. The chauffeur is also his servant, a silent and taciturn man with a smooth, expressionless face. His name is Lukas, and people know that he was once in prison and that he did dreadful things. He is the only servant in the huge castle, and they don't get any information out of him. Before him there was a servant whose name was Olsen. He had been in prison too, and probably went back to prison because he stole some of the squire's silver. Now it seems he's in Copenhagen, according to what people say.

It's probably out of goodness and compassion that the squire takes people who have done time under his wing and gives them employment in his house. After all, they say he does good deeds in secret and is interested in the Salvation Army and the Prisoners' Aid Society and other charitable organizations.

They know that the pastor is a regular visitor at the castle. And Henningsen, the old tailor from Præstø, who is a religious fundamentalist and the author of small religious pamphlets, often comes over on his bicycle for a visit. He's probably a friend of the squire's from the days when he only had a small shop that sold ribbons and thread. Old Henningsen is interested in all kinds of charities and the rehabilitation of wayward girls and the Prisoners' Aid Society. He has a son who is on the staff of a prison and who can point out the prisoners who have behaved well and deserve to be helped.

The tailor from Præstø may be the squire's only friend. So few guests come to the castle, and the squire isn't interested in entertaining. He doesn't even drink wine, and he doesn't smoke either.

He rides around in his car looking after his numerous enterprises. To Præstø, to Vordingborg, and to Næstved. He has factories and establishments everywhere, and he needs a good head on his shoulders to keep track of it all.

They rarely see him. But they feel his presence everywhere. When they buy a pair of navy pants or a suit of overalls, the clothing is from his factory. And when they pay their interest and service fees on their property, it is to the Præstø Savings, Loan, and Mortgage Association, which he directs. And when they are looking for work or want to buy firewood in the woods or peat in the bog or vegetables at the store, they run into the squire everywhere.

They feel his presence but they don't know him. They know practically nothing about him. But they can certainly talk about him even though they don't know a thing. They can certainly talk about his wife too, because it's a good bet that not everything is the way it should be between her and the squire.

She is delicate and aristocratic, and people have to wonder

why she chose a husband so far beneath her station, who once ran around on the roads as an ordinary Jutland wool peddler. But she probably chose him because of religion. They say that when she was young she wanted to study for the ministry and go out into the world and become a missionary to the savages. And they say that she really wanted to die for her religion and be eaten by cannibals. To each his own. She always was rather high-strung. But her parents wouldn't hear of this business with the cannibals, so she had to settle for evangelical work at home. And that's where she met the wool dealer and married beneath her station. Not that he isn't a capable man, with enough money and enough land and the resources to buy a couple of castles, so she didn't have to suffer any hardship.

But they really don't get along well with each other; there are scenes and melodramas and arguments almost every day, according to the maids. And there certainly isn't much left of her Christian faith either, because she never goes to church but makes the squire sit alone in his reserved pew.

The castle sits there—huge, red, forbidding, and historic. With thick walls and tiny windows. Frydenholm—"Isle of Delight"—is its name, but not everything is all that delightful up there.

Surrounding the castle are the park and the nursery. At an appropriate distance is the actual working farm—with a huge barn and elegant stables and machinery—and the manager's residence and garden. Along with little clay-walled houses for the workers, the feed master, and the herdsman. The long, low clay-walled house farthest away is leased out to the county as a poorhouse. Four entire families with a lot of children live here. This is where feeble-minded Jenny lives with her eight brothers and sisters, as well as her mother, who has bad legs. And there are even a few more children at the Institution for the Mentally Retarded that the county has to pay for too. That way it's not hard to make taxpayers' money go down the drain. That's obviously what it's all about these days. "It's the system," says Niels Madsen.

And Jenny runs around on the road not doing any work. Even though she's simple-minded, she could still make herself a little useful in return for her food, couldn't she? There are so many weird things going on these days. There are young people bicycling around putting bad ideas in people's heads and wanting to have the Athletic Association reestablished. Lord only knows whether Martin, who lives out there next door to Jens Olsen, isn't one of them. He was such an avid soccer player once. And once he was fresh and impudent and talked back to the pastor. "That's the kind of person we prefer not to have too many of in Denmark!" the pastor said.

Rasmus Larsen, who used to be called Red Ras, has to admit that the pastor is right; he is furious at Martin for his opposition within the union. Rasmus himself is the chairman of it, and he recognizes his responsibility and the limits of what's possible and knows what was achieved in the old days. He knows that now is not the time to be making demands. The main thing now is to hold on to the gains made in the past. If Martin isn't able to understand this, it's because he is a man of dissension and has an un-Danish frame of mind.

There are conflicts and antagonisms in the little village. And dissatisfaction with a number of things. That's the way the system is. "But maybe someday they'll come and teach people how to work in this country," says Niels Madsen. He has gotten himself some long black boots and a leather belt and a military cap and is waiting for the new times to come.

At night that crazy Panty Marius goes sneaking around the village. Things have reached the point that people hardly dare let their laundry hang out to dry at night. That's what the times have come to.

# [ 24 ]

THINGS HAD ACTUALLY been better when Marius's mother was alive to take care of him and make him stick to his work. After the police had picked Marius up, there was none of this running around outdoors at night.

"It's time for you to go to bed now, Marius," his mother would say. "It's nine o'clock."

She was just a tiny woman, but he had respect for her. And when she sent him to the store for groceries, the really important thing was for him to get the exact change. What he was supposed to buy was written down on a slip of paper. "And then I'll need 5 øre's worth of hard candy for myself too," Marius would say.

"Oh, is that so?" the grocer would ask. "Did your mother say you could?"

"Of course she said I could!" replied Marius. Then he left, a tall man sucking on hard candy with snot in his mustache.

Marius is 50 years old now; his mother was over 80 when she died. You can't live forever and take care of your children. Besides, Marius really ought to be able to make it on his own. He inherited money and he's big and strong. And he's not afraid of working either. He takes care of his farm and keeps it running well and doesn't throw his money away. And if it weren't for that peculiar inclination of his, he probably would have gotten married and had children to help him.

It's not that he has given his heart to the Devil either. He makes sure to go to church every Sunday and takes part in the life of the congregation, its Bible-study sessions and everything. And he says his prayers every night, loudly and clearly, so that in the beginning his housekeeper thought that he was talking to somebody in bed with him.

That's the way it was even before the new pastor came. Marius isn't one of those new converts who has been caught up in the latest wind to sweep across the region. For half a century he has maintained his childhood faith. But there are a lot of other people who didn't jump on board and give their hearts to Jesus until quite recently.

Pastor Nørregaard-Olsen came into the parish like a terrible swift storm and an apple of discord. "People are going to have to be awakened and shaken up here!" he said on his first day. "I haven't come to make peace, for peace is not the best thing — it's better for people to have the *will* to act!"

Pastor Nørregaard-Olsen isn't like the old pastor, who went around puttering in his garden, a kind and pleasant man who just let things happen around him. But he's no hellfire-and-brimstone preacher or fanatic either. He's an intellectual. He's the pastor for the New Age. A modern spirit. A practical man. An organizer and strategist. He is, so to speak, a "modernistic" pastor.

Here was the old pastor poisoning the air of the parsonage with his foul-smelling pipes. Good-natured and old-fashioned, with modest, harmless interests. He collected meerschaum pipes and owned pipe racks made of carved wood with embroidered fabric and fringe on them. He liked to work in his garden and he loved roses.

There was a Maréchal Niel rose on the south wall that he took special care of, pruning it and fertilizing it from his chamber pot.

"Oh, please be careful," his wife would tell him. "People can see you from the road when you stand there peeing on the Maréchal Niel rose."

"Just let them look," the old pastor would say. "They certainly can't see anything more than what the good Lord Himself created. It does the rose a lot of good. See how green and lush its leaves are! And smell the fragrance from those yellow flowers!"

"Yes, but people can see you," his wife would say. "And besides, you should save a little for the other roses too."

"No," the pastor would say. "Maréchal Niel is going to get it all. He's my favorite child."

Pastor Nørregaard-Olsen doesn't have those kinds of interests. He convinced the church council to hire some energetic people to clean up the old garden. Away with winding walkways with their boxwood and ivy borders! None of those small, old-fashioned musk roses, but long-stemmed, modern varieties. Danish varieties. Hardy, vigorous bloomers. Straight, wide walkways and elegant rectangular lawns. Stone curbs and flagstones. And if the Maréchal Niel rose on the south wall can't do well without its daily dose of urine, it will have to be dug up to make room for fast-growing Japanese ivy.

There was controversy and discord when the old trees were to be cut down. The church council was divided into two hostile factions, whose members showed up and forbade each other from touching the trees and accused each other of illegal logging

and "crop theft." They wrote letters to the editor about each other. There were lawsuits and arguments. But the pastor prevailed.

A man of action. A soldier and general for Christ. The cleansing and the new order.

"I love to throw myself into battle for a cause," the pastor told his wife. "Oh, how fresh and alive I feel! A divine storm is going to sweep across this parish."

"You're an idealist!" said his wife.

The pastor managed to get a majority on the church council, and it voted him 40,000 kroner to rebuild the old parsonage, which was no longer up-to-date and which was not a worthy setting for Pastor Nørregaard-Olsen's activities. The old thatched roof was torn off, and an attic area and gables were erected. Central heating was installed, and an all-electric kitchen with tile, chrome, and stainless steel. And a bathroom with a built-in tub and shower so the pastor could begin his day's work with a refreshing sprinkling of water. Doors were walled up, and windows were chopped out, and partitions were moved. Flush doors and plastered ceilings were installed. Beechwood parquet was

laid on the floors, and sheets of insulation were put on the walls.
There was a glassed-in porch and a terrace. And a laundry room
with machines and a garage with water faucets.

"Ah! Now we can breathe!" said the pastor. "Now we have
space and air and light! Now we can move around! I have to
have a large room to be able to work. I have to be able to wander
about in my room in order to think clearly."

There was criticism because of the rebuilding. It was too
expensive and extravagant, the pastor's opponents said. "Does a
pastor need to have eighteen rooms? How did Christ and St.
Paul live?"

"Where am I going to put my confirmation classes?" the pastor asked. "And the people who come to see me? Aren't they
supposed to be received properly? Isn't a parsonage supposed to
be a place that can elevate and ennoble? Shouldn't there be space
here for Bible study and the sewing circle and the Youth Division and those many, many other things? Where am I supposed
to put my furniture? And my books?"

There was room for Pastor Nørregaard-Olsen's beautiful furniture. Bookcases were put up and filled with leather bindings.
"Nothing looks as beautiful and cultivated in a room as books!
There they stand, volume upon volume from floor to ceiling,
creating warmth and comfort. People should be able to see that a
pastor is a cultivated man. A man who reads and keeps up with
intellectual life. Now how would this home look without books?"

Everything was new and elegant. And certainly everybody
should realize that this parsonage was a showcase for the region
and a worthy focal point for the life of the congregation. And
Pastor Nørregaard-Olsen wasn't afraid of pitching in some
money of his own. Where the church council couldn't grant him
any more, he paid the costs himself. He probably had the financial resources through his wife, who was well-off, and who in
fact was related to Squire Skjern-Svendsen.

The town helped too, constructing a driveway with a granite
curb and a sidewalk and parking area so the parsonage would
present a good appearance.

"There we are!" said Pastor Nørregaard-Olsen. "Now we can
get going! Now we can get to work!" A new age had come to the
parish.

# [ 25 ]

IT WAS THE WOMEN who cared for Jesus Christ, preparing his meals and anointing his feet with ointment of nard from alabaster jars.

And it was to the women that Pastor Nørregaard-Olsen turned first.

Once the women were won over to the Kingdom of God, the men were sure to follow. That's why the ladies' sewing circle and the YD were the cornerstones of the new House of God that Pastor Nørregaard-Olsen was going to erect.

Old Emma was the first to arrive. She certainly wasn't one of the trend-setters or leading members of society. But he couldn't be particular in the beginning. "A simple soul," the pastor said. "But one of God's children nonetheless. If only she would wash more often and be a little more reserved and not talk right in my face!"

"My dear woman," he told her. "Since my office hours are from 3:00 to 4:00 p.m., you really must observe them. A pastor has an enormous amount of work to attend to, and his hours must be respected."

But Emma was the first one, and he couldn't cast her aside. "She was the first swallow to fly in," Pastor Nørregaard-Olsen would say.

"It's wonderful how elegant you've made things, Pastor," Emma says. "I hardly recognize it, the way the garden has changed, with flagstones and rocks every which way. I guess that's the way people do things now. But aren't you going to have any vegetables at all, Pastor? The old pastor had so many vegetables and herbs."

"Legumes aren't worth the effort," Pastor Nørregaard-Olsen says.

"Oh, yes they are," says Emma, not knowing that you're not supposed to keep contradicting your pastor and teaching him things. And she doesn't notice the impatient expression on the pastor's face. "Yes indeed, they're worth it! I just have a small plot of land myself. But I get leeks that are *this big*! Just as long as you take good care of them with your chamber pot."

"Of course, of course," says the pastor. "Nature is abundant. But we get our produce from the gardener. He's kind enough to send us what we use in the household. It's no bother for him, of course; he has so much in his vegetable garden."

"Oh, I see," Emma says. "That makes more sense. Because it certainly is worth it. Big, fat leeks like that are one of the best things I know. But you do have to take care of them."

"Yes," says the pastor, "it is a miracle. A tiny seed is put into the ground and it sprouts up and unfolds and turns into nourishment and healthful food. It grows from nothing and puts out leaf after leaf and flower after flower, more beautiful than King Solomon in all his glory."

"But it needs a lot of manure," Emma says. "It's no good skimping on it." Then she happens to think of the Maréchal Niel rose on the south wall that was the apple of the old pastor's eye and received such meticulous care. "Oh my, where is it? The rose bush? Oh no, was it taken away? How could you let that happen, Pastor? It really looked so nice with its yellow roses. And the old pastor was so fond of it and watered it himself and —"

"Yes, I know, I know. But it really wasn't doing well. And I like red roses better. 'Red roses and eyes of blue,' that's what we sang in the student club," the pastor says, humming, proving that a pastor certainly doesn't need to be a sourpuss but can be lively and cheerful too.

And other ladies come to the sewing circle. The gardener's wife and Niels Madsen's wife. And Panty Marius's housekeeper comes because she doesn't know what to do with herself in the evenings and doesn't have anybody to talk to. They regard her with interest and would like her to tell them what it's like living with Marius, and what goes on behind the small windowpanes of his house.

Naturally the pastor's wife is the focal point of the sewing circle. She is friendly and charming and quite straightforward, as if she were just like everybody else.

They begin with a song, which unites, uplifts, and brings them closer together. Then they say a prayer, and the pastor says a few words. Then they sing again. Then they start sewing and knitting industriously. It's truly incredible the number of charming table mats and useful little crocheted items that these diligent ladies manage to produce.

Afterwards they refresh themselves with some coffee. In the little Sunday newsletter, Pastor Nørregaard-Olsen invited the nice ladies of the sewing circle to bring along some home-baked goods. The nice ladies have certainly complied with his invitation, so there are baked goods in the parsonage for the entire week.

Only Panty Marius's housekeeper is not allowed to bake anything, because Marius is so stingy with his margarine and flour. So she has to buy a whole coffeecake at the bakery instead, and that's quite costly considering the wages she makes. But it isn't really necessary for her to buy a whole coffeecake every time. All in all, there are certain indications that the new housekeeper suffers a little from delusions of gentility, although God only knows there's nothing very genteel about working in the house of someone like Panty Marius.

But the whole matter of pastry for coffee vanishes the day baker Andersen's wife joins the ladies' sewing circle. She has easy access to baked goods and takes the pressure off the others. She represents a social coup for the circle in her own right. Because wherever Mrs. Andersen goes, everything is done elegantly. Several more ladies of the town join along with Mrs. Andersen.

"Ah yes, things are going very well." And Pastor Nørregaard-Olsen rubs his white hands together so his knuckles crack.

# [ 26 ]

BUT EVEN MORE IMPORTANT than the ladies' sewing circle is the YD. The Youth Division. The Corps.

"The YD, they're my elite troops, my Guard!" says Pastor Nørregaard-Olsen. "With the YD I am going to conquer this parish. These cheerful young people will not be stopped by anything. They are the incarnation of healthy, young life, which demands its rights and pushes its way forward."

It's a glorious sight when the YDers march into church in their handsome uniforms. Straight-backed and cheerful they arrive in one body and take their places—the place of youth in the ancient church. Doesn't the singing from their young throats sound grand!

"YDers! Assemble for a demonstration in church this Sunday," Pastor Nørregaard-Olsen writes in the little Sunday newsletter where the YD has its own column. Because it *is* a demonstration when the YDers march in wearing their uniforms. A demonstration and campaign for the Kingdom of God.

The YDers are recruited from among the girls going to confirmation class. The seeds must be sown in young, receptive minds. And the YD does have an awful lot to offer. Fellowship and entertainment. Energetic marching trips and bicycle excursions and open-air devotions. And meetings in the magnificent parsonage garden with singing and games. And YD coffee with YD cake in the pastor's living room. "Remember to bring some coffee beans along, YDers!" the pastor writes in their column.

The uniform costs 8 kroner, which is actually quite a reasonable price, considering that it can also be worn off-duty so they can save on their civilian clothes.

There's the gardener's daughter, for instance, who works in her father's little shop weighing potatoes and making wreaths and crosses out of bands of straw and wire, nice moss from the forest, and varnished red berries. She always wears her pretty YD blouse with its kerchief and emblem so people can see what she is and see that she dares to acknowledge her God. Of course she does look self-conscious and ill-at-ease, so perhaps it's just that her good parents decided she should wear the uniform and campaign and save her other clothes. But everyone can see that the YD uniform is more stylish and better-looking than the dress she usually wears.

She's a tall, pale girl with a pretty face. She's rather shy and bashful and can't really look people in the eye. "That's because she doesn't have a clear conscience," says her father.

"We have to keep watch on our thoughts," says her mother.

"Even though we might not be sinning on the outside, we can certainly be sinning on the inside."

Every Saturday afternoon the gardener's daughter distributes the Sunday newsletter to various houses. But her parents know that she does it without joy. "Her heart's not in it," says her mother.

"It's because I'm afraid of the dogs," her daughter says.

"In covenant with the Lord's Prayer you'll never have to falter," the gardener says. "Remember all that Jesus suffered for your sake when He died on the cross! So can't you do this little job for Him?"

Eight kroner is actually cheap for a uniform. But there are still some people who don't feel they can afford it. The feed master's daughter, Anna, is taking classes from the pastor for her confirmation in the fall, and she is invited to join the YD just like the other girls and show the world that she dares to take a stand for what she believes in. But no, she doesn't think . . . she doesn't really know . . . and the pastor has to have a serious talk with her and ask her whether she has any faith at all, because he *certainly* can't stand in the church in the presence of God and confirm a heathen.

Anna does have faith, of course, and she'd like to join the YD too, where they have so much fun and bicycle in the countryside together and sing songs and enjoy good fellowship. But the next day she comes in and says that her mother won't let her because the uniform is too expensive.

So the pastor's wife has to go out to the feed master's house and talk with Anna's mother. Because when a person has said yes to something, that's the way it is. "A man's only as good as his word." And as far as the 8 kroner are concerned, that can be paid in monthly installments, of course. The pastor's wife is friendly and straightforward, and it's not easy for Anna's mother to stand up to her and handle the situation. In this way, Anna joins the Youth Division too. She joins on the installment plan. Eight kroner isn't a lot of money, even though it only covers the blouse and the kerchief and doesn't include the belt or the emblem or the hat guard or the sash or the badges that the patrol leader and other non-commissioned officers have to buy, if they ever get that far.

It's the pastor's wife who orders and buys the uniforms, because her brother in Copenhagen owns a sporting goods store. He supplies all the YDers in the whole country, and the fabric comes from Uncle Skjern-Svendsen's textile mills. So, in a sense, the money stays in the parish.

Naturally there are some people who are so petty that they talk about percentages and profits for the pastor's wife. "Oh, just let them talk!" her husband tells her. "Shouldn't we be able to endure opposition and irritations? Haven't Christians been defying persecutions and crosses and burnings at the stake and wild beasts for 1900 years? Are we going to let ourselves be stopped by a bit of spite?"

And the YDers bicycle out into the Danish summer. Straight-backed and cheerful. What a glorious sight, these suntanned young people singing together, so warmhearted and sincere.

# [ 27 ]

THE WORK OF THE YD has been greatly blessed. God has crushed the Athletic Association, which had opposed it and was tempting young people with worldly emptiness.

The way things were before, you might see young girls running around on the roads in suggestive gym outfits when they were going out to play handball. Short pants and bare legs reigned supreme. Titillation and sensual arousal.

Pastor Nørregaard-Olsen has managed to overcome this too. The Athletic Association has been disbanded. If young people want to participate in sports, which certainly can be a good, healthy thing, they can do it only through the YD now. YD gymnastics and YD handball have become established institutions. They have engaged YDers from other parishes in many splendid tournaments. Our spirited YDers have brought home many triumphs and trophies. It certainly *is* possible to play handball wearing stockings. Our YD girls have proven that.

And what joyous summer camps the YDers have had! In

cheerful camaraderie and merry fellowship. Up early in the morning to raise the flag. Then a hymn in the bracing morning air and a short devotional service before they start in on their oatmeal. How magnificent oatmeal tastes when you've made it yourself!

And what an atmosphere there is in the evening when they're sitting around the campfire, and their young faces are tinged by the fire's enchanted glow. How stirring the old Danish hymns sound in the still summer evening. And how intently they listened to the words of the gospel and Pastor Nørregaard-Olsen's speech. These were words that became fixed in the young people's minds and were not forgotten. Ah yes, we brought something home with us from those summer camps. Something that no one can ever take away from us, no matter how we fare in life.

Occasionally Squire Skjern-Svendsen invites the entire corps up to the manor and gives them a tour of the old, historic castle. Not only is it interesting and educational to delve into our nation's history, it's an exciting and fantastic experience too. So it was in surroundings like these that those old noblemen lived, who made our fatherland so beautiful and wonderful and erected those proud fortifications that still mark the scenery of Denmark and harmonize so intimately with the Danish landscape.

It was like a journey back into the history of the fatherland. Here bands of rebellious peasants tried to storm the ramparts but were annihilated by ironclad horsemen. And here knights fought among themselves in celebrated battles. We can still see the old suits of armor standing on display in the stairwells and the long corridors.

Squire Skjern-Svendsen has returned everything to its original state. The baronial hall with its marble fireplace and beautiful tapestries. Yes, they certainly did appreciate beauty back then. Such taste! Such culture! Shouldn't we be grateful to these bluff old lords of the manor for the things they left to us? They spared no sacrifice in making everything as magnificent as possible. All the peasants of the region were forced to haul stones and work on the construction for more than a year. There wasn't any harvest *that* year! But a monumental work was created that would endure above and beyond the worries of daily life.

What banquets must have been held in this hall! Here they sat

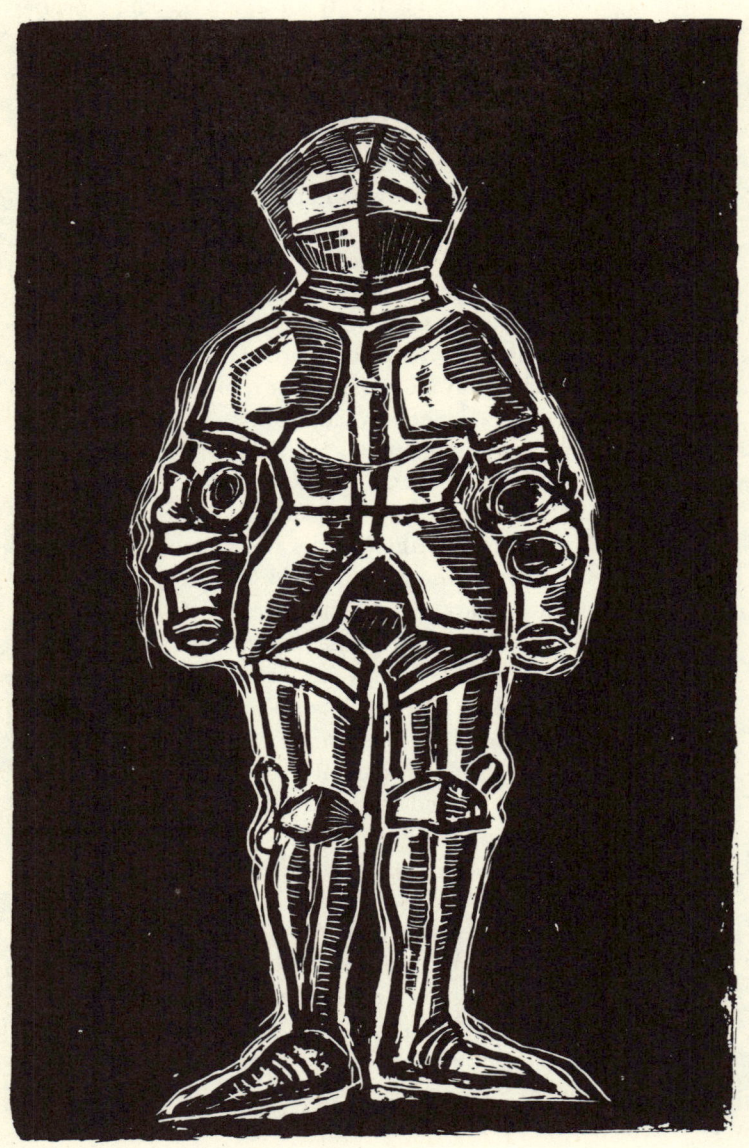

wearing sable and marten fur and scarlet cloth, eating and drinking, attended by pages and servants. There was once a count
here at Frydenholm who commanded twelve trumpeters to blow
a fanfare every time he emptied his glass. And that happened
often.

Pastor Nørregaard-Olsen is a cultivated man who is familiar
with our country's history and can bring the past alive for young
people. In a lively and graphic manner he tells them about
manorial life in the old days.

"And believe me, elegant dishes were served when there was a
banquet and the king came to visit. Entire stags were carried in.
And there were boars roasted on spits, and pheasants. Once
there was a cook who happened to scorch the meat, and the lord
of the manor had him seized at once and spitted and roasted in
the fireplace so he could feel what it was like to be scorched.
They did have a sense of humor, those old knights. They were
high-spirited back then!"

It's a long walk through the old castle's many rooms and
passageways. Here was the ladies' bower where the women sat
embroidering silk with gold thread as they sang beautiful old
folk songs. Here is the Blue Room where a lord once had his
wife walled up. And here is the room where, in a fit of temper,
Count Johan accidentally killed his brother. And under these
flagstones the countess concealed the body of her husband after
she had put poison in his nightly beer.

Every stone can tell a tale. Every nook and cranny has its
story. Each piece of furniture bears witness to everything that
once was. The history of a people is a precious treasure that they
can never lose. "May God grant you a future as he granted you
memories!"

In the days of the Swedish War, the officers of the Swedish
military were quartered here. Colonel Sparre lived here with his
dragoons. Even the Swedish king himself spent the night here
once, and the bed that he slept in is still here. The squire has
been kind enough to let us see it.

Colonel Sparre and the Swedish king were hospitably received. The Danish manorial lords were not petty. They served
the best wine and had the best food set on the table. They were
smart; they knew that resistance would do no good. If they had

started an insurrection, the castle would certainly have been burned to the ground just the way the farms had been, and all its abundant memories would have been lost. It was a good thing that the Danish noblemen knew their duty to the fatherland and let these cultural memories come down to us as our legacy.

But out in the forest, the Gjønge partisans lay in wait, harassing the enemy and ambushing Karl Gustav's convoys. The Gjønge partisans were poor people and menial peasants who had nothing to lose. They were irresponsible people who couldn't understand that their imprudent resistance would bring unimaginable misfortune to Denmark. Who knows how the war might have turned out if these bands of Gjønge partisans had observed the decrees of the authorities and hadn't destroyed our relationship with the Swedish military power?

Their irresponsible resistance brought much misfortune to the fatherland. It's just not a good idea for the common man to try to determine the politics of the kingdom by himself. The Danish noblemen did what they could to preserve good relations with Karl Gustav, but the irresponsible masses destroyed what had been achieved.

All these memories stand before us large as life in this old castle. Here is the dungeon that insubordinate peasants were flung into. And the young YD girls can peer into the forbidding hole and shudder. And here in fact is the wooden horse! Well, unfortunately it isn't the original wooden horse. That was burned by the peasants 150 years ago. Back then people didn't have any feeling for the memories of the past. But Squire Skjern-Svendsen had a cabinetmaker manufacture an exact replica of the wooden horse from old engravings and drawings. It now stands in its historic place, and anyone can imagine what it was like to sit on it and remember the Denmark of bygone days.

No doubt some of you are tired after the long walk through the castle. And no doubt it would feel good to lie down and rest on the large lawn in front of the garden stairway. But what's this? Now there's a surprise. The squire is serving soft drinks to everybody. All for free. Oh, it tastes so good! Now let's all give the squire a rousing cheer!

Then they eat the lunches they have brought with them and drink the soft drinks out on the lawn, laughing and having a good time. And afterwards, when the lunch wrappers have been gathered up, Pastor Nørregaard-Olsen holds a brief devotion. Could any setting be more beautiful for the devotion than the scenery in this wonderful park?

The squire himself comes out onto the stairway, nodding and smiling to the young people. He watches them line up in their ranks for the march home. They give him one more rousing cheer and thank him for his hospitality. Then the YDers march off singing the YD song: "Cheerfully, cheerfully, onward friends!"

It was a day we won't forget for a long time. We got good and tired. But does anyone regret going along?

# [ 28 ]

IT HAS BEEN A GREAT blessing to the parish that a man like Squire Skjern-Svendsen is among those who have given their hearts to God.

For many years he has had "The Clothing Warehouse" in Præstø send out his little Christmas calendar to thousands of homes. Clothing Warehouses in other towns have sent it out to thousands of other Danish homes. The calendar hangs in living rooms everywhere, a useful item for the farmer with its market days and gestation tables. Its little Bible verses are good for holidays as well. "Buy quality at low prices at The Clothing Warehouse" is printed on it. People have been eagerly buying their ribbons and buttons and socks and undershirts at Skjern-Svendsen's stores, putting money in circulation and creating employment and helping to work for the Kingdom of God without even knowing it.

Even before Pastor Nørregaard-Olsen arrived in the parish, there was a new evangelical meeting house there. Red and solid with Romanesque windows and Gothic balustrades. It was made possible only through Squire Skjern-Svendsen's extraordinary generosity. A collection was taken up for it, of course, but it only brought in a pitifully small amount. Back then most people still belonged to the world. Not even the old pastor was all that interested in the evangelical meeting house. In fact he was practically antagonistic.

Only Pastor Nørregaard-Olsen's eminent organizational skill and refreshing gospel message have made it possible to turn the parish into a Christian one.

"Have you forgotten your baptismal covenant?" he would shout. "Have you forgotten the promise that was made to you at baptism? We have God's own word that the promise will be fulfilled. So take God at His word!"

What Squire Skjern-Svendsen could do in the business world, Pastor Nørregaard-Olsen could do in the spiritual world. And it was fortunate that the two men knew each other and wanted the same thing and were able to work hand in hand.

People know that the squire is a frequent visitor to the parsonage. His big car is often parked in the parking spot in front of the new driveway. But the squire doesn't come to Bible reading where the Gospel According to St. John is studied and interpreted. And he doesn't come to the parties that Pastor Nørregaard-Olsen gives for the prominent people of the region either. Squire Skjern-Svendsen doesn't drink red wine or liqueur and doesn't smoke cigars. He's not the sociable type.

He pays only brief visits in the evening, just like Nicodemus, to discuss practical matters. There doesn't seem to be any real friendship between the two men. But they seem to be in agreement on the ways and means of establishing the Kingdom of God.

It strikes many people as odd that Mrs. Skjern-Svendsen never accompanies her husband. She never goes to church. She never goes to the ladies' sewing circle or bazaars or any of the other special arrangements for women. And it's regrettable that she of all people doesn't want to be in the vanguard and set a good example for the ladies' efforts in the struggle for the Kingdom of God. They know that she once wanted to be a missionary and wanted to die for Jesus and be eaten by cannibals. So why has she turned her heart away from God?

There seems to be a lot about that marriage that isn't what it ought to be. And then they've never had children either, whoever's fault that might be. And they say that the squire's wife isn't quite right in the head sometimes, and that the squire has threatened to have her put away in an institution.

But Mrs. Julie *is* so much younger than her husband. And it *can* be hard for a young wife to have an old husband. And since the squire is so busy with all his factories and projects, there probably isn't much time left to devote to his wife.

That squire must be a strange man. Solitary and unapproachable, and yet full of enterprise and plans for his fellow human beings. He is modest and ascetic, but he does live in a castle that cost a fortune to restore and bring back to its original state. He works in silence and without vanity, but in the little village churchyard he's having a mausoleum built that costs more than the whole church.

He stays in the background and doesn't want to be seen or noticed. But it is a fact that he had an artist come and paint a pretentious life-size portrait of him.

The artist was the young painter Hakon Brand, who became a member of the Oxford Movement and painted altarpieces and decorated evangelical meeting houses. He later died in Paris under mysterious circumstances. They remember him well around here. He had long hair and a full red beard and resembled the Savior Himself, amazing everybody who saw him.

The squire posed for him sitting in a tall Renaissance chair with lilac-colored silk draperies as a background. "I look rather good, don't I?" he said to the painter, gazing at him with his innocent pale-blue eyes.

Hakon Brand lived in the castle for one whole summer working on the large painting. In the upper corner the squire wanted to have an aristocratic coat of arms painted with a spinning wheel and part of a loom as symbols of his trade.

Later, however, the artist and the squire had a falling-out. And Hakon Brand, who was a temperamental artist, slashed the canvas with his dagger.

Now Hakon Brand is dead. But the large portrait is still hanging in the castle, with its coat of arms and lilac background in its enormous, resplendent gold frame. The slash in the canvas was patched up and repaired by experts from the Academy of Art. And when the squire was honored with the Knight's Cross on his sixtieth birthday, he sent for another artist to paint the Knight's Cross on the portrait.

Life-sized and lifelike, the picture hangs in the squire's private room, looking at him with pale-blue eyes. The squire looks at his portrait. And their eyes meet in a strange way.

Work on the burial mound is making good progress. It looks as if it might be completely finished in the fall so that it can be consecrated by Pastor Nørregaard-Olsen before the frost sets in. A large work force is busy digging and pouring concrete and shaping granite boulders, and every once in a while the squire shows up and stops his car outside the cemetery, where he gets out to inspect things and urge the workers on. It's as if he knows that he will soon need his burial mound and is impatient and anxious that it won't be ready.

Special workers have arrived from Copenhagen to make the marble floor and the mosaics. There are also skilled craftsmen from the porcelain factory who set up tiles with religious pictures on them. They have a Catholic and alien appearance, but they must be Protestant, since it was the squire who commissioned them. The artist who painted the tiles drives out in his car in person to watch them be set in place. He definitely does not look Catholic; he is an elegant man who wears spats and white chamois gloves.

There's going to be grass growing on top of the mound. But the grass isn't sown in the ordinary way. Gardeners arrive with large rolls of sod under their arms, and they unroll the grass as if it were a carpet. They water it and trim it and show the castle gardener how to take care of it.

The actual burial vault is made of reinforced concrete one meter thick. If war or times of unrest should come someday, the grave will be safe from aerial bombardment and that sort of deviltry. Nothing bad can happen to the interred. He will lie there safe and sound until Judgment Day, when the last trumpet sounds and the resurrection of the body takes place.

"It's not right to tell jokes in a grave," Rasmus Larsen says. "We should respect the dead."

"Well, damn it, he isn't dead yet," the other workers say. "Besides, it's a bunch of crap to decorate a burial mound with marble and bronze and spend several thousand kroner, when there are other people who can't even scrape together enough to pay their rent. Does a corpse need to be surrounded by all this luxury with electric lights and pictures? No, it's just plain nuts!"

"This costs about the same as enough land for almost a dozen tenant farmers!" someone says. "His servants live worse than his livestock. His barns have got to have tiles and be nice and clean. And his grave has got to have art and modern conveniences and electric lights. The hell with that!"

But Rasmus calms them down with sober words. "You can just go home if you don't want any part of earning this money. Nobody's forcing you to stay here. It's a free country. But I do think it's a good thing there are rich people too, who aren't afraid to start things going and create jobs and profit. And besides, there's also something called 'cultural treasures.' Even though some people don't understand culture, some of us think it's a good thing to make something beautiful, both for tourists and for our descendants."

But the workmen would like to know what this has to do with culture. Burying valuables in the ground and putting in electric lights for a corpse—how much culture is there in that?

"Well, anyhow, it's pretty," says Rasmus, "the stuff they're doing here. Real nice pictures and everything. Of course there's always somebody who's not satisfied and has to object. But luckily there are enlightened people who stand guard over our culture and realize that there are things that are more valuable than stuff you just eat."

Rasmus is an articulate speaker and is used to making speeches. He has turned out to be a level-headed man. He raises the Danish flag on the new flagpole in front of his house. He is the chairman of the labor union and is on the board of directors of the voters' league. He knows his responsibilities to society. He knows what's what about education and progress, and nobody had better say otherwise. He is a man of advancement through compromise, who knows that it is awfully easy to tear things down but so hard to build them back up.

And the work goes on. The specialists file and polish and hone things inside the burial chamber. And Rasmus and Martin mix cement and lug heavy boulders and shape them and pound them smooth and put them together. Sometimes the squire comes into

the cemetery, without a sound, and suddenly stands there looking at them. He peers into his grave and smiles and is satisfied
with the work being done.

Short and gray-haired, he stands there smiling, this strange
man who is a Christian and an ascetic and is building himself a
sepulcher like a pagan Egyptian. The squire, who rules over
tracts of land and woods, this big manufacturer who supports
textile mills and spinning mills and button factories and shops.
He owns a historic castle. But he only has one servant to wait on
him. An ex-convict with a smooth, empty, and expressionless
face.

He has rooms full of tapestries and paintings and suits of
armor and a replica of a wooden horse in the courtyard. And he
has a little embroidered prayer stool with a white dove on a blue
background in his bedroom, where he kneels in the morning and
in the evening and begs God for forgiveness for something or
other.

It is noteworthy that only one marble sarcophagus is being
placed in the burial chamber. Isn't his wife going to lie in the
mound? Is she going to be buried out in the cemetery or be
deposited in an urn in a strange place far from her husband's
sarcophagus?

There's a lot that's peculiar and incomprehensible about this
marriage, and it would be a real blessing if people knew a little
more about it.

# SORCERERS

## [ 29 ]

*Shortly before the monarch is strangled, when a comet is seen, copper-tinted Castor and Pollux shall be seen by all over land and sea.*

*The highest one is strangled by night in bed because he has tarried too long with the blond elect. The Empire, after three rulers, having forced its way into the rights of others and worked to subjugate, will deal cards to the game of Death, and the packet has not been read.*

So wrote Nostradamus in his *Prophecies* in the year 1555 about things that are to happen sometime far in the future.

"Can anything be expressed in more crystal-clear terms and more convincingly?" asks Kados.

A series of events may occur at different places in the world. And apparently they have nothing to do with each other. One day a diminutive gentleman walks into an office and donates large sums of money for charitable causes. A little later an elegant lady drives up in a long blue car and pays a visit to a doctor on the outskirts of the city. She confides surprising and intimate things to him. And in the inner city Olsen is going around trying to borrow 20 kroner from a friend because he intends to take an important trip to a place in southern Sjælland. And in a Chinese crystal ball the poetess Sylvia Drusse sees things that are hidden from other people.

*The holy lady has heard the faint voice beneath the earth and sees the human flame shine as the divine. This causes hermits to color the earth and the holy temples with their blood to destroy the impure!* writes Nostradamus.

The things that are happening are neither trivial nor random. There is a relationship and an inner connection among the various incidents. Not everyone can see this relationship. But Kados, who is familiar with Kabbala and Nostradamus and the occult sciences, feels that he can see the relationship and the meaning in the world and can draw conclusions from seemingly random events in nature and in people's lives.

"Just don't call him Kados!" says his mortal enemy, the little astrologer, Sjögren. "Call him the Beast of Østre Farimagsgade!" Sjögren talks this way because he is a lowly and envious man, and Kados has no regard for him at all.

"He is a windbag and a fop, that Sjögren," Kados says. "He is a pure dilettante. His horoscopes are unscientific drivel for the entertainment of the mob."

There is nothing superficial or frivolous about Kados. He has received schooling from the French masters and acquired for himself the sum of medieval and Hellenistic science, knowledge of secret things and forces transmitted down through the centuries to a few initiates. Knowledge which would be dangerous and fateful if it were misused and which therefore must remain secret and can only be confided to the chosen few of an especially high moral caliber.

Kados reads Nostradamus in Provençal and Paracelsus in Latin and the main work of Kabbalism, *Zohar Hakodosh*, in a nearly inaccessible, incomplete Aramaic text. His collection of books is unique. He owns books that the libraries of Europe would envy. He has the first edition of Nostradamus, with one half of his *Centuries* from 1555, which is regarded as lost and which the main library in Paris would give a great deal to acquire. "They have to make do with Benoist Rigaud's printing of 1568 down there," says Kados. "And it is full of errors and distortions."

He owns the rare 1642 Amsterdam edition of the *Sepher Yezirah* — the book of creation concerning the 32 ways of wisdom, the 10 numbers and the 22 letters. He owns books by Raimund Lullus and Knorr von Rosenroth which no one suspects exist. He has a manuscript by Johannes de Luna and a bundle of letters from Strindberg.

He corresponds with Hasidim in Poland and with Shabbetaians in France and with Freemasons in Holland. What is a man like Sjögren compared to him? A worm that it isn't even worth the trouble to squash. An unworthy who cobbles together a horoscope for a measly 10 kroner on the basis of a mere birthdate. A mountebank and a charlatan who has gleaned his knowledge from weekly magazines and dream books!

Occasionally the two of them meet in Damascus's shop. And fat little Sjögren grows red in the face with excitement. But Kados rarely grants him a word. He only gives him a single glance with his black flashing eyes, and the little man is paralyzed and writhes in impotent indignation.

"He is the disciple of Satan, the Beast from Østre Farimagsgade! He is in league with Lucifer!" Sjögren hisses.

But nothing is further from the truth. He has not made a pact with evil or the principle of evil. On the contrary. Defiant and intrepid, he fights with all his magical resources for a higher justice. It is true that he has tried to communicate with Lucifer, who is not the Prince of Evil but the Bringer of Light, the ousted one. The falling, creative light that was cast out into the most profound condensation of primordial substance. The creative idea, born of the dual light, the twilight. The world of the nature spirits and the elemental spirits.

Lucifer, or Satan, is not the enemy. He is the solar force, the fire spirit, exhaled in the bubbles. The light that falls down into matter in order to animate it. Lucifer, who is chained to the earth just as Prometheus, the Fire-Bringer, was chained to the cliff. The creative light chained in material conditions.

This world simply would not exist without Lucifer and the effects of light. And along with Lucifer, the Angel of Light, an entire host was thrown into the abyss. And could these angels be anything other than creative spirits and intelligences?

"Depart from me!" Sjögren shouts. "Depart from me, you who stand together with the Prince of Darkness!"

"But it's not Lucifer who is the Prince of Darkness. Belimod is darkness. But what is darkness other than light's shadow? And what is Lucifer other than the light that works within us?" If Sjögren weren't an ignorant cheat, he wouldn't be uttering this nonsense.

"Yes, but is Satan not the Serpent?" shrieks Sjögren. "Is not Lucifer the Dragon referred to in the Revelation of St. John the Divine? And is not the Dragon darkness?"

"The Dragon was the sun god of the past," says Kados. "Shining during the day and its own opponent at night, since it was the producer of the darkness. It was the symbol of God, who is both night and day. Only by the falling of light upon the earth does darkness come about. The light within us is the creative, fructifying power. And the light is Lucifer!"

"No! No!" shouts Sjögren. "Lucifer is Satan! And Satan is God's enemy! Satan is the Tempter!"

"Lucifer is both the Tempter and the Savior! Without the Light of Lucifer, we would be like beasts. Lucifer is Thought and Spirit. And you, my dear sir, are but a beast without Lucifer! An insect. A worm. Without cognition. Wriggle away, worm, and hide yourself in the darkness!" And Sjögren falls back impotently before the flashing gaze of Kados.

Bravely and resolutely Kados has joined Satan's opposition against that Jehovah who is an unworthy demiurge, under whose misrule the entire solar system is languishing.

# [ 30 ]

KADOS OWNS A DAIRY SHOP on Østre Farimagsgade. In number 32, right at the corner of Lundsgade.

But Kados isn't a practical man, so his wife looks after the dairy shop for him. He himself is incapable of weighing out a pound of butter. And he gets into arguments with the customers. "You've got to stay out of the store!" his wife says.

"You're right," says Kados, "I can't cope with it. And I should have foreseen it. When I bought this ill-fated dairy shop, Mars was just entering Libra. How was I ever supposed to learn how to weigh out a pound of butter under those circumstances?"

The family has an apartment up on the sixth floor. The roof of the building is adorned with a kind of slate and tin tower that

has an iron fence on top of it, as is common for corner apartments on Farimagsgade. There used to be an artist's studio in
the tower, and it is part of the Kados family's attic apartment.

Kados has his study in the tower. He calls it the "seventh
tabernacle" even though there are only three rooms plus a
kitchen in the apartment. It's a lucky thing that the building's
architect made the tower five-sided, giving it the form of a pentangle, which is precisely what Kados needs. It was the shape of
this tower, plus the fact that the building was number 32, the
sum of whose digits is exactly five, that made Kados buy the
dairy shop and rent the apartment.

Because five is the number for the planet Mars. It is the
number of fire and of creative intelligence. The number five, the
five-sided shape, and the five-pointed star symbolize the human
being with his five senses. It is also the symbol for the star of the
falling light, which as it falls turns its point downward—the
sign of Lucifer. It's a good thing to live in a building whose
numbers add up to five.

Kados has painted symbolic characters on the walls in the
five-sided tower. The twelve signs of the Zodiac and the symbols
of the seven sacred planets. Through the window of the studio
he can see the North Star. A little iron spiral staircase leads up to
a trap door in the ceiling through which he can get out onto the
roof. Kados often climbs up here at night and stands staring at
the firmament in his long black overcoat. And his wife shouts up
to him not to lean against the railing because it's old and rusty.

A furnace of fire—an athanor—burns day and night in
Kados's tower. And it is very hot having an athanor at this time
of year when the chestnut trees are blooming on Østre Farimagsgade. But there has to be a fire burning for the sake of the
salamanders—the elementals of fire which Kados wants to
create and develop contact with.

His books and papers are arranged on shelves along the walls.
If he's not careful with the athanor and there's a fire, irreplace-
able treasures will be lost.

He has a small table with bottles and flasks and distillation
apparatuses. As well as a small alcohol stove, because his wife
doesn't want him using the gas hotplate in the kitchen for his
experiments. Kados is busy working with the spagyric art, the

art of separating and uniting. And he isn't working with alchemy because he covets gold, but because he is an intellectual seeker. He owns old formulas which could obtain for him the grand *Magisterium. Lapis philosophorum* — the philosophers' stone. But he lacks the financial means to procure the necessary materials of a sufficient purity.

Kados buys his chemicals at a shop on Skindergade. He isn't able to spend large amounts of money on these purchases. The grand *Magisterium* will have to wait until better times. But even the lesser chemical experiments that Kados is able to perform in his pentangle tower have their significance. When he dips his pocket knife in a green copper solution, so that the blade is covered with copper, he is doing something that is dangerous and reprehensible to speak of openly. It symbolizes Mars removing his armor and putting on Venus's clothing. And he chases the red lion through the gray wolf whenever he cleans an old gold filling with antimony sulfide.

His wife comes in with coffee and puts a cup, sugar, and a

bottle of cream on the table among the crucibles and flasks. There is also a slice of pastry on a saucer. Kados eats it in silence and stirs his coffee as he continues his work.

On this table he also lays out his cards among the coffee cup and boiling flasks and sits reading and writing down ciphers, and consults his tables and sees the mystery of the numbers revealed to him.

There is a child's skeleton on the table. He brought it back from Paris, where it had been dug out of Madame Montvoisin's garden behind the building at rue de Beauregard 25 where this lady used to conduct her black masses. When Kados was in Paris, there was a bed factory in the building, but he was given permission to go inside and was able to ascertain that the ceiling in one of the rooms was still painted black.

He also has a little wooden sword that is called Shibulah. He put it together himself, and it looks clumsy and childish because he isn't a handy or practical man. But Shibulah's symbolic meaning is the same even though it was clumsily made. The same is true of the high-priestly headdress which he puts on his head on special occasions. It is awkwardly and naively made too, out of an oval margarine box that has paper pentangles and magic characters pasted on it. But the way the workmanship has been carried out has no bearing on the symbolic meaning.

Occasionally one of the children will come rushing into the dairy shop where Mrs. Kados is standing weighing out butter. "Mother, mother!" the child will shout. "Come quick! Father's gone crazy again."

But Mrs. Kados doesn't let it interrupt her. "Go out and shut the door," she says simply. And she calmly smacks a lump of butter with her long, flat wooden spoon and pours water on the paper to add weight. She is a practical woman who pays attention to her own business. She sends the children out into the city with fresh-baked goods and bottles of cream in the morning, and she knows that you have to put a lot of water on the paper when you're weighing out butter.

She has jelly rolls and rose-glazed pastries and little round butter cakes in her shop. Under a glass cover she has licorice whips and cinnamon sticks and chocolate frogs and colored suckers that the schoolchildren buy in the afternoon. And when

word comes that her husband has gone crazy again, she takes it in stride and acts as if nothing has happened.

"It's not right to say that your father is crazy!" she tells her children. "Especially not when there are strangers listening."

Kados is up in his five-sided tower. He is standing in the middle of the room in a magic circle which he has drawn around himself with chalk. He is swinging the sword Shibulah over his head and shouting strange and portentous words to invisible powers. And on his head he has the high priest's oval hat with its pentangles, numerology, and signs of the Zodiac. And he is mumbling and conjuring and shouting in ecstasy.

"Now you cut that out," his wife tells him. "And try to settle down. The children think you're crazy, and there are customers in the shop, and they can hear you in the apartment downstairs. We'll end up being evicted."

"Go, woman! Go away! Do not come too close!" he shouts. "Do not tread on the pentagram!"

And Mrs. Kados leaves. "Just don't let it go on too long," she says. "And don't shout so loud."

Down on Farimagsgade there are streetcars running. People are going into stores and buying everyday items. People are taking care of their own affairs; they are ordinary and normal. And no one knows what's going on up in the five-sided slate tower in the corner building at number 32.

The furnace of fire is burning. Black smoke is coming out of a chimney at a time of year when nobody stokes up a stove. It is stupefyingly hot inside the five-sided tower. Kados is sweating so much it drips off his large nose. He is pale and overwrought. He hasn't slept for several days. But he doesn't know what sleep is. His black eyes are animated and flashing.

"You'll get sick before long," his wife tells him, "if you don't ever sleep and if you don't eat properly."

"There have been adepts who neither ate nor slept and who lived to be 150 years old," Kados says. "Don't disturb me now! These are important matters I'm working on."

"And it's so suffocatingly hot in here that we can hardly stand it in the other room. And all that expensive coal! What's the idea of having a fire in the stove in the summer anyway?"

"Go! And let me work in peace!" says Kados. "Can you really

feel the heat all the way into the next room? You're right, it's actually very hot in here. But it's necessary."

"You'll end up getting heat stroke," Mrs. Kados says.

But up on the roof it's cool. The nights are bright and they're not really suited to observations of the firmament. But Kados climbs up there every evening anyway and lets the breeze cool him off as he follows the developments in the heavens.

On the other side of Østre Farimagsgade the buildings are very low and have small, artless gardens. Kados can see far and wide with his sharp gaze: out across Queen Louise's Children's Hospital, Holmens Cemetery, and Østre Anlæg to the warehouses and masts and smokestacks of Frihavn. He can also see a glimpse of Øresund and the blinking of the lighthouse towers at Trekroner and Middelgrund. Toward the north he can see out across the lakes and parks, out to distant rows of houses and factory smokestacks. And at one particular spot to the northwest, his eye lights upon one certain smokestack. And here his gaze encounters that of another sorcerer.

The other sorcerer lives far away. In a little town on the outskirts of the big city. But when he is standing on his balcony looking toward the southeast, he can see the same smokestack from the other side.

The gazes of the two sorcerers meet at this factory smokestack in the bright summer night. With firmness and resolve each one looks at his own side of the smokestack. Neither of them blinks or lowers his gaze. They test their strength against each other and prepare themselves for what is to come.

And above them shine the stars, whose significance and secret influence they both understand.

# [ 31 ]

IN THE DAYTIME it is pleasantly cool in the dairy shop. Sometimes Kados comes down all those stairs, exhausted and dripping with sweat, and walks into the dairy shop to refresh himself with a glass of cold milk. And he holds the ice-cold milk bottle against his hot forehead and breathes deeply.

Sometimes he even takes a walk and enjoys the sunshine on his way to the Royal Library, where he has old books brought to him in the reading room. He looks things up and jots things down on little slips of paper. The library staff treats him haughtily and without enthusiasm because he doesn't have a Doctor of Philosophy degree. But Kados doesn't let it upset him. If he wanted to use the powers and forces at his disposal, the librarians would be in a very bad way. But Kados is tolerant and forbearing and doesn't misuse his power.

He is also fond of strolling around and looking in the windows of the used book stores in the narrow streets around Frue Plads, hunting for books in the bins set up on the sidewalk. Sometimes he finds a book he can use and goes into the store to bargain about the price. But as he walks around looking at books, he is sometimes seized by anxiety that his wife will let the athanor go out up in his five-sided tower, and he hurries home with long strides.

Directly across from the dairy shop on Østre Farimagsgade there is a little shop that sells birds and goldfish. It also has a jar with salamanders in it that cost 15 øre apiece. "A child's best playmate," a sign on it reads, "easily tamed." And Kados stands looking at the little spotted animals that are climbing up and down in the jar. Now why were these wet, tailed amphibians that live in water and mud named after the spirits of fire? Perhaps it's because foolish people believe that amphibians won't burn when they're placed on hot coals. More likely the fact is that these resilient aquatic animals can stand more heat than most other living creatures.

Their flat heads bespeak a low intelligence. It is foolish and unbefitting to name these backward and material amphibians after the luminous spirits of fire! But that's the way natural science is. The Age of Philosophers is over, and there is only a very small circle of truth-seekers who keep the old occult sciences alive and carry on the medieval, kabbalistic, and neoplatonic philosophy.

And charlatans and ignoramuses like Mrs. Drusse and Sjögren desecrate the ancient sciences with their ignorant groping and depraved misuse of words and symbols.

Kados has no peers in this country with whom he can discuss the highest matters. He is a solitary man. An adept. An initiate and a loner. A superhuman being. And it is the fate of the adept to be lonely.

He can correspond with adepts in other countries in a language that the chosen few understand. But at home he is alone and misunderstood.

He has no disciples. He has no one he can train and consecrate to the call of the adept. And when he dies, perhaps his knowledge will die with him.

He feels that the times are against him. He is a prophet and a seer. But he doesn't see that the times are in the process of changing. He can read things in the stars, but it has escaped his notice that the world is in the process of becoming more receptive to the teachings of adepts. Cold reason no longer reigns supreme. Legend and myth are on their way to becoming a philosophy of life. Kados is a seer, but he doesn't see what is about to be realized. He is a lonely man who hasn't noticed that he is about to become timely. His gaze is turned inward, and he hasn't discovered that mysticism is about to come into vogue. He does not see that darkness is spreading.

He is a soothsayer who can predict the future. But he does not foresee everything. He doesn't realize that the time is about to come when people will read the Revelation of St. John the Divine and the large *Dreambook* of Cyprianus as fashionable reading material.

He walks around in the sunshine on Østre Farimagsgade wearing his old long black overcoat. His overworked eyes are dazzled by the sun, and he blinks into the sharp light. He is unable to see the approaching twilight.

He is alone with his thoughts and signs and symbols. But there is another man who, through strange channels, has gotten hold of some of the same secret and dangerous knowledge that Kados is trained in. But this man is more harmful. He does not possess the old adept's moral principles or scruples, but is ready to use his insights in a cynical and ruthless manner in order to consolidate his own power.

Kados knows this man. And he has watched with apprehension as he developed into an adept and took the occult forces into his service. Someday it may be necessary for Kados to bring his power to bear against this younger man and oppose his dangerous necromancy.

The other sorcerer lives far away from Kados. But in the evening, after Kados has gone up onto his roof to cool off in the night air, their gazes meet at a factory smokestack someplace out in the northwest.

The days pass. The furnace of fire burns. The sun bakes the tower's slates. But inside the hot tower, vapors are beginning to stir in a fat, tightly corked bottle. They are so distinct that even Mrs. Kados can see them, although she is unable to grasp their significance.

Things are happening. And all things are dependent on each other. Everything is an interactive totality.

Kados can see the connection and interdependence and relationship among things and people and events which to the uninitiated don't seem to have anything to do with each other.

On the basis of this knowledge plus an ingenious technique, he is able to make his computations. He lays out his tarot cards on the table in a significant pattern among the cake crumbs and spilled coffee. He has to shove aside bottles and flasks and coffee cups and rose-glazed pastry to make room.

On the street below, an organ grinder is playing the latest new tunes: "In Great-Grandma's Parlor" and "Beside the Old Chapel." But Kados doesn't hear it and doesn't let it disturb him. The radio in the next room is broadcasting a program with songs and melodies about old memories from our grandparents' days. But Kados works on calmly and isn't bothered by the noise.

But if he would listen to what the radio was saying, he might also be able to find out something about what is in store. The radio waves that are being transmitted via Copenhagen-Kalundborg must have their significance as well, affecting people and preparing the future. It might do a prophet some good to pay attention to the radio waves.

But Kados is preoccupied with his fire salamanders. He is studying his tarot cards, the cosmic aspects, and the kabbalistic numerical series and number systems. He looks into the future,

but the things that absorb his interest are specialized and particular. There are other things that he is overlooking.

Concerning the relationships on Stengade out in Nørrebro, though, there *is* something that catches his attention. He arranges his cards and peers at his tables. And he is astonished and disturbed. He adds up certain numerical quantities and calculates the sum of their digits and does some very unusual and ingenious things with them. The result makes him apprehensive. He has a foreboding that fateful and ominous events are going to take place. Dark and sinister clouds are gathering over Stengade.

"No, no," Kados mutters. "It mustn't happen if there's any way to prevent it! I must intervene. I must act. It is my duty to warn Damascus!"

# [ 32 ]

A SMALL NEW TOWN has been built on the outskirts of Copenhagen. It has long, freestanding apartment blocks with spacious balconies and flat roofs.

There are green lawns and trees and playgrounds and sandboxes among the apartment blocks. It is a parklike area without closed-in courtyards. Modern apartments with wide windows and sun and light. Garbage chutes and bathrooms and handy electric laundry appliances in the basement.

A small town on the outskirts of the big city. Beautifully and rationally planned. With room for many residents who ought to be happy and contented people. The fact that they aren't has its own special reasons.

There are flower boxes with nasturtiums and sweet peas on the balconies. And there are colorful parasols and sunshades. In the evening people light small lamps on their balconies and sit drinking tea or smoking an evening pipe or playing their radios and listening to the nostalgic programs from Copenhagen's Industrial Exposition Year of 1888 or looking at the view. Around them are grassy green open areas and allotment gardens. Electrified trains run along a raised embankment. Behind the embankment they have a view of distant natural-gas tanks and the gables of buildings with neon signs and chimneys.

Everything was pleasant and idyllic. But one day a sorcerer arrived and settled down in the town. And from that day on everything was changed. The town is enchanted. Life in the long buildings has become difficult and dramatic. What good does it do for an architect to plan everything in the best and most practical manner with nice rooms and pretty balconies, when there's a sorcerer sitting on one of the balconies breathing discord and disorder out over the little town?

"There are no normal people!" says the sorcerer. "Everybody is my patient. Ha, ha!"

Young newlyweds unsuspectingly rent an apartment in the

parklike town. They buy furniture and curtains and move in, happily thinking that they will live a long life together.

But the sorcerer is sitting on his balcony puffing his breath out over the town. And the newlyweds don't like each other anymore and want to get a divorce. They discover peculiar defects in each other and in themselves and realize that it was only a delusion for them to believe that they were normal people.

"There are no normal people, ho, ho!" the sorcerer shouts.

People who have been in love with each other and lived together and slept together and had good times with each other suddenly no longer know how they are supposed to behave. They have to go to the doctor and ask for his advice and guidance. "So now what do we do on this or that occasion? Why have we lost our desire and urge and pleasure?"

"I can fix that," says the doctor. "You need a series of treatments. It will take time, but if we work on it, I'm sure we'll achieve some results. We'd better begin right away!"

"Is this psychoanalysis?"

"No, no! Not at all. The psychoanalyst is passive. I am active. The psychoanalyst just sits there and listens. I work actively with my subjects. The analyst prefers to sit with his back to his patient. I don't do that at all. On the contrary!"

Things that used to be simple and straightforward have become problems that people can't solve by themselves. What people had thought was easy and innate can only be done after treatments and instructions and exercises and theoretical preliminary work in study groups.

"Ho, ho!" the sorcerer says. "You think you're happy with your wife. But it's an illusion. You think you're satisfied. But it's only because you don't know what it means to be satisfied. How do you go about it? How does it feel to you? How long does it last? Yes, just as I thought. It's an incomplete and unhappy experience." And the sorcerer convinces his victim and takes his vitality away from him.

"Please give me back my vitality, dear sorcerer!" the victim says.

"Ho, ho!" says the sorcerer. "I can indeed. But it'll cost you."

"I'll give you anything you ask," says the victim, "if only you'll give me back my sex drive!"

A woman comes to him and says, "Help me, doctor. I'm still young. But I'm lonely and neglected. And it's spring now, and all that. I can't stand it!"

"Come right on in," says the sorcerer. "Come into my clinic and take off your clothes." And he makes her happy again, and she becomes his disciple and his supporter and a participant in the study groups and a member of his league. And she brings all the money she can earn to the sorcerer and buys treatments and help for herself.

Madness and disorder have gripped the little town. It's called "Sex Park" now. But that's not a good name. Because the people in the town have lost their sexuality and have placed themselves in the sorcerer's power to get it back again.

There used to be young people who went walking in the woods on Sunday and strolled along holding hands and feeling good. But now they don't want to touch each other anymore because they have discovered that they are different than they thought they were.

"I'm a sadist!" the young man says. "I didn't know it before. But I know it now. All my earlier life has been a mistake. Look, I'm stepping on black forest slugs and slipping on them! It's because I'm a sadist. I used to think it was disgusting when I happened to step on a slug. But now I know that I want to do it, and I do it on purpose."

"And I'm in love with my old father!" says the girl. "I used to think he was crabby and old-fashioned and unreasonable. But now I know that was only because I'm in love with him. When I didn't like him, it was a sign of love. I'm in love with my father and I'm jealous of my mother. I want to go home to my father and don't want to walk in the woods with you anymore and watch you squash forest slugs."

"All right, let's go home," the man says. "This is a misunderstanding. We didn't know it before but we do now."

People have gone mad and taken leave of their senses. It's the sorcerer who is sitting and breathing insanity out over the neighborhood. He sits up on his balcony beneath an orange parasol looking out across the bewitched town. And he rubs his hands and smiles, saying "Ho, ho!" because odd and crazy things are going on in the town.

# [ 33 ]

THE CHILDREN ARE PLAYING on the lawns and in the sand-boxes between the apartment blocks in Sex Park. The sorcerer is sitting on his balcony watching them.

"These are problem children, ho, ho!" he says. "Should I cure them? Let them come to me. I know how to do it." But he doesn't mention that he was the one who bewitched the children and cast a spell on them.

There is an orange parasol on the sorcerer's balcony. Orange is the color that emanates from the planet Mars. But there are green parasols on the other balconies. Green is the color of Venus. There are also striped parasols that combine the colors of several planets, making things involved and complicated. The idea was for everything to be functional, simple, and rational in the long yellow apartment blocks. But life has become complicated and convoluted and dramatic because a wizard is living in one of the buildings.

The adept, Dr. Robert Riege, lives in building number 6. This is not just a random number. The Latin term for this number is *sex*, and it has lent its name to his profession and science. *Six* is the same thing as *sex*. And the number 6, the hexagon, and the hexagram stand for love, copulation, and union.

The number six is the union of two threes. Two times three is six. The six-pointed star is formed from two triangles placed on top of each other. One of the triangles, the one that points upward, symbolizes fire and the masculine principle. The other triangle, which points down, represents water and the feminine principle. The upturned triangle, upturned force, is man, the father, the spirit, electricity, heat, fire, and centrifugal force. The downturned triangle, water, is woman, the mother, magnetism, and centripetal force. Fire is expansive and masculine. Water is contractive and feminine. Positive and negative, which seek each other. Fire and water are opposites in cosmic nature and begin their metrographic manifestation according to a triangular and hexangular system.

That is why the number six is the symbol of copulation, sympathy, connection, psychism, satisfaction, release, orgasm. So it's no accident that Dr. Riege has taken up residence in building number 6.

He lives on the top floor. Unfortunately there are only five stories, but five is a good number too. He has rented two apartments, which he has joined together. In addition to his residence, he has the editorial office of *Sex News* here, as well as a clinic that has a wide couch with good springs, and a nice little laboratory that his supporters and disciples paid for when the Rockefeller Institute refused to put a room at his disposal for his sexual-cosmological experiments.

The plate on his door says *Sexpol Office*. And the mailman, the milkman, and other non-initiates wonder about just what sort of thing a "sexpol" is and are surprised that people are allowed to write words like that on their doorplates. People come and go all day. Clients and patients, disciples and sex politicians. Subjects and assistants. Study group leaders and sub-adepts.

Riege the adept is not a solitary man like Kados the adept. There is life and activity around him. He crackles with electrical charges and high tension. He organizes things, puts them into effect, and sets them in motion. He doesn't have a dairy shop like Kados or any wife to take care of the shop. He is a bachelor and is perfectly capable of taking care of his projects himself. He is practical and economical. His activities bring in a good income. He does not cultivate the spagyric art like Kados. He doesn't know how to make gold, but he certainly knows how to make money.

Outwardly he doesn't look like a sorcerer. He doesn't have a long beard or a black cape. He is clean-shaven and elegant and works in a cool white smock coat. He doesn't have a sword called Shibulah or any magic headdress. There are no signs of the Zodiac or pentangles or numerology painted on his walls.

But he has a nice collection of surrealistic and abstract paintings whose symbolic contents and occult significance are the same as Kados's magic signs.

"Cosmic Water" is the name of one picture. Other titles are "Yellow Object" and "Magic Fissure." The pearl of his collection is a large painting called "Static Object." It depicts a red ring on a violet background, and in its simplified artistic form it represents the symbol for the womb itself, chaos before conception, the egg of the universe, macrocosm, bubbles of the solar system, the egg into which the monad is to be introduced, the still untouched auric egg.

Another gripping work by the same artist shows a blue-green circle with a red dot in the center. In its simple beauty it is the symbol of space and eternity. The picture is called "Dynamic Object, or the Dawn of Manifestation." The red dot represents the spermatozoon in the egg of the universe. Potential space within abstract space. The focal point for all motion. And the present and moving cosmic fire.

On Dr. Riege's birthday his grateful disciples presented their master with a huge painting by a well-known abstract artist. The artist called his picture "Cosmic Force," and Dr. Riege's disciples were so enthralled by its grandiose concept that they immediately took up a collection so that they could purchase the painting. It shows a black vertical stripe on white canvas. The symbol of the masculine. The creative force in the universe. Saltpeter and fire. The vertical force that functions in the bodies of the stars as the axes around which the orbs rotate. It is also the symbol of the will, the monad, humanity's upright posture, and the erective force. The masculine creative force.

A famous painting whose unveiling stirred up a great sensation and much discussion. Many people interpreted and explained it. But many people were catastrophically wrong in expounding upon its symbolism. Yet the artist himself once provided the correct explanation in a catalogue. And this explanation was cut out and pasted on the frame.

It is only in his private apartment, however, that the doctor has paintings. In his laboratory and clinic the walls are white and businesslike. He doesn't have a child's skeleton on his desk like Kados. Only a jar with a small fetus in alcohol.

And he has an athanor—a slow-combustion oven—in his laboratory. Here he heats up sand and iron oxide until they're red-hot, and he combines and reshapes these materials. He does not have the formula for *lapis philosophorum*. But he knows about the transmutation of metals and is able to transform minerals. His master in America could produce organic matter out of inorganic chemicals. Life and cells from lifeless minerals. But his discovery didn't create the stir that its significance should have warranted. "Maybe he didn't wash out his flasks properly before using them," said the skeptics. Now Dr. Riege wants to carry on his master's work—work that will mean the solution to the mystery of life itself.

There is a large, fat flask in his laboratory. It contains a liquid the composition of which is Dr. Riege's secret. But his most faithful disciples have been given permission to look at the flask. And some of them could clearly see life stirring in the milky fluid. Small bubbles rise up. And dark shadows move. Things are stirring in the flask that will one day astonish humanity and disgrace a bald-headed professor at the Rockefeller Institute as well as the entire skeptical scientific establishment.

Dr. Riege looks on with a smile. Charged up and energetic. In America, where he studied chiropractic, he learned how to give a toothy smile. There was a time when he cured people of many different kinds of ailments by blows to the spinal column. He still understands the importance of the spinal column as the seat of human electrical forces even though he is no longer engaged in the chiropractic business. He knows that cosmic rays, waves, and vibrations primarily affect the spinal column. He knows that the primeval cosmic force, which we also call electricity, magnetism, and energy, is nothing more than sexuality. He is the father of Sexual Cosmology. He has studied many things even though he isn't as learned as Kados. And he doesn't have Kados's strict moral principles. His goal is to gain power over people. And his power is already so great that Kados can feel it and is aware of the danger.

In the evening Dr. Riege sits on his balcony looking out over the neighborhood. Across the S-train rails, the common, and the little allotment gardens. And he sees the gables of buildings and distant smokestacks. Far out to the southeast he can see a certain factory smokestack. Here his gaze meets that of Kados, who is standing in his pentangle tower looking toward the northwest.

Two sorcerers and adepts. Two experts on hidden forces and secret knowledge.

# [ 34 ]

PEOPLE COME AND GO at the Sexpol offices. Subjects for experiments present themselves at the laboratory to have their life energy measured and recorded as curves on a rotating cylinder. And life energy is nothing but sexual energy. A bio-electrical charging and tension which is discharged and measured.

The subject sits peacefully and patiently on a chair. Electrical wires lead from him to the recording instrument, which has a drum where the curve of his sexual energy is plotted. The doctor stimulates him in a variety of ingenious ways and produces tension and excitement and registers the degree of excitement. Afterwards there is a release of tension, relaxation, and exhaustion, and the subject has to rest on Dr. Riege's couch for a while. Being a subject is hard work, but there are unemployed people who can be convinced to do it for the price of a meal. There are also enthusiastic disciples who willingly and without payment put their sexual energy and bio-electricity at the master's disposal.

A cordial relationship prevails between the master and his disciples. He likes to be in their midst, and they are grateful beyond all bounds when he smiles at them. He has nice white teeth and knows how to give an American smile. They come to him and ask his advice on all aspects of life. They know him, and he knows them, and they have no secrets from each other.

And the master is not too proud to ask the advice of his disciples either. When he is going to give a speech or write an article on new points of view for *Sex News,* he will often submit the question to a study group and have them work on the material.

They are like a league. A working fellowship. A congregation assembled around the sexual idea. A community preoccupied with the administration of their common sexual energy. A family busy balancing the libido's household budget.

Strictly speaking it's not an actual organization. The disciples are assembled in study groups that are concentric with each other. A wheel within a wheel like the one Ezekiel saw in his vision. The innermost study group is like a grand council where the master himself presides.

Power emanates from the master just as solar energy and cosmic sexual energy emanate from the sun. The sexual-cosmological idea is enormous and all-encompassing.

It has brought to life a great number of new sciences. And it must be assumed that more will follow. Bion-research and bion-cancer research. Anal rhythmics. Oralogy.

Chiromancy was an old science that explored the lines of the hand and read a person's character and future fate from lines and furrows and elevations. But oralogy is a new science that can read the same things from the shape of the mouth and the folds and wrinkles around the mouth. How many people have turned into incomplete and inhibited neurasthenics because they were taught to keep their mouths convulsively closed during the first years of their lives? A relaxed, open, receptive mouth is a precondition for health and happiness in life.

Many children suck their thumbs or their pacifiers dully and mechanically without any real conviction to their sucking.

"His orality is inhibited!" says the sorcerer. "The mouth as pleasure zone has been neglected. This child was already a neurasthenic in the maternity ward, when they tried to force him to regular feedings at fixed times. The first eight days of life were fateful because of the violence and compulsion in the maternity ward. It will take a long time to repair what has taken place."

"What the hell is this?" a child asks. "Your left breast is hardly giving any milk at all. What's the big idea?"

"I can't help it!" says the mother. "You've sucked so much there isn't any more."

"But that's exactly the reason there should be more! Because I'm sucking and stimulating it!" And the child is indignant and insulted. And his parents are worried about what will happen when their child has to go to school next year and can't breastfeed whenever he feels like it.

Because children have their own rhythm, and mealtimes and regularity are compulsive and unnatural, destroying that rhythm and the feeling of pleasure and leading to neuroses. So, better gastritis than depression! And if some parents are so caught up in their conservative prejudices that they won't let their children gobble up all the chocolate their pleasure requirements demand, but serve them other food once in a while despite the demands of the child, they are directly to blame if their child becomes re-pressed, fearful, and sexually unsatisfied.

Pedagogy is not possible without sexual cosmology. A child's rhythm must be respected. And if, without thinking, a mother tells a child who has sat down in a mud puddle that he shouldn't get so filthy, it is only natural for the child to answer, "Are you out of your mind, Mother? Are you trying to inhibit and ruin me?"

Worried parents bring their children to the sorcerer and ask for his help. "This is little Søren. He's five years old but he doesn't want to masturbate. We've tried everything, but it's impossible to make him do it."

"That's bad," says the sorcerer. "But we mustn't lose heart. Patience is required."

Some children say, "Ah! Ah!" and beg to be put on the potty. "So what are we to do?" ask the parents.

"Well, if the child absolutely insists on doing it in the potty instead of in his pants, there's nothing to do but give him a potty," the sorcerer says. "But at least make sure that he dumps the contents on his head and smears it on the walls afterwards!"

"We'll do what we can," the parents reply.

In the study groups, mothers exchange experiences and work with the material. "I'm afraid my little Jørgen has grown so peaceful lately. What do you suppose the reason could be? What could have inhibited him?"

"He's peaceful? That's not so good. Are his muscles tight? Does he have lines around his mouth?"

"My little Anna throws the most delightful temper tantrums. Her aggression is so violent that we have to be careful she doesn't beat her little brother to death. Is this wrong? How can we give her aggression free reign without harming her little brother too much?"

"Wouldn't it be a good idea to give her a big cloth doll that she can take out her aggressions on?"

"Yes, but if the cloth doll doesn't cry or bawl or put up a fight, that won't completely satisfy her, will it?"

"Just as long as muscular tension and tightness are dissipated, does it mean that much if the object of her aggression is capable of complaining?"

"But what about the psychological factor? Muscular relaxation alone isn't enough, is it? The object really ought to be alive, shouldn't it?"

"Just have the child pound on inanimate objects with a hammer! That will provide satisfaction in most cases. Another good thing is stabbing a knife into a shiny tabletop."

Many problems are urgent and need to be dealt with in the study groups. There is plenty of material to work with. "Is it proper to forbid children from playing on window ledges? Or out in the street?"

"Prohibitions can inhibit the child. On the other hand, falling from the fifth floor or being run over by a truck can be dangerous too. What should we do?"

"The child must learn for himself what is dangerous for him and use self-regulation to adapt to the law of gravity and other unavoidable evils."

"But how will the child learn about the danger of falling from the fifth floor?"

"Well, try letting him fall from low, harmless heights. Let the child learn that hurting himself is painful."

"But then won't the child also learn that these falls aren't potentially lethal?"

"Prohibition is an evil thing! Self-regulation will certainly save the child's life. Let him burn himself slightly on the heating pipes. And run into him with a bicycle. Cautiously and slowly, so that he won't be harmed but will learn that vehicles mean danger."

There are many questions that have to be cleared up. "We work with the material and learn more and more every day. Our study groups have produced good results."

Questions can also be asked in the question-and-answer column of *Sex News*. Dr. Riege gives concise answers, which, it is hoped, have brought consolation and guidance to many people in matters of sexual doubt.

They work with the material and they work with the children. They give them tickling treatments so that the children practically have convulsions from laughter and excitement. And when a couple has a little boy who, in spite of all his sexual-cosmological upbringing, sits at the table, nice and quiet, meticulously eating his jam, it is understandable that the worried mother feels compelled to grab the jar and smear the jam in the child's face.

"Or wasn't that the right thing to do?"

"Oh yes, it was, absolutely! How did the child react?"

"He howled."

"That's splendid. Just let him howl away. Your child is entitled to have people respect his right to cry."

This is the way life goes in Sex Park, with work and studies and experiments. It is alien and peculiar to the uninitiated. A group of young uniformed girls wearing bathing caps comes marching along between the apartment blocks. These are the "P-Girls," Sex Park's "flying squad." Volunteers that Dr. Riege can call out quickly and send into action wherever sexual aid is required.

And a group of young people is heard singing from a balcony. With solemn determination they are singing the Jazz-Pol party's fight song:

C'mon, we gotta relax,
C'mon, we gotta relax,
Why do we gotta?
Well, 'cause we oughta.
Ah, ah, didelee-delee lideleee . . .

# [ 35 ]

ONE DAY A CONSPICUOUSLY elegant, long blue car drives up between the blocks of yellow buildings in Sex Park.

It stops at building number 6, right behind a little cream-colored sports car which belongs to Dr. Riege and which looks completely insignificant beside this very long blue car.

An attractive lady steps out of the car. She is delicate and slightly pale and is wearing a custom-tailored suit. Proper and discreet. She looks around somewhat apprehensively. She is still free and can turn back. Once she has entered the sorcerer's building, she will be in his mysterious power. Then there will be no turning back.

In the old days, distinguished ladies wore veils or masks when they visited sorcerers or witches. That was when ladies sought diversion and variety by participating in Black Masses. Now they go to sex-political study groups. And they no longer wear masks.

The lady in the blue car is from the provinces, and she doesn't think anyone will recognize her even though her car is conspicuous and unusual. She doesn't know that a man by the name of Olsen has seen her car. He is interested in cars and motors and has noticed its unusual appearance. He thinks he recognizes it. He notes that there is an H on the license plate. So it's Præstø county. That fits.

The lady in the blue car has probably long since forgotten the existence of a man by the name of Olsen. But he hasn't forgotten her. And he recognizes her easily enough.

In the house of the witch Madame Montvoisin in the rue de

Beauregard in Paris, where distinguished ladies went for the stimulation and diversion of Black Masses several centuries ago, the ceiling and the walls were painted black. The ladies burned black candles that were made from human fat. And dreadful, macabre symbols were displayed.

That's not the way things are at Dr. Riege's. Everything here is white, cool, and chromed. And only the cosmic symbols of the abstract paintings on the walls suggest the occult activities that are conducted in the building.

"Ho, ho! I've been expecting you," the sorcerer says. "Consul Cederbusk's wife has talked about you."

"Yes, Consul Cederbusk's wife is my best friend. Both she and her two grown daughters are so pleased with you. She thought that you could help me too."

"Sit down, madame. Relax and don't worry. Trust me," the doctor says. And when he touches her lightly, she can feel an electrical force emanating from him, and she senses his strange power and feels limp and light-headed.

"Can you remember that I wrote to you once?" she asks. "Anonymously. To your question-and-answer column in *Sex News?*"

"Ho, ho!" says the doctor. "That question-and-answer column! People criticize me for it. The scientific establishment doesn't think that one can give an adequate answer in such a limited amount of space. But isn't a short answer better than no answer at all?"

"Yes, you gave a very short answer," the lady says.

The doctor looks at her. Energy streams from his blue eyes. A charging process is taking place. The room is electric.

Dr. Riege is not a hypnotist. But he knows how to create a mood. An atmosphere that alters the patient's consciousness and makes the patient receptive to the impressions he wishes to evoke. The surrealistic symbols on the wall emphasize the mood.

"Do you think psychoanalysis would help?"

"No, no! Psychoanalysis is only able to uncover subconscious psychic mechanisms. I am not a psychoanalyst. I am a sexualist. Psychoanalysis is passive. We are active. Psychoanalysis only wishes to ascertain. We wish to liberate."

"Can you cure me?"

"Cure you? There's nothing to cure. We must accommodate our inclinations. Our inhibitions must be dissolved. Life has only one purpose: the pleasure experience. The only urge of elementary life energy is the pleasure experience."

"Ah!" says the lady.

"Old psychoanalysis was indirect and made use only of language and language associations. We, on the other hand, intervene directly! Purely physical influences and acts must precede linguistic communications."

"But shouldn't I even tell you about my . . . about my case?"

"Oh, yes! Do tell me. Unburden yourself and loosen up and tell me freely and without inhibitions." He takes her hands, and again she experiences the magnetic force that emanates from him. She feels limp and strange. And she tells him. She has read Dr. Riege's brochures and knows the right terminology. She confides intimate and amazing things to him. And every time the sorcerer touches her, his electricity flows through her. Strange sensations run through her. And she relaxes and surrenders.

Dr. Riege has gained a new, faithful disciple. A patient whose case demands a peculiar and unusual treatment. They agree that for the time being she should come for treatment twice a week. Mondays and Wednesdays at 2:00 p.m. And the doctor doesn't forget to tell her what the first session has cost either. The pale lady takes a checkbook out of her purse and writes a check. Regarding future sessions, he will let her have a discount according to the number of sessions and the length of the treatment.

The doctor gives her a couple of new brochures in which she can do some further reading about the gospel of sexual cosmology. She thanks him and stuffs them into her purse.

"Just a moment," the doctor says. "I think the price is on the back. Let's just see," and he takes a look. "Yes, here it is." And the lady gets out her coin purse and pays him.

Everything might have been just fine if the blue car hadn't been seen and recognized as an "H" car from Præstø county.

In the evening two sorcerers sit and write.

One of them is sitting in his five-sided tower on Østre Farimagsgade printing his letters neatly and meticulously by hand.

The other is sitting in his modern office in Sex Park typing on a flat, silent typewriter.

Simultaneously they fold up their papers, put them in manila envelopes, and address the envelopes to: Mr. Damascus, Printer, Stengade 41, Copenhagen N. Simultaneously they go down to the street and drop their letters in the mailbox.

# [ 36 ]

THINGS HAPPEN. They have repercussions and make more things happen. One thing leads to another, then spreads and branches out.

One person commits an act, and his act has consequences and causes other acts by other people. What is liable to happen is impossible to control or anticipate.

A man goes around giving away large amounts of money to charitable causes. Perhaps he feels that good deeds can offset and neutralize other deeds. But Kados knows that this isn't possible. Actions cannot be undone. Once a thing has happened, it has happened, and its consequences must continue *ad infinitum*.

A word is sent out into the world, and what it may bring about is absolutely unpredictable. It starts working, releasing things and setting processes in motion. Two sorcerers are sitting in their respective parts of the city sending their words out into space. And their words move about at random, having their own special consequences.

Printer Damascus has received two manila envelopes. "This is to be set in 14 point," Dr. Riege writes. "And would you send me the proof sheets right away?" The material that is to be printed in 14 point is cryptic and brings Nostradamus to mind. Everything is symbolic, and nothing is accidental. And these mysterious printed words will be sent out and have an effect on many people.

But Kados too writes about symbols. It is not accidental or haphazard when his tarot cards line up in a specific order or sequence. Someone who can decipher the symbols can discern the meaning of things. Kados does not write articles. His writings are private and are sent only to Damascus, because someone who has insight also has the duty to warn people. "Watch out for the six-tongued dragon, the enemy of nature! And beware of the man who steals Saturn from the type case! Watch out for the 17th of July!"

It is obvious that the six-tongued dragon can be none other than Dr. Riege, and that the man who steals Saturn must be Olsen, since Saturn is the alchemical symbol for the lead that Olsen swipes from the type case. Damascus understands the warning clearly and does not dismiss it. But how is he supposed to approach the matter?

As for Dr. Riege's envelope, in addition to the manuscript it contains a small slip of paper, which has great power and significance because it is a check in payment for the latest issue of *Sex News*. This check is welcome and indispensable for Damascus. *Sex News* is actually the only periodical he prints that shows a profit. Kados's warning doesn't mean that Damascus shouldn't print Dr. Riege's magazine, does it?

Now at least the most pressing bills can be paid. The telephone bill can be paid, but it would be better if that confounded telephone didn't exist. And Olsen can have the 20 kroner he needs. Then he probably won't do anything risky and get himself mixed up in any trouble. "Actually, I can give you a little more, Olsen. The day after tomorrow is Friday anyway."

"Thanks, that would be real nice," says Olsen.

And Olsen smiles cryptically because he received a letter too. It's an answer from the man he wrote to recently:

Dear Olsen,
    You can meet me at "The Stag" rooming house on Lavendelstræde. Don't come before dark. Don't let anybody see you. Use the prearranged knock on the door.
                                                    Hans Christian Andersen
                                                    from Odense

But before Olsen can meet Hans Christian Andersen, there is something he needs to take care of. He has to buy a heavy envelope, the kind people use to send cash through the mail. He borrows a piece of sealing wax from Damascus. He writes something on a slip of paper that Damascus is not supposed to see.

Damascus can see only the word *Danielsen*. Olsen puts the slip of paper in the envelope and seals it carefully and puts his thumb-print on the wax seal. Olsen's fingerprints are registered at police headquarters and don't look like anybody else's, so it would be impossible to forge his seal.

It's midsummer, and it takes a very long time to get dark. Olsen has to hang around in the streets and wait. Why the devil does it absolutely have to be dark before he can meet the writer Hans Christian Andersen?

Not until 11:00 p.m. does he walk over to Lavendelstræde and look for "The Stag" rooming house. It is a particularly gloomy and sinister-looking place. Why the hell does Hans Christian Andersen always choose these kinds of places when he can actually afford to stay in better ones?

He asks the obese landlord whether a writer named Andersen from Odense is staying there.

"Up on the third floor facing the back," the landlord says. "Number 21. It's the worst room. Mr. Andersen asked to have it reserved several days ago. As long as he's paying for it, he's entitled to have his fun. God only knows what he's up to. I imagine he's an idealist, this Andersen?"

"Yeah, he's an idealist." Olsen walks up the narrow staircase and knocks at number 21.

There's no answer.

He knocks again and tries the door. It's locked. Then he remembers the letter: the prearranged knock on the door! Now how did it go? Three short knocks and three long ones, then one long one and one short one three times. It's a veritable percussion concert and it attracts attention in the rooming house.

Finally the door is opened. "Come inside quickly, Olsen! And lock the door! I'm afraid somebody'll spy on us."

"Hello, Mr. Andersen," says Olsen. "I don't recognize you at all with that beard."

Hans Christian Andersen is standing in the middle of the room. He has a long black beard and a big nose. Olsen can see immediately that the beard is fake. But the nose is certainly real enough. Hans Christian Andersen has an old seaman's cap on his head. And he has on a pea jacket and sailor's workpants.

"Why do you have that beard on, Mr. Andersen?"

"You can't tell it's not real, can you?"

"Well, yes I can, sort of," Olsen says. "Since I know you, after all."

"Hm, that's not so good. But it won't do to switch beards again. It would be too conspicuous. I have several beards in my bag, by the way. Do you think the landlord was suspicious about my beard?"

"Heck no."

"Sit down on this chair, Olsen. There's only one chair. So I'll sit on the bed. Wait a minute. I'll spread a newspaper out first. There we are. You never can tell who might have been lying on this bed. And even though I can switch my beard, I'd hate to get lice in it."

"That makes sense," says Olsen.

"And now you'll have to talk very softly. The walls in this building have ears. You never can tell who might be listening."

"Right," says Olsen. "This won't take very long. See, the thing is, I've got something cooking out in the provinces that I can't really talk about. I mean, it's not illegal or anything like that. Still, there is a risk, and something might happen to me. So that's why I wanted to give you this envelope first. Of course, I *can* trust you, can't I, Mr. Andersen?"

"You can. No one has ever doubted my word," says Hans Christian Andersen.

"I know you're a fine man who can be trusted. So I won't play games with you. See, here in this envelope, which is sealed by the way, there's a note for you. But you're not supposed to read it unless something happens to me. If I don't come back from what I've got going, then you open the letter and publish what it says in your newspaper. It's something that will interest your readers, believe me! But if I come back within a week, and nothing has happened to me, don't read the letter or publish it in your newspaper."

"Right. I won't read it. You can trust me. I'll only open it if I don't hear from you within a week. And I trust that what you've got going is nothing illegal?"

"It's completely legal. Rest assured about that!"

"That's good. And if you disappear, I'll break the seal on the envelope. And if the message inside is suitable to be printed in a newspaper, I'll publish it."

"Exactly. I've put my thumbprint on the seal. So of course I'll be able to see if someone's been monkeying with it."

"I won't monkey with it. And the envelope won't fall into anybody's hands but mine. You can trust me." And Hans Christian Andersen takes off his cap and hides Olsen's manila envelope inside the double lining. "Pretty clever, huh? Nobody'd think of looking for it there."

"Great!" says Olsen. "So, not a word to anyone, Mr. Andersen."

"My discretion is known all over Denmark and in large portions of Sweden."

"I know you're a fine man."

"So when are you leaving, Olsen?"

"I'm leaving next week. The 16th or 17th. So why don't we say that if you haven't heard from me by the 24th of July, you'll go ahead and open the envelope."

"And until that time, it will remain secure in my fire- and burglar-proof safe. Depend on it. No human eye will see it," says Hans Christian Andersen.

"That's fine."

"Then I suppose there isn't anything else, Olsen? I assume that in due time you'll give me a satisfactory explanation for all this? And there's nothing illegal involved in this business?"

"No, there isn't. And you'll learn everything in due course."

"Then we'd better part company. Leave the building as unobtrusively as possible. I'll just wait a little longer. A taxi is waiting for me out on the street. The important thing is not to attract attention. Goodbye, Olsen."

"Goodbye, Mr. Andersen, and thanks."

# UNREST IN THE PARISH

## [ 37 ]

JUNE HAS BEEN COOL. And the grass in the meadows is damp and tall. There will be a lot of hay this year. And after Midsummer Eve the hot weather arrives. That's exactly the way things are supposed to be.

People are trimming their hedges bordering the road. Niels Madsen's boys from the children's home are hoeing and raking the soil in front of the hedge all the way out to the asphalt, so that everybody can see that the man who lives here likes order and neatness.

Old Emma walks around with her bucket fertilizing her leeks. They're still only small and thin, but in time they'll be as thick as your wrist.

Everything is thriving and growing. Jens Olsen's large sow has had a litter of sixteen piglets. They all survived, and they're cute and well-formed. But of course she is an exceptional sow who deserves to be scratched and tickled and spoken to nicely. Jens Olsen gazes fondly at her offspring, almost as if he could have been their father himself.

After Midsummer Eve the quaking grass goes to seed and isn't nearly as pretty. And the flowers of the water avens turn into fuzzy balls. The cuckoo should have stopped singing by now, of course, but it's still cuckooing over in the forest. And if anyone asks how long they're going to live, it cuckoos a great number of years. There will be time enough for everything. Summer has only just begun.

But the squire, who rides off all by himself in his car, probably hasn't asked the cuckoo how long he's going to live. Maybe he thinks life will go on forever. He has so many irons in the fire, and he rushes around inspecting his numerous projects and his factories and his shops and his burial mound and tells the workers to hurry up. But his burial mound will probably be ready in plenty of time.

It has been hardened with reinforced concrete and will be secure against bombs and artillery shells in the event of war. And if there is a war, agricultural products will probably command good prices. They say that the squire has begun buying up horses. He's a man who seems to know what's coming.

But everything is peaceful. The countryside smells of new-mown hay. And little roosters are crowing all around, on all the farms. It's only on the radio at night that anybody talks about war, and statesmen argue heatedly with one another in foreign languages.

It's not only the hay harvest that's going to be so incredibly good this year. The grain harvest promises to exceed all bounds. The winter was mild, and spring came early. All of Denmark was already planted by the middle of March. The crops are standing tall and thick and lush. If warm weather comes now, there'll be a record harvest. Farmers look nervously at their fields, because with all this abundance and surplus, prices probably won't hold up. In America they have so much wheat that the farmers are practically starving to death, and they have to burn their wheat just to stay alive. Things haven't gone that far in Denmark yet, but we did receive livestock destruction orders. And it must have cost the state quite a bit of money to destroy so many cows and pigs, but we did manage to get prices up. Maybe it really would be better if there was a war, since there's too much of everything.

Jens Olsen's family has taken in a vacation child from Copenhagen. Panty Marius would have liked to have one of the older vacation girls himself to help out his housekeeper a little, but they wouldn't let him have one in view of the fact that the police have been after him for his strange inclination. Niels Madsen, on the other hand, isn't interested in vacation children. He has his boys from the children's home, and he gets 3 kroner a day for each one; they sweat and slave running his place to make it a model farm.

The schoolchildren who rode the bus to grammar school are on vacation too, but they have to be careful not to forget their learning during these six weeks. The village school, though, delays vacation until the harvest so the children can help out and make themselves useful. Towheaded children wearing wooden clogs and rubber boots hike their long ways to school. But they only have school every other day, and their homework isn't so bad because the entire school only has two classes. The worst part is the long hymn verses, which are so obscure and enigmatic. They walk along the road practicing them:

> Learn thusly by past lesson,
> All ye who are God's chosen.
> Jesus calls: watch and pray
> That thou shalt never fall away.

In fact, it isn't necessary for the evangelicals to set up a Sunday school. The town makes ample provision for religious education. And even if some fanatics did consider getting their children excused from the school's religion class, there are still morning prayers, hymns during music class, scriptural passages in their copy books, edifying stories in their readers, and miracles and wonders in the history of their fatherland.

But there's a Sunday school anyway. And Pastor Nørregaard-Olsen agitates diligently for people to join and offers prizes to the children who can bring the most friends along. If they come three Sundays in a row, they get a shiny sticker with a picture of God on it. And if they make it through an entire season, they get fruit juice and cookies. "Close ranks! Close ranks!" Pastor Nørregaard-Olsen says. "And don't forget the children's worship service in the church either. What we learn in our youth, we don't forget in our old age. And truly these seeds that are now being sown in these small hearts shall one day take root and bear fruit."

And the children trudge off to learn about Original Sin and the Atonement and the mystery of the Last Supper and the Holy Spirit and to get a shiny sticker of God and a share in the Danish national treasury of hymns. The children are so small and short that they only stick up a little ways above the grass at the roadside ditches. They're so close to the ground that they see little tiny things that big people don't notice and can follow little tiny ants and beetles on their tortuous journeys.

There are so many insects and small animals and little green snakes living in the grass. They're all busy and have someplace to go and something they have to do. They creep and crawl and walk over obstacles and press onward. Maybe everything they do has a purpose.

The frogs aren't croaking in the pond next to Martin's house anymore. They have finished their mating, and their eggs have turned into tadpoles that scurry about under the duckweed. And thousands of other aquatic creatures are swimming and wriggling around. Jens Olsen's fat white ducks are slurping up the duckweed and having a wonderful time.

At night a pair of hedgehogs comes out and walks around in the grass grunting and coughing. Martin's wife puts a saucer of milk out for them, and they come all the way up to the door to drink, growing tame and bold. The children are allowed to get out of bed to look at the two hedgehogs, which have friendly eyes and cute little snouts and drink out of the saucer just as neatly as the cat.

During the day there is a baby carriage standing outside Martin's house. His youngest child is lying in the carriage making noises. The three other children play nearby, rooting in the pond with sticks. They don't go to Sunday school even though the two oldest ones are certainly big enough. They won't get any shiny stickers with a picture of Our Lord on them.

Martin and his wife don't belong to the Kingdom of God. They don't even go to church on Christmas Eve. Their children are growing up without Sunday school and children's worship services and get-togethers at the evangelical meeting house — as if they were Turks or heathens. "Nyaa-nyaa," say the other children, "you're not going to be saved!"

"What's being saved?"

"That's just something you're not going to be! And you won't get a picture of Jesus either!"

# [ 38 ]

THE GARDENER HAS BEEN SAVED and is a true believer who belongs to the Kingdom. But he's not a happy man. Salvation hasn't brought him peace or contentment. He has a heavy heart in spite of his faith in the Divine Promise, and his life is full of worries and speculations.

Every hour of the day he can observe God's creative powers and can see wonders performed before his eyes. But he takes no delight in it. Things sprout and grow and flourish in his nursery. This has been a year of fruitfulness and blessing. Tiny flat seeds have turned into swelling cucumbers in his hotbeds. And his tomato plants are growing at tropical speed in his greenhouses and bearing several levels' worth of fruit. But the gardener waters them without joy and looks with melancholy eyes at the luxuriance and profusion of nature.

They have been divinely blessed with plenty of asparagus this year. But now, after Midsummer Eve, asparagus season is about over, and pretty soon the gardener will have sent the last bunches to Pastor Nørregaard-Olsen. Which is too bad, because the pastor is so terribly fond of asparagus. But he can send tomatoes to the pastor every day. It's only reasonable to give your pastor a slight token of your esteem. The squire approves of it as well and deducts it from the accounts.

If this warm weather continues, the strawberries will really take off. The gardener's daughter has already shown up at the parsonage in her YD uniform with the first basket of ripe berries.

The pastor says, "Oh, my! The first strawberries! What fragrance! Oh, what bliss! Sunshine and health and vitamins have been concentrated into a little red berry. What a wonderful artist God is, to be able to make this from soil, water, and sunlight. Try to imitate him in this, all ye learned and intelligent men at the university!

"Wouldn't you like to taste a berry yourself, Johanne dear?" he says. "And will you say hello to your father and give him our kindest regards for thinking of us?" Then the pastor calls a maid and says, "Take this basket and show it to your mistress, Kristine. Then put it out in the icebox."

The nursery is an extensive operation, and gardener Holm has a lot of people working under him. The situation is most advantageous with the young nursery apprentices, who receive no wages, and they pay for their training plus room and board besides. Then there is the estate's large permanent staff, which he naturally can put to work where they are needed.

The large park is the gardener's responsibility too, and there are people constantly at work trimming the lawns, raking the pathways, and removing leaves. The flower borders are tended with seasonal plants, and the hundreds of fruit trees have to be sprayed and dusted and pruned. Even if the squire owned nothing more than the nursery, he would still be a wealthy man.

Every morning the gardener sends a truck to the produce market at Grøntorvet in Copenhagen, and on Wednesdays and Saturdays a truck goes to the market in Præstø. The flowers and vegetables that aren't sold at the market are culled out and sold in the little shop in town. Johanne works there, weighing things out, conscientious and accurate with the scales, and not squandering God's gifts. When there are birthdays or funerals, a lot of money can be made selling flowers and wreaths. There are also attractive cross arrangements out of moss, pine cones, shellacked berries, and everlasting plants. Johanne is good at going into the woods and gathering lichens and moss and putting them together with wire. In the old days people wanted to have wreaths made out of glass beads and wax palms. But the enlightened education of the last few years has elevated their taste. Now they know that nature is more beautiful, and moss wreaths with pine cones and varnished holly berries have become popular.

It's been a long time since there was a good funeral, though. And since the squire turned 60 last year, they haven't sold many flowers. The squire's birthday was a big day. All the flowers the gardener could get his hands on were sold. There were five people in the shop tying bouquets and taking telephone orders. Even the flower borders and the rose beds in the castle park were cleaned out. And as the bouquets and arrangements were taken up to the squire in the castle, the squire had Lukas carry them back to the gardener so they could be retied and sold one more time. God loves a cheerful giver. And the squire didn't want to deprive anyone of the joy of giving.

Squire Skjern-Svendsen made over 2,000 kroner just on flowers to himself on his own birthday. He has a lucky hand. Everything he touches turns into money and prosperity.

Gardener Holm is an able man in his profession; he does things properly and settles his accounts with the squire precisely and punctually. There are no conflicts or disagreements between them. They both belong to the Kingdom and have given their hearts to Jesus. And yet there might be something in their mutual relationship that should have been different. The gardener gets a fixed wage, and he doesn't begrudge anyone anything, and he intends to render unto God that which is God's and render unto Cæsar that which is Cæsar's. Besides, you should be content with the place God has put you in and do your duty and be a faithful servant like Eliezer.

But Holm's heart is heavy, and he has many thoughts to wrestle with. Mrs. Holm is serious too and doesn't like ill-timed laughter and frivolity in her house. She dresses in dark colors and isn't one of those women who make an effort to be pleasing and alluring with frippery and finery. And she watches over Johanne and sees to it that the Devil doesn't get hold of her.

Johanne is a modest, quiet girl who is shy and bashful the way young girls ought to be. But it's impossible to search the heart and reins, and how can someone really know what a girl like Johanne might be walking around thinking about or dreaming of at night or unconsciously longing for? Once the Devil gets the slightest hold on a person's heart, damnation and the eternal torments of hell lie ahead.

> A little bit of yeast
> Can leaven all the dough.
> Once those urges do catch fire,
> They are very hard to slow.

Johanne is good at making crosses out of moss, and on Saturdays she goes around distributing the Sunday newsletter. But it's as if her heart really isn't in it. And Mrs. Holm admonishes Johanne to keep a close watch on her thoughts and to remember what Pastor Nørregaard-Olsen wrote in her hymnbook about yeast when she was confirmed.

But Mrs. Holm knows that the Devil is so cunning that it's precisely the thing we're trying so hard *not* to think that he will slip in among good and innocent thoughts. After Johanne has gone to bed at night, Mrs. Holm sometimes goes into her bedroom and wakes her up. "Johanne, I've told you that you're supposed to sleep with your hands on top of the comforter!"

"Yes, but my arms are cold."

"Then you can put on your long mittens. And besides, it's better to be cold now than to burn in hell later, isn't it?"

Now the warmth of summer has arrived. And it's easy enough to sleep with your arms on top of the comforter. Things are growing and blossoming in gardener Holm's garden. Bees and hornets are buzzing around, creeping into the flowers, tickling and pollinating them. The asparagus plants aren't being cut anymore, so they grow out of their earthen ramparts and turn green and look like tiny Christmas trees. The beans are twining around their poles, and the peas are clinging to their stakes. Cucumbers of the "Langeland Giant" and "Green Torpedo" varieties are cut and carefully placed in boxes and sent to the city. The ones that have gotten a little shriveled and can't be sold at market show up in the gardener's little shop, where Johanne gets 40 øre apiece for them and wraps them up in newspaper. These 40 øre are written down, because the squire is an orderly and meticulous man who inspects every entry in the account books and checks the cucumber box.

The young apprentice gardeners are trained to pick hundreds of pounds of strawberries, and Pastor Nørregaard-Olsen can look forward to these good berries and the bounty of the Creator every day.

But gardener Holm is somber and heavy-hearted in spite of all this fertility and joy of life that he sees around him. He has pollinated his melon blossoms with a little brush and has seen to it that each yellow flower got what it needed. He takes care of his plants and makes sure that they are doing well. But there isn't much joy or comfort in his own life.

He is the father of a seventeen-year-old girl, and there were no children after her. There was no opportunity for more either. Mrs. Holm sleeps alone; she is strict and pure and doesn't want to have anything to do with sensual or carnal desires. And she makes no effort to be pleasing.

Lonely and withdrawn, the gardener walks among his plants. Sometimes the squire comes into the nursery, checking up on him and inspecting things. "Now what's this? A flower pot's been smashed. A flower pot doesn't cost too many øre, but it's the little things that count, and they add up."

The squire may arrive silently like an inspector or an auditor. He might just take it into his head to count the bundles of radishes that have been placed in boxes to be sent to market. He has a lot of things to attend to. He has a button factory and a clothing factory and textile mills and stores and a bank and a loan association, and he isn't even a gardener and doesn't know a thing about horticulture. But he is everywhere, taking care of things and inspecting them, because it's the little things that add up.

Squire Skjern-Svendsen is a strange man. It's incredible what he finds time for and what he manages to get done. He's everywhere. But nobody knows him. He belongs to the Kingdom of God, but maybe he isn't very happy either. His wife lives in the other end of the castle, and the maids over there can tell a lot of strange and interesting stories. His wife doesn't belong to the

Kingdom of God and doesn't go to church, even though she once wanted to be a missionary and die for the heathens. It was probably after she made the acquaintance of that mysterious doctor from Copenhagen that she turned away from religion. Because he's supposed to be a veritable anti-Christ, according to what people say. God only knows what those two are up to. Why, they say he whips her on the bottom and he gets 25 kroner each time for doing it. It's pretty hard to believe people would spend money on that, though, even if they are high-strung.

The gardener is a quiet man. He doesn't talk to many people and he doesn't listen to what is being said. Sometimes Mrs. Skjern-Svendsen comes into the nursery and asks to have some flowers cut. She asks politely if she can see the greenhouses and whether it would be all right for her to pick a rose. And she's modest. You'd never believe that she owned the whole thing and could go around picking whatever she wanted.

"It must be wonderful to be a gardener," she says. "Things grow and blossom, and it's so quiet and peaceful in your garden." She says "your garden" and behaves as if it were the gardener alone who made all the decisions here.

"If I were young, I'd want to be an apprentice gardener," she says. "I could get an apprenticeship with you, Holm. Do you think you'd have me?" She makes the somber gardener smile.

She is delicate and rather pale. And you can see that she's aristocratic and has blue blood. But she's straightforward and friendly like an ordinary person, and she's not too good to sit down on an old crate. "What's this flower called? What kind of rose is that?"

And when she sits there pointing at things and asking questions, the gardener keeps thinking of the verse from the Easter hymn:

> An angel sits on the stone of the grave
> Amid the lilies of the garden.
> With a frond of palm the angel shows
> Where Jesus from the grave arose.

The squire's wife is still young. She is slender and has nice legs, a delicate face, and mournful eyes. And the gardener looks at her and thinks of the angel.

And the bees are buzzing and crawling in and out of the nursery's flowers, gathering pollen and passing it on so that things can happen and life can go on.

# [ 39 ]

ONCE THERE WAS A STRAWBERRY in gardener Holm's strawberry bed that was as big as a child's head. This giant strawberry was photographed with a matchbox beside it for comparison. The county newspaper published a picture of the Frydenholm strawberry, along with a picture of Squire Skjern-Svendsen, the owner of Frydenholm.

Other especially noteworthy products of the nursery have been in the paper too. An incredibly large squash and a giant potato that weighed no less than 4½ kilos made their way through the newspapers of the entire country. Each time it said in the captions that these incredible things were from Squire Skjern-Svendsen's nursery.

Now you would think that gardener Holm would be proud of all the flattering publicity in the press. But gardener Holm is not a vain man. Besides, the gardener's name wasn't even mentioned in connection with the huge strawberry or the giant squash or the potato. The squire got all the credit. And the stories said that Squire Skjern-Svendsen's nursery at Frydenholm was a model nursery and that the squire had always shown a hearty interest in the horticultural cause and that he deserved the utmost recognition for his interest.

Perhaps the gardener is a little bitter about this; he knows that the squire isn't interested in horticulture at all and doesn't know a thing about it. Perhaps he's also bitter that several times the squire has been awarded silver trophies and certificates at horticultural exhibits, and once even received the Queen's Grand Prize for an exceptional chrysanthemum of the same variety that sold so well on the squire's birthday.

But gardener Holm is a man of few words who never complains

or lets off steam. He doesn't tell people what he's thinking about. It might be better, though, if he could swear and blow up at people instead of letting his thoughts fester.

He also knows that you should be content with the place that God has given you in life. He has a steady income, which is certainly enough to live on, and it is written that a man should not lay up for himself goods upon earth which moth and rust can corrupt. Gardener Holm settles his accounts with the squire punctually, and he knows that the squire earns ten times as much from the nursery as he does. But are we supposed to gather up riches for other people? Are we supposed to gather them up in another person's barn? Holm gets 40 øre for each cucumber. He passes on the 40 øre to the squire. He feels that he is being investigated and watched. He has to account for every bunch of radishes, which he has sown and watered himself and nursed along and pulled up and tied with twine. He is given fuel for the greenhouses and chemicals for spraying, in allotted portions. The squire decides on the meals for the young apprentice gardeners who board with him, and Mrs. Holm is allotted the food she will prepare based on the bargains the squire has made.

Gardener Holm has the right to call himself Head Gardener or Palace Gardener if he wants to. As far as that goes, he would be able to enjoy the same social standing as the head forester. But he is not vain about the titles and trifles of this world.

As far as the certificates and silver trophies for exhibited vegetables are concerned, this sort of thing also belongs to the empty delusions and deceptions of this world, which you're not supposed to strive for. There was a time, though, when he loved his profession and felt that the occupation of gardener was the most beautiful on earth. But now it's almost as if his work is without joy. He grafts and prunes and sprays and fertilizes and sows and plants. But the results don't really mean a thing to him. He is successful and things are thriving, but he is melancholy and his heart is heavy.

It's not proper to rebuke your superiors. And you should not criticize the man to whom God has given the authority of command. It is not for gardener Holm to judge what the squire does. But he can't hold back his thoughts. He thinks and thinks about

how strange the squire is—who is one of God's children, who
has built the evangelical meeting house and has a prayer stool in
the privacy of his room, but who is also building a burial mound
and mausoleum like a heathen and has his portrait painted
against a purple background, wearing his Knight's Cross.

Sometimes the squire will take some of his own silver and
stick it among his servant's things so he can surprise the servant
later and accuse him of theft and intimidate him into doing
whatever he says. Lukas tells him that he has to go through his
belongings and his pockets every evening and put back the
things that the squire has sneaked in and planted.

"Judge not," the Bible says. But a person can't stop all his
thoughts. And it isn't always easy to determine whether a
thought has come from God or Satan.

Mrs. Holm is happier. She doesn't do any thinking. She is
focused on another world and she doesn't wish to take a position
on anything that happens in this interim place. She is looking
out for her soul, and she is looking out for her daughter's soul,
so that they won't be damned. She knows that whatever she
renounces here will be repaid to her a thousandfold in her salvation. It is simple and straightforward. She has known this since
she was a child. When other girls were going to dances or parties, she didn't envy them. She knew that they were dancing
their way into damnation and that one day she would receive a
bounteous reward. Because life is only a transition and a prepa-
ration for eternity.

But the gardener feels that it might be selfish to think only of
your own soul's salvation. What if it were possible to save other
people's souls by sacrificing your own? It's hard to be a human
being. You don't know what your responsibilities are and you
don't know how much free will you have. You do what you
think is your duty, but maybe you're really doing the work of
the Devil.

You have Original Sin in you when you're born, and the fear
of hell and eternal torment is linked to everything you do your
whole life. But if you attain redemption and salvation by faith
and grace and by the sacrificial death of Jesus, is it possible to
enjoy salvation completely when you know that so many other
people are damned for eternity?

Gardener Holm has never doubted the words of the Gospel. There is nothing the matter with his faith. But his conscience is uneasy. Should he be a party to all this? Should he save his own soul and look on as so many other people are lost? And can he accept a redemption that comes from another person's death on the cross?

Gardener Holm believes in God. But there are times when he can't love Him and be on His side. He isn't acquainted with Kados, the adept on Østre Farimagsgade. But perhaps, just like Kados, he might take it into his head to join Lucifer's opposition to Jehovah. The gardener isn't as learned as Kados and hasn't scrutinized so many books and sciences. But sometimes he does have thoughts like those Kados has.

He struggles with his thoughts. And he grows more gloomy and mournful. He is a man of few words who doesn't find it easy to talk to people about his problems. He might find help and consolation if he talked about these things with Pastor Nørregaard-Olsen. But he can't bring himself to do it. He is alone with his many thoughts. He sends strawberries and fresh vegetables to the parsonage kitchen and hears the pastor's words in church. But that's as far as it can go.

# [ 40 ]

BUT THERE ARE OTHER PEOPLE who don't do so much thinking about God and eternity—people who are busy with ordinary earthly things.

There's Martin Olsen, who lives in Jens Olsen's clay-walled house. His mind is on a coffee set that he would like to give his wife as a present. She saw it at the grocer's and talked about it and thinks it's pretty. It would be nice to come home with it someday and say, "Oh, by the way, here's that coffee set you were talking about."

Martin's wife is just like a young girl even though she has four children. She wants to have pretty things and have a pleasant life. Her name is Margrete. She has close-set eyes, a large, pretty mouth, and black permed hair. And if she didn't have four children to take care of, she wouldn't mind going to a few parties and having some fun.

But they could certainly pay old Emma a krone to sit in their house and look after the children some evening, Martin thinks. Then they could bicycle over to Præstø and go to the movies.

"That would be fun," Margrete says.

Or maybe they could get Jens Olsen's vacation girl to look after the children. She's a big, sensible girl they could certainly depend on. She's doing very well at Jens Olsen's, and it's a real pleasure to see her putting on weight.

Jens Olsen is a good-natured man. He's not an unreasonable landlord and doesn't take it all that seriously if they're a little behind in their rent. He really likes Martin and Margrete, even though Margrete is a little skinny for his taste. He is plump and good-humored and likes to see abundance and plenty around him. His own daughters are fat and firm. And his pigs are so incredibly prolific that it's a joy to behold. He's good to them and pampers them. Over time he has come to look a little like a pig himself.

He is a widower. But when his wife was alive, she was so stout that they almost couldn't slice through her when she had an operation over at the hospital. "She was a wonderful woman," Jens Olsen says. "It's a shame she died."

But even though Jens Olsen is a decent landlord, it would really be nice if Martin and Margrete could have their own house, just like Rasmus Larsen. But they can't even consider it, and it's never going to happen since they have four children and will probably have even more. Rasmus doesn't have any children. His wife can go out and work and help bring in money. And Rasmus has a lot of little jobs and duties. Even at that it's difficult for him to manage the interest and installments on his new house.

"He's tied down," Martin says. "And he'll never be able to get away from here. The rest of us can move if things get too hot here because of the holier-than-thous, or if there's better work to be had someplace else. And we can strike and go our merry way. But Rasmus is stuck. And he's got to stay on everybody's good side and toady to the squire and the evangelicals and wheedle. He has to work for what they want to pay him and slink around and wheedle because he's stuck with that house."

The most bothersome thing about Jens Olsen's clay-walled house is that it doesn't have a yard. There's just a little bit of grass between the house and the pond, along with an ancient elder tree that barely produces enough berries for a few bottles of juice. It would have been nice if there had been room for some potatoes and vegetables. Now Margrete has to go to the gardener's little shop to buy the things that couldn't be sold at market. Johanne weighs out the vegetables for her; she's so shy and silent that it's almost impossible for Margrete to make her smile a little.

But even though they don't have their own house, it's still possible to have a nice, pleasant life. There is always a slightly musty odor in the old clay-walled house, and it never disappears entirely because the house is built right on the ground. But there is also the aroma of coffee and fresh-baked bread from the kitchen. There are pretty plants on the windowsills, and there are white curtains. The furniture is new and shiny, with lots of small doilies and embroidered table runners.

The new coffee set will be a nice surprise. "Be careful," Martin says as he comes in with the large package. "This is fragile."

Margrete unwraps it piece by piece from the paper and excelsior. This is just what she wanted, the one with the delicate little roses on it. "Why, it must have been awfully expensive! Where did you ever get the money?"

"You're right, it wasn't exactly cheap. Now let's make sure the kids don't break it. Don't touch a thing!"

"It's certainly not for everyday use," Margrete says. "Only for company." The children look at the unwrapped porcelain. A little gray cat plays with the excelsior and sits down in the paper.

The radio in the living room is broadcasting popular dance music loud enough for it to be heard out on the road. The latest new dance tunes are "In a Corner at the Old Inn," "Grandmother's Spinning Wheel," and "Under the Parson's Pear Tree." When the dance music is over, a pastor gives a talk called "Our Old Danish Village Churches" in the "Old Memories" series.

The radio is playing in the houses of Jens Olsen and Niels

Madsen and old Emma too. Old Emma is happy and grateful for the radio, which brings back her younger days and makes her memories come alive.

Rasmus Larsen is a member of the board of directors in the Radio Listeners' Association, and in some ways he feels partially responsible for the programs. "This is culture that's coming to us," he says. "It comes right into our living rooms, in the city and out in the country too."

Rasmus is a gifted speaker. People say that he'll probably be voted onto the Parish Council at the next election. "And he sure wouldn't be the worst one to get in," says Jens Olsen, who is a member of the Liberal Farmers' Party. "He's not so bad. It was in the old days that he was so red and hotheaded. Now at least you can talk to him."

He can probably expect the most opposition from his own people. Naturally there are always those who have to criticize and be dissatisfied with things—the unemployed people who come to register and have to stand outside Rasmus Larsen's house and aren't allowed inside because Mrs. Larsen doesn't want her new floors messed up. Rasmus has been given a telephone that the union is paying for, but you can't even go in and look at it.

"We have the best social welfare laws in the world," says Rasmus. "A protective shield has been erected around the life of every single Danish citizen. It's not right for a good Dane to sow suspicion and discord!" Rasmus is a good speaker. And at the general assembly meetings he knows how to rebuff the opposition with authority.

"Rasmus Larsen is unquestionably an idealist," says Pastor Nørregaard-Olsen. "We must respect him even if we don't share his political views. He is a man who dares to stand up for his convictions and doesn't let himself be bound by old party dogmas and slogans. The time is past when the worker looked askance at the church and its men."

Rasmus Larsen isn't afraid to appear in church Sunday after Sunday. He has the courage of his convictions. He's a real man. Maybe it's possible to cooperate with Rasmus Larsen. Maybe by working together with him they could come up with the ways and means to engage the workers in a dialogue.

"Come up and visit me at the parsonage tonight, Larsen, and let's discuss the matter. And give my regards to your wife. I know her from the ladies' sewing circle. She's one of its faithful members."

Rasmus and the pastor agree to hold a meeting at the inn, where the pastor will speak about the workers' attitude toward Christianity. Afterwards anyone will be free to speak. There will be an opportunity for them to buy coffee and make closer human contact with one another.

"Yes, at the inn it shall be," says Pastor Nørregaard-Olsen. "Truly, that's where it shall be. We shall defeat the enemy on his own turf! A pastor in an inn. Ah yes, yes indeed. It will be known far and wide!"

# [ 41 ]

THE HISTORIC INN has been having hard times since Pastor Nørregaard-Olsen transformed the parish. Balls and parties and amateur plays are a thing of the past. The bowling alley is silent. The garden swing and the ring-toss game in the yard are no longer used.

There are pictures on the walls of Svend Gjønge's exploits: Lord Mayor Nansen of Copenhagen and the Gjønge chieftain in Jungshoved Forest with white sheets over their shoulders. And valiant Ib atop the smooth copper roof of Gjorslev Manor. And Palle's tame raven that comes to him with food. And the Swedish dragoons, who are looting and greedily gulping down the good Danish food and drinking wine from the barrels of their pistols. And the traitors, Tam and the witch Kulsoen.

But no one comes to look at the pictures anymore and have a quiet glass of beer and recall the improbable events of old. Only an occasional traveling salesman finds his way to the inn to eat the ever-present ham and eggs. The bus driver brings his lunchbox to the inn, but he's a teetotaler and drinks only non-alcoholic beer with it.

On summer Sundays there is sometimes a little life in the garden when cars stop by. And sometimes families arrive with picnic baskets which they unpack in the garden, ordering a cup of coffee with their food while their children play on the swing or toss the rings at a nail in the old linden tree.

But it doesn't provide enough business to be noticeable. The innkeeper is getting thin, and the waiter is getting depressed.

Things were different in the old days. Back then people would drive to church in their carriages from far away and stable their horses in the large travelers' stable at the inn and have themselves a glass of aquavit after the church service. In the winter they would come in sleighs and would have to go inside and warm themselves up both before and after the sermon. And when there were funerals, the whole procession had to go to the inn and have themselves a sandwich and a shot and a little funeral beer.

And there were harvest festivals and wedding celebrations, and people who would get together in the evening and sit talking about things over coffee with aquavit in it.

Before Pastor Nørregaard-Olsen came to the parish, there were Grocery Cooperative dances and Health Insurance balls and Tenant Farmer banquets and Veterans' Club parties and Athletic Association and Young People's Association dances. And there were amateur plays and Punch-and-Judy shows and lectures and music.

But this is all a thing of the past now. On an occasional evening the hall might be rented out for an educational slide lecture on Greenland. But not many people are really interested in that sort of thing.

But now the pastor has come to the inn, and perhaps a new day will dawn for the historic place. The lecture about the attitude of workers toward Christianity couldn't be expected to fill the hall completely, of course. Still, 23 cups of coffee and 18 slices of pastry were sold, and that's a beginning, at any rate. Now Pastor Nørregaard-Olsen has decided that missionary Poulsen, who was supposed to speak at the evangelical meeting house about the work of the overseas mission in the Dutch East Indies and show slides from the field, should deliver his evening speech at the inn instead. This will unquestionably bring in people who don't go to the evangelical meeting house. "If they won't come to us, we'll have to go to them!"

Missionary Poulsen did have a few misgivings about it at first, but he gave in. "I think you're right after all," he told Pastor Nørregaard-Olsen. "We should go to them and imbue them. Jesus spoke to sinners and publicans and harlots. So why shouldn't I be able to speak at an inn?"

Pastor Nørregaard-Olsen and Rasmus Larsen agree to resume their thoughts about meetings and discussion evenings for workers in the winter, when the evenings aren't as warm and bright any longer, and when people are running low on firewood and kerosene at home. "I'm sure that we'll get a grip on your workers, Larsen," the pastor says. "The Danish worker is decent enough at heart. He just needs the opportunity to hear us. We'll find a format he understands. Won't we, Larsen?"

"Absolutely," says Rasmus Larsen. "Of course you're right, Pastor. But we mustn't forget that there are a few unfortunate elements who trade on dissension and unrest."

"Quite so. There are black sheep in every flock. But I'm counting on the fact that the Danish worker is sound at heart."

"I hope you aren't disappointed in your good opinion of us, Pastor. We'll try to show ourselves worthy of your confidence."

In this way Pastor Nørregaard-Olsen is constantly expanding his field of action and bringing new tracts of land beneath his plow. "I just hope you don't overexert yourself," his wife tells him. "I just hope your strength is up to it."

"I've never felt as strong and healthy as I do now. I sense growth and vitality everywhere. Things are growing beneath my hands. I feel so fervently that my work has God's blessing!"

"You're an incorrigible idealist!" his wife says.

"I hope so," Pastor Nørregaard-Olsen replies.

He sees to his numerous projects and pulls his strings. He has no doubts or scruples like the heavy-hearted gardener. He throws himself into his work. He writes his Sunday sermons. He prepares his confirmation classes. He baptizes children and buries the dead. He takes care of the YD, the sewing circle, Bible reading at the parsonage, meetings at the evangelical meeting house, and lectures at the inn. And once a week he drives his car to the hospital in Præstø and visits the sick from his parish,

whose names he has written down on a list. Nothing is as re-
warding as working with the sick. He can get even the obstinate
ones to talk to him when they are lying there in sickness and
fever and full of anxiety. Pain and fear are some of the means
God often employs to get the soul to talk to Him. "I have had
many blessings from visiting the sick," the pastor says. "I
wouldn't miss these hours by the sickbed for anything in the
world. What splendid results I've had!"

Pastor Nørregaard-Olsen gets up early in the morning, does
morning calisthenics, and takes a cold shower, singing loudly
while he towels himself off. He's in fine fettle for the deeds of
the day. After he has eaten a soft-boiled egg, toast, fresh-baked
rolls, and some stewed prunes for his stomach, he throws open
the veranda door to the garden and greets nature. And he puts
his dear old student's cap on his head and goes out into the dewy
morning, smoking his morning cigar while his wife has the maid
vacuum the books in the pastor's study. And he sees how everything in the garden has grown during the night, and he picks a
flower and puts it in his buttonhole.

This half-hour stroll in the garden is his morning devotion
and meditation. It's also excellent for the stomach if the stewed
prunes haven't worked. Regularity is an extremely important
matter for both body and soul.

Then when his wife calls to him that his study is cleaned and
vacuumed, he shuts himself in with his work. And the children
are told not to get too close and disturb him while the pastor is
reading the *Daily Times* and the *County Journal*, which one of
the maids has picked up at the post office.

During these morning hours, Pastor Nørregaard-Olsen also
likes to write his little articles for the Sunday newsletter. This is
the time of day when he is most inspired and at his best. To be
sure, the Sunday newsletter is merely a modest little publication; nevertheless, he has to have his heart in what he writes for
it. And sometimes the pastor calls his wife and reads her a
particularly well-written article.

Maybe he could have become a writer, the way one of his
fellow university students did, well-known and talked about
across the land. Or simply a critic and literary historian like his
friend and classmate Harald Horn. He had the talent, no doubt.

But there's no time, if he is to fulfill his place in life and do the work he has chosen. That living, creative, and organizational work. The current struggle. But isn't it marvelous to be standing in the midst of the din and the breakers and the foam!

For wherever there are deeds to be done, there is also opposition and struggle. There are also unyielding, old-fashioned people in the congregation, and in the evangelical movement in fact, who don't like Pastor Nørregaard-Olsen's style or hearty manner. It has come to his attention that a private devotional service was held out at Lauritz Nielsen's farm. An anti-worship service, so to speak. A demonstration against Pastor Nørregaard-Olsen's special gospel. And there are people who have taken their children to other, distant churches and had them baptized by unfamiliar pastors as a protest and an affront to their own parish pastor. And there are still conflicts about money for the rebuilding of the parsonage and about the old trees that were cut down without the consent of the church council.

"Just let those stiff-necks and sourpusses grumble," says Pastor Nørregaard-Olsen. "Their persecutions can only steel and purify me. Did not Jesus Christ and his Apostles have to endure great persecutions? Just let them come."

But if there are enemies and opponents, there are certainly also friends, supporters, and admirers so faithful that people accuse them of hysteria and ecstasy. And they will know how to stand fast as a group in the struggle for their ideals. "Just let our enemies rage in impotent hatred! Just let them spread rumors about the YD. And about the midnight worship services. Just let them hold their anti-worship services and protest baptisms!"

And Pastor Nørregaard-Olsen negotiates with Rasmus Larsen about new tasks and new fields of action. And he negotiates with the squire about battle plans and strategy. It is a great advantage and a blessing to have a man like the squire on your side.

# [ 42 ]

B UT THE SQUIRE has his worries too.

There have been work stoppages and unrest at the garment factory in Præstø where the nationally known, strong-as-iron navy pants are produced. And even though the law forbids walkouts, and even though the workers were served an immediate court order to resume work and pay a fine plus damages, it still caused losses and annoyance. And some unpleasant things were written about the garment factory and its owner.

There has also been some unrest concerning the squire's purchase of some farms that cannot simply be annexed to his estate. The squire has been forced to put some farm hands on these annexed farms and designate them as managers, taking measures to give the appearance that the farms are being run separately and independently. Even though these maneuvers haven't cost an awful lot, they're still a waste of time and are irritating to a practical and enterprising man like the squire.

Squire Skjern-Svendsen is a solitary man in the midst of his many businesses. He doesn't have Pastor Nørregaard-Olsen's ability to make himself loved or to gain power over people and make them devoted to and dependent on him. He doesn't have a phalanx of faithful followers who will die for him like the pastor does. After Pastor Nørregaard-Olsen has taken the YD girls into a room one at a time and made them kneel down and swear that they will give their hearts to God fully and unreservedly, that from now on their lives will be devoted to the Kingdom of God, they are his, body and soul.

The squire sees this ability in the pastor and admires it. But he does not possess it himself. He is not able to acquire disciples and supporters. The only person he has who is devoted and dependent on him is his servant Lukas, but the squire probably only has power over him because he knows something about Lukas.

The squire doesn't even have power over his wife. She is under the influence of other people. A mysterious doctor in

Copenhagen who seems to have the same abilities as Pastor Nørregaard-Olsen. A sorcerer and psychic researcher who can cast a spell over his fellow human beings and make them follow him blindly. His phalanx is no less faithful than that of the pastor. His disciples and supporters are no less fanatic. Pastor Nørregaard-Olsen may have his YD corps, but Dr. Riege has an equivalent in his P-Girls—his auxiliary corps that is always on call and ready with support and guidance in sexual matters.

If only Pastor Nørregaard-Olsen had come to the parish a few years earlier, perhaps Mrs. Skjern-Svendsen would have been one of his disciples. But it was that strange sorcerer who gained power over her instead. And every Monday and Wednesday she starts up her blue car and drives to Copenhagen to have herself treated by him, and she pays him 25 kroner each time for his trouble.

Squire Skjern-Svendsen is a rich man who can have a mausoleum and an evangelical meeting house built and give away considerable sums of money for the salvation of his soul. But he knows the value of money and knows what small amounts mean. All his life he has been frugal and modest in the conduct of his affairs, and he doesn't like the way his wife spends money. When he sees a pin lying on the ground, he bends over and picks it up. And he checks the kitchen and pantry to see that nothing is going to waste. And he inspects the leftover cucumbers in the gardener's little shop and frets over a smashed flower pot in the nursery. Twenty-five kroner isn't a lot of money for him, but he doesn't like to see it spent ineffectively and mindlessly. And he doesn't understand Dr. Riege's therapy.

Human life is strange and complicated. Mysterious powers play their games with people. A new pastor comes to a parish and he makes everything change. He speaks words, which are only sounds and vibrations. But the vibrations have an effect on other people and change them and make them do things. Flour wafers from a baker and wine at 2.25 kroner a bottle are transformed into flesh and blood at the word of the pastor. And young girls kneel down and submit in obedience and are no longer able to make their own decisions.

And a doctor arrives in a small town on the outskirts of a big city. He sits on his balcony looking out over the world, breathing out sorcery, and people get strange and irrational. They give their little children to him and they give themselves to him. And married couples get divorced, and lovers break up, and good-natured people become vicious, and sensible people become disturbed.

And on Østre Farimagsgade the wise Kados sits in a little apartment above a dairy shop. He draws a magic circle around himself and swings the sword Shibulah over his head, conjuring up a world that other people can't see and forcing the spirits to submit to his will. If he wants to, he can kill or injure people by sticking pins into clay dolls. And he can pronounce maledictions next to globes and wheels so that the maledictions will propagate and spread in rings and act through all eternity.

Pastor Nørregaard-Olsen is sitting in the assembly hall of the evangelical meeting house holding a study session. He is reading with a group of serious men and women. They are reading the Revelation of St. John the Divine, about the lamb and the seven seals and the great whore and the four beasts at the throne and the seven thunderings and the first and the second and the third woe. And the great, fiery red dragon that had seven heads and ten horns and on his heads seven crowns. And his tail drew the third part of the stars of heaven and did cast them to the earth. And the dragon stood before the woman which was ready to be delivered, and when she had brought forth her child, he then could devour it. And the great beast, which was like unto a leopard, his feet as the feet of a bear and his mouth as the mouth of a lion. Here is wisdom. Let him that hath understanding count the number of the beast, for it is the number of man; and his number is six hundred threescore and six. And they that dwell on earth shall wonder, whose names were not written in the Book of Life from the time the foundation of the world was laid, when they behold the beast that was and is not and yet is. Here is needed a mind which hath wisdom. The seven heads are seven mountains on which the woman sitteth. Even the kings are seven. Five are fallen, and one is, and the other is not yet come. And when he cometh, it is meet for him to continue a short space. And the beast that was and is not, even he is the eighth and is of the seven and goeth away into perdition.

The pastor expounds on these ingenious words and prophesies

what is to come and explains the inner meaning and the mysteries of life to the serious people in the evangelical meeting house.

At another location Dr. Riege is sitting with his disciples
around him leading a study group and explaining what resides
within them and what their thoughts and dreams and unconscious actions symbolize and what currents and vibrations emanate from the heavenly bodies and minerals and animals and
people. Concerning the mystery of life, he has discovered that
too. He himself has created life from inanimate chemicals. He
has iron oxide and lead and lifeless substances in a flask, and
they have turned into living cells. And if people will give him
time and let him work in peace, he will organize the material
into a minuscule human being in the flask. It is still far from
finished, but you can just make out its incipient form. The ladies
in the study group can clearly see it as a small, transparent worm
that is in the process of assuming the shape of a tiny fetus. And
they look at the flask and listen to the doctor's explanation and
are no less serious and devout and enraptured than the pastor's
listeners in the evangelical meeting house.

But out on Østre Farimagsgade, Kados sits reading Nostradamus, which isn't all that different from the Revelation of St.
John the Divine. He has his tables and his tarot cards and is
making his calculations, writing things down, and seeing what is
going to happen in the future. He has insights into the spagyric
art and has penetrated the secrets of nature and drawn the forces
of nature in under his command. He is not making organic life
or tiny human beings. But he is producing a salamander out of
sun and light and fire. Not some transparent worm like that of
Dr. Riege or Dr. Paracelsus, but a charming little lady who sits
in a bottle and lives on the rays of the sun. And even though his
wife can't see this lady, he himself can both see and talk to her.

Three strange men with power and influence and secret forces
at their disposal. Each one of them has attained insight and
explained the mysteries of life. It probably can't be proved that
any of them is right, but their followers have faith in them, and
it probably can't be disproved either. Everyone has to believe in
what he finds most expedient. The squire has chosen Pastor
Nørregaard-Olsen, while his wife has chosen Dr. Riege. The
squire does not possess the legal authority and the forcible means
to drive his wife from the doctor to the pastor. He considers

whether he might be able to have her declared insane, deprive her of her legal rights, and have her committed to a mental hospital. He has spoken with his doctor about it, but his doctor doesn't think it would be easy to arrange.

The squire has his worries. He owns a castle and over 50 square kilometers of land. He has influence on boards of directors, in banks, and in loan associations. He pulls strings and sets wheels in motion. But he doesn't have the power or the authority to put his own wife away.

He sleeps alone in his historic canopy bed where the Swedish king once spent the night. But his wife sleeps in another wing of the castle and won't talk to him and doesn't want to have anything to do with him. Every Monday and Wednesday she starts up her long blue car and drives to Copenhagen, and the squire anxiously watches her go and thinks about the 25 kroner that will be spent so uselessly and unreasonably.

And things go on. People mow their lawns and trim their hedges. In the evening they turn on their radios and listen to lectures about old memories. But when they turn the dial, they can also hear that the air around them is filled with threatening words. There is the sound of drums, the sound of horns, and the sound of heavy boots tramping. And people are screaming and shouting in foreign languages, and applause roars out of the loudspeakers. The squire is buying up horses and adding land to his property. He sets up a flax scutching mill and decides to plant certain areas in fiber flax next year. And he bomb-proofs his burial chamber. He is preparing himself for what might come.

Printer Damascus on Stengade feels that eating raw fruit and vegetables and vegetarianism could save the world, since it is the meat-eaters who turn people into predatory beasts that tear each other apart and wage wars. But there are other people who feel that bare feet or sandals or Esperanto are what could secure peace and happiness for mankind. Dr. Robert Riege teaches his disciples that sexual liberation and systematic sexual housekeeping will free the world from imperialism and war. And Pastor Nørregaard-Olsen propagates the Kingdom of God and reads the Revelation of St. John the Divine with his faithful and prophesies about what is to come.

# [ 43 ]

THERE IS UNREST in the parish. Some people don't have enough to do with their own affairs, so they pry into things that other people are doing and meddle in matters that don't concern them.

Pastor Nørregaard-Olsen has stated that there are "certain people in this parish that we could do without." And Rasmus Larsen, who has many duties and holds positions of trust and knows a lot of people, says that there are undesirables who only want to sow dissension and discontent.

Niels Madsen would also like to be left in peace and be spared from having the wrong kind of people meddling in his private affairs. He owns a model farm with newly whitewashed walls and freshly tarred half-timbering. His hedge is nicely trimmed, and the gravel in front of it is neatly raked. There are flowering geraniums and clean white curtains in his windows. And everyone knows that order and neatness prevail at his farm.

But now one of his boys from the children's home has broken his nose. That kid always was sticking his big nose where it didn't belong anyway, and he was impudent and rebellious. But if he had simply stood still and hadn't turned his head when Niels Madsen gave him a couple of well-deserved slaps in the face, nothing would have happened to his nose.

It was just an accident. But the boy squawks and hollers and runs away. He comes screaming into Jens Olsen's house, causing a panic and an uproar. Jens Olsen is a good-natured man who is kind to his farm animals, and he doesn't like to see people suffer harm either. He lays the boy down on the sofa in his living room, and his fat daughter comes in to help and puts cold compresses on the boy's nose and tries to get him to eat some cookies and drink some raspberry juice. And since she doesn't know what else ought to be done, she runs over and gets Martin Olsen's wife from the other side of the pond.

"Why, that's a disgraceful, shameful thing to do," says

Margrete. Jens Olsen and his two daughters think that it's disgraceful too and that something ought to be done about it.

"We'll have to call the doctor right away so he can come and look at it," says Margrete.

Fortunately Jens Olsen has a telephone so they won't have to run very far. "But I'd prefer not to make the call," he says. "I'd hate to get mixed up in anything. I want to live in peace and harmony with my neighbors."

"Well then, I can certainly call if I can borrow your phone," says Margrete. So she calls up the doctor and tells him what happened.

"Hm," the doctor says. "That doesn't sound so good. Are you quite sure his nose is really broken? It's so easy to get a nosebleed, you know."

"Well, you can come and see for yourself, Doctor," says Margrete.

"Well, yes," the doctor says. "I could, of course. But the thing is, it really ought to be Niels Madsen who sends for me. I'd really hate to intrude and barge into something before I was asked."

"So you're not coming?"

"Oh yes, of course I'll come. And I will, too, as soon as Niels Madsen sends for me. And he'll probably call soon, if it's really as bad as you say. It's not something critical that needs immediate attention, after all. Just keep putting those cold compresses on his nose. That can't hurt. There really is nothing else to be done right away. And then get hold of Niels Madsen and have him call me."

"That's a fine thing!" Margrete says to Jens Olsen. "He won't even come. He wants us to have Niels Madsen call him first."

"Well," says Jens Olsen. "Then we'd better carry the boy over to Niels Madsen's and get him put to bed."

"But we can't just take him back to that monster!" Margrete says. She is irate and excited and wants something to be done. "It should be reported to the police too. It should be reported right this minute! May I borrow your phone again?"

"Yes, go right ahead if you want to. But don't mention me. I don't want to get mixed up in anything."

Margrete calls the police and notifies them that Niels Madsen, the owner of the farm, has broken the nose of a boy who works for him.

"What's your name?" the policeman asks. "Are you related to the boy?"

"No."

"Where do you know him from?"

"I don't know him at all."

"Are you absolutely certain that a fracture of the nasal cartilage has occurred?"

"I don't really know for sure. It looks like it."

"So there hasn't been a doctor to look at the nose yet?"

"No, the doctor didn't want to come until Niels Madsen himself sent for him. Does he have the right to refuse to come like that?"

"Now that's a different matter. It kind of depends on the circumstances. I can't really see what we can do either. Does the boy have parents?"

"I don't know."

"Uh-huh, because it really should have been his parents or guardian who notified us about the matter."

"But isn't Niels Madsen going to be arrested for what he did?"

"We'll see. I don't know yet. First we have to find out more about the whole thing. In any case there has to be a doctor's affidavit to the effect that abuse is involved. And we'll have to hear from the boy's guardian. Maybe it's not as bad as you think. But if we hear anything further, we'll be sure to check into it."

So there is nothing more Margrete can do. She has to go back home and take care of her children and wait until Martin comes home from his job at the burial mound.

And of course the boy can't stay with Jens Olsen forever but will have to go back home. He doesn't want to be carried but can walk all right by himself. And Jens Olsen goes along with him so that no harm will be done to the boy. "I don't want to get mixed up in anything," he says. "But, by damn, it does look pretty awful."

"You shouldn't swear," Niels Madsen tells him. "But thanks for taking care of the kid. Yes, it was an accident—these things happen. I just wanted to slap him one, but he turned his head on purpose.

"So now I suppose you can't work anymore today?" he says to the boy. "You're welcome to go in and lie down." And since the boy has had juice and cookies at Jens Olsen's house, Mrs. Madsen doesn't feel she can do any less and grudgingly gives him a glass of juice and a cookie. She changes the compress on his nose too and thanks Jens Olsen for his help.

No harm has been done to the relationship between the neighbors. Jens Olsen is reassured and can go inside and see to his pigs and give the big sow a little tickle under her chin and on her teats. She grunts with pleasure, and Jens Olsen calls her "old girl."

# [ 44 ]

"OH, SO THE POLICE weren't interested," says Martin. "Of course if the boy had stolen a piece of firewood from Niels Madsen, they would have raced right out there."

"Yes, it's a fine thing," says Margrete. She is still indignant and excited and insists that something be done. "Maybe we should talk to Rasmus Larsen about the matter. He's a member of the Child Welfare Agency and involved in so many things. It would be too bad if a child abuser like that was allowed to continue. And it's not the first time he's abused the children."

Martin and Rasmus work together on the squire's burial mound. They are coworkers from seven in the morning until four in the afternoon. But when you pay a visit to Rasmus in his new house after working hours to talk about official business, Rasmus is a man of authority who doesn't appreciate a tone that's too familiar. He weighs his words and talks in complete sentences, as if he were composing an official letter.

"Now as far as this business of Niels Madsen's boy from the children's home is concerned, of course it appears that Madsen lost his temper and made a mistake. But we mustn't take hasty or rash measures. Niels Madsen is known to be a sober-minded and steady man, and what happened was probably just an accident.

"But of course we'll look into the matter," says Rasmus. "And if it should turn out that a mistake has been made, we'll call attention to that mistake and rectify it."

"But it's not a question of any mistake," says Martin. "It's simply that Niels Madsen is a monster who has boys from the children's home working for him for free. And then he abuses them and breaks their noses. It may be that he's regarded as holy and known as sober-minded and all that. But he's also a child abuser. And he shouldn't be permitted to have children at his house!"

"We supervise the boys at Niels Madsen's, of course," says Rasmus. "And nothing objectionable has occurred. Whether he actually did break the boy's nose, I can't really say. But as I mentioned, the matter will be looked into. In the meantime, it doesn't benefit anyone to make a big fuss and to-do and turn it into an incident and get the public mixed up in it. Something like that can only harm the child-welfare cause. In this country we have the world's best child-welfare system. Everybody agrees about that. Mistakes can happen, since nothing is perfect, and to err is human. But if an error has been made, it will be rectified. In the meantime, it is imperative that calm prevail about the work of the child-welfare agency. A calm work atmosphere is a requirement for a good resolution. It serves no purpose to create unrest or discord, but it can cause irreparable harm, especially to the children."

"So, you're not going to do anything? You just want to cover up for that monster?" says Martin.

"I don't want to cover up for anyone. The only thing we at the Child Welfare Agency insist on is to be able to work in peace. I'm well aware that there are people who aren't ashamed to exploit these orphaned children as a means of agitating for inappropriate purposes. I can only say that *that's* not the Danish way of doing things!"

"You don't have to go to the bother of making a speech to me," Martin tells him. "And I have no more to say to you. You're so damned high and mighty. I bet you think you're going to be a government minister someday!"

"I have taken on the tasks that my colleagues have had the confidence to entrust to me. And I carry them out to the best of my ability," replies Rasmus.

"But your abilities are pretty damned limited!" says Martin. "And I don't feel like talking to you anymore."

The pastor is the chairman of the Child Welfare Agency, and Martin goes to the parsonage to talk to him about Niels Madsen's boys from the children's home. "The pastor only receives people between 3:00 and 4:00 p.m.," the black-clad maid tells him.

"But I'm at work then."

"You can see, it says so right here on the door: Office Hours 3:00–4:00. The pastor insists that people respect his work. The pastor doesn't want to be disturbed at any old time." There's nothing he can do about it, so Martin has to wait until the next day.

"I already know about the matter," says Pastor Nørregaard-Olsen. "I've spoken with the owner of the farm, Mr. Niels Madsen, and I've spoken with the boy, who is feeling fine now and bears no grudge toward his master. What happened was a regrettable accident, and farmer Niels Madsen has given me his word that it won't be repeated. Believe me, Niels Madsen is a good and honorable man who only wanted what was best. He wanted to punish the boy because he was disobedient. Discipline and order are necessary, you know, where so many boys are gathered together. And in this case, as we know, the boys are especially difficult. The farmer happened to hit the boy's nose by accident, and no one could be more upset about what happened than he is. And I have the impression that Niels Madsen and his wife are trying to outdo each other in pampering the boy. They were treating him to juice and cookies. They just couldn't do enough for him. I actually think the other fellows are rather jealous of him."

"And have you informed the police about the matter?"

"The police! No, what are you thinking of, my good man? No, no. It would certainly be a crying shame, especially for the boys, if the police were to get mixed up in this, and if the home that Niels Madsen has made for these orphans were to be tarnished by gossip and notoriety. I can tell you in confidence, my friend, that I certainly punish my children too, whenever it is necessary. Perhaps you would like to report me to the police as well? Furthermore, I can tell you that I have spoken with the laborer, Mr. Rasmus Larsen, who is also a member of the Child Welfare Agency. He is in complete agreement with me that no dust should be stirred up over this insignificant matter. And if you, from your point of view, do not agree with me, laborer Larsen is your colleague and comrade, after all, and I would assume you have confidence in him."

The pastor is an eloquent man, and it isn't easy for Martin to get a word in edgewise. The pastor is in his own home too, and is full of confidence and power. He has his large desk in front of him with papers and other items on it, and he has many meters of books lining his walls, which lend him a background of erudition and authority.

Martin is sitting on a stiff-backed chair and has no desk in front of him for support and cover. He doesn't want to interrupt the pastor, and when he does start to say something, the pastor raises his voice.

"It wouldn't be because you wish to do harm to someone that you're pursuing this matter so vigorously, would it now, Martin Olsen? I would prefer to believe that it springs from idealistic reasons. From sympathy with the orphans. It is so terribly easy to do harm if one does not know all the ins and outs of a matter. Especially if one has a preconceived point of view. I think it would be a shame for the children if they were to be misused for inappropriate propagandistic purposes. I think we should leave the children in peace! We may disagree on many a matter, Martin Olsen. But I wonder whether we don't actually agree on wishing the best for our children?"

"Yes, of course," says Martin. "But that really wasn't—"

"I'm glad of that! I'm inutterably glad that the two of us agree on that point! We will not work against each other but will work together to obtain the best possible outcome. Let us never forget that our children's well-being is the most important thing for both of us."

"I just feel that when children are abused, we ought to—"

"Children must not be abused!" says Pastor Nørregaard-Olsen vigorously, striking the desk with his white hand. "They must be watched over and defended. Here I sit to watch over

and defend them. Count on me, Martin Olsen. I do not wish
little children any harm!"

"Well, then what about Niels Madsen? You'll have to do
something to prevent—"

"I know Niels Madsen extremely well. And I know how genuinely good he is. Like the two of us he wants only what is best
for the children. You can have faith in me when I vouch for
Niels Madsen."

"No, I don't have faith in you, Pastor Nørregaard-Olsen, if
you want to cover up for Niels Madsen."

"I can do without your faith, my good man. I can get along
without it. But no one is going to keep me from doing my duty.
And my duty is to protect these little children. Against one thing
or another. Against poor treatment and against being exploited
by rabble-rousers. Now I see where I've got you, Martin Olsen.
And I'm not alone in my opinion of you. Your own coworkers
feel the same way I do. Laborer Rasmus Larsen shares my
opinion."

"Well, as for Rasmus Larsen, it's always—"

"I don't think we have anything more to discuss," Pastor
Nørregaard-Olsen says, getting up. "I have sacrificed quite a bit
of my time for you. I have listened to you and taken the trouble
to explain to you the way things are, even though I certainly
don't have to stand accountable to you. I can't say that you have
any authorization to get involved in the activities of the Child
Welfare Agency. You're not the legal custodian or the guardian
of the boy you feel justified in taking care of."

Martin picks up his cap and says goodbye, realizing that
there's nothing to be done here.

"Goodbye, Martin Olsen," says the pastor. "And I hope that
you will go about your deeds with a purer heart next time.
I hope it will be sympathy and goodness—yes, goodness—that
impels you when you wish to plead the cause of children and
orphans."

"In any event I won't be troubling you next time, Pastor,"
says Martin. "Now I know what the result will be."

"I hope you will turn your heart to Him who said, 'Suffer the
little children to come unto me.' He had no ulterior motives. He
was pure."

"He was killed by priests too," Martin says.

"Goodbye," says Pastor Nørregaard-Olsen.

# [ 45 ]

THE DAYS ARE LONG AND HOT. People are eating strawberries and red currant pudding with cream. Everything is flourishing in great abundance.

The flies are reproducing in Jens Olsen's manure pile; it's amazing and incredible. They swarm in and out of people's living rooms, alighting in sugar bowls and crawling on the red currant pudding. People hang up flypaper and drape protective gauze around their brass lamps. The flies get stuck on the flypaper and buzz and buzz, taking a long time to die. But new flies are constantly coming out of the manure pile.

"Nature is rich and wise and full of purpose!" says the pastor.

"Nature must be overcome and controlled!" says Kados.

"Nature isn't natural at all!" says Dr. Riege.

White moths swarm in the sunshine, laying their eggs on people's cabbage leaves. Old Emma glowers at them and chases them away and pours salt on the green caterpillars, making them writhe and tumble down off the cabbage.

The bees are swarming from the gardener's hives, buzzing and sucking nectar and pollinating the flowers of the nursery in an efficient manner. But the gardener himself is taciturn and gloomy. And his wife is dressed in black and makes no effort to be attractive.

The gardener's daughter stands in the little shop making funeral crosses and wreaths out of moss and wire. She is seventeen years old and has to go around wearing her YD blouse to save her civilian clothes and to make propaganda for the Kingdom of God. She is embarrassed and bashful as young girls ought to be. And her mother admonishes her to be careful with her thoughts.

The evenings are mild and light. People sit on benches in their yards and leave their radios going with the windows open so the program on old memories from the days of the steam trolleys can be heard out on the road.

Old people take evening walks on the road, checking to see if there have been any new developments in the neighboring gardens. Some people have planted New Zealand spinach and Chinese cabbage. "That's the way they do things these days. But you know where you stand with the old-fashioned kind of spinach."

The young people are out to take bike rides and stand talking and giggling over their bikes. They're eating ice-cream cones out in front of Andersen's bakery. And the ones who aren't in the YD buy cigarettes from the vending machine at the grocery store and smoke and horse around in the summer evening.

But when people turn the dial on their radios, they hear about arms budgets and naval readiness and air-raid precautions and preparations. "There definitely has been some talk of unrest in Central Europe," the Prime Minister says on the radio in his calm, deep voice. "But this talk of unrest will not involve Denmark in any way, for the relationship of our country to other countries is the best possible. But if it did happen that this talk of unrest should approach Denmark's borders, the listeners should rest assured that the government will take under advisement making all necessary preparations for a discussion of those problems which in this connection might at any given time be expedient and desirable. And these discussions will in any given event take place to the extent that it is deemed to be requisite with regard to the prevailing conditions at any given time, and insofar as it may be deemed reasonable and imperative. But first and foremost it is necessary and appropriate for everyone, in both urban and rural areas, to exhibit calm behavior. Daily business should proceed, and daily tasks are to be carried out, and calm and order should prevail. Preparations for every reasonable and desirable precaution will be discussed at the appropriate time by the responsible authorities to the extent that, after sound consideration relative to the prevailing circumstances, they are found to be justifiable and requisite."

But if they turn the radio dial a little, they hear another voice that isn't calm and deep, but shrill and uncontrolled. And the applause and exultation roar when it screams loudly. There are the sounds of military marches and drums and tramping boots. And the squire, who knows how to listen, buys up horses and has his gravesite bomb-proofed.

"There is so much in these times that leads our thoughts to that which was foretold about the last days," the pastor says. "There are signs in the sun and the moon. And in America a meteor measuring four meters in diameter has fallen to earth. Who cannot help but think of the words of the Scriptures that 'the stars shall fall from heaven'?" He is reading The Apocalypse with his faithful in the evangelical meeting house. About the white horseman and the red horseman and the black horseman and the pale horseman which is death. And the faithful nod and say, "It all applies to our time. It is all being fulfilled and carried out as it was foretold in the Holy Scriptures."

But the country is peaceful and quiet with its elderberry bushes and green fields and far too much grain. What's going to happen to prices if the harvest is just as large as last year's? It's all well and good that Jens Olsen's pigs are thriving and multiplying, but how can they get up to a decent price with all this richness and profusion?

"It's the system that's wrong," says Niels Madsen. "We've got a lot to learn here in Denmark. But it will come. We can't live on subsidies and softness!" And Niels Madsen looks quite militant and stalwart in his new cap and high, shiny boots.

Jens Olsen's vacation girl is growing and thriving, and every week she is weighed on the pig scales and writes home about how much weight she has gained. Her parents are a little afraid that she won't want to stay at home with them on Dannebrogsgade in Copenhagen anymore, where there isn't any heavy cream for the red currant pudding. "And don't forget to thank Mr. Olsen," they write.

Niels Madsen doesn't weigh his boys. He teaches them industry and order and discipline. There isn't anybody getting mixed up in his private affairs and domestic discipline anymore. The boy with the broken nose is feeling fine and can go about his work again. Every Sunday Niels Madsen and his wife go to church. Mrs. Madsen has a hat, gloves, and a pocketbook and looks refined and urbane and gives everybody a friendly nod. No one can tell by looking at them that they don't talk to each other at home and lie in bed with their backs turned to each other and have to take pills to get to sleep.

The unemployed men are waiting outside Rasmus Larsen's house. They're out of work and can't afford to buy anything because there's too much of everything. "But at least they could work for their relief money, couldn't they?" the farmers say. And maybe that's the way it will be someday. The farmers are getting emergency relief, and pretty soon it won't be worth the trouble to be a farmer in Denmark. But if something really does come out of this war they're talking about, a lot of things sure will be different.

There is unrest and dissatisfaction. Even old Emma is angry and indignant. She has run afoul of a new law that was enacted for the conservation of nature, and her habits and time-honored rights have been infringed upon. Every summer she has picked raspberries in the woods because she doesn't have raspberries in her own garden, and because forest raspberries are sweeter and more delicate. Nobody else is interested in these wild raspberries, and you would think they belonged to everybody. But Emma runs into a forester who tells her that berry-picking is prohibited and that venturing off the paths and trails is also prohibited. And he takes Emma's basket and dumps out the raspberries and stomps on them with his big boots. And Emma should actually be happy she's getting off without a fine or a citation. But she scolds and screams and spits and sputters, and the forester has to threaten her with his oak walking-stick and tell her to leave the forest.

Emma complains to the ladies of the sewing circle and to the pastor. But they can't help her, and the pastor doesn't want to register a complaint with the squire. The law has to be respected, after all; it's the same for everybody, and Emma did actually commit a sort of "forest poaching." They're no longer all that enthusiastic about Emma in the sewing circle anyway. And since baker Andersen's wife joined, they would just as soon be rid of Emma. She isn't particularly clean or appetizing, and it can certainly be tedious to listen to her chatter on about the old pastor. If Emma really wants to be insulted, this might be the perfect chance to get rid of her.

"So I'm a kind of poacher, am I?" Emma says. "Well, I don't want to inconvenience the sewing circle or be a burden on anybody. But in the old pastor's day this sort of thing wouldn't have happened!"

Johanne, the gardener's daughter, goes into the woods to gather moss and lichens for crosses and funeral arrangements. She's a hard-working girl, and it's amazing how much she manages to gather. And even though Mrs. Holm knows that it doesn't do children any good to be praised, she does have to show some appreciation of Johanne's willingness to gather moss in the forest. But it's probably a good thing that Mrs. Holm can't see Johanne sitting on a forest embankment with a young man whose name is Oscar and who works at the dairy.

There is a meadow in front of the embankment, and there are only a couple of calves looking at the two young people. Johanne is pretty and blonde and long-legged, and she is sitting very close to the young man and looking at the calves. The man is looking at Johanne and holding her tight. "What lovely little breasts you have," he says.

"Do you really think they're pretty?" she asks.

"They're just about the prettiest things in the world." He touches them beneath her yellow YD blouse. Johanne is a quiet girl who isn't used to saying much. And she isn't used to protesting about what people do to her. She is sitting on the forest embankment with a young man and leaning against him. In front of them stand the calves looking at them, glad that there are people there with them.

The grass in the meadow is fragrant. Tiny beetles and bugs are crawling in the grass and have things to do and places to go. And other insects are whirring around in the air, buzzing and busy.

The calves are standing in a semicircle looking at the girl and the young man. And the girl is calm and lets things happen to her.

# THE MURDERER

# [ 46 ]

On Wednesday the 17th of July the astrological conditions are as follows:

The sun has entered the sign of Cancer, whose planet is the Earth with its satellite the Moon, the intermediary of the lower forces in the period when the Sun has culminated and is on the descendant toward its December point. But since the Earth cannot be openly acknowledged as one of the sacred planets, it has been interchanged with the melancholy planet, Saturn. Wednesday is ruled by Mercury and is therefore light blue and vibrates in the key of D during the first quarter of the day, which is why the entire day reverberates in D major with two sharps.

That's how matters stand. But apart from the conclusions that can be drawn from these portentous facts, Tycho Brahe created a special entry for the 17th of July in his catalogue of inauspicious days on which one should not begin any project or set out on a journey.

Furthermore, on the basis of his own special calculations, Kados felt himself compelled to pick up his pen and send an urgent warning to Damascus. And even Sjögren, who is otherwise a mortal enemy of Kados and Lucifer, has to admit that in this case Kados is right and that the day actually is inauspicious. "But this must in no way be regarded as an endorsement of Kados and the Luciferan principle in general," Sjögren says.

"I'm afraid that an injustice has been done to Lucifer over the course of time," says Damascus. "There's probably something good in him too." And he tells Olsen, "Go on the 16th. Or go on the 18th. But don't take the train on the 17th of July. Haven't you had enough bad luck in your life? Won't you ever listen to warnings?"

"Just tell me I'm an ex-con," Olsen says. "Go ahead, hold it against me."

"Oh no, that's not it," Damascus says. "I don't want to hold anything against you. And you know that very well. I only want what's best for you."

"But you're always mentioning my 'bad luck.' You're always telling me that I've been inside. Every day you have a nasty remark ready for me."

"Oh, you really don't mean that, Olsen. Now how can you say such a thing?"

"Just keep it up. You know I've got to put up with it. Just keep telling me about my past. Just remind me that I've been up the river."

"It wouldn't occur to me, Olsen. I merely want to ask you to go on a different day than the 17th. Couldn't you do that for my sake?"

"No," says Olsen. "No. You've done enough carping at me."

Olsen takes the first train in the morning from the main station. And even though the day may be inauspicious, the weather is wonderful, and the sun is shining, and it's going to be a beautiful, warm day.

He is fresh from a good night's sleep. Freshly shaved and cool with brilliantine in his hair, wearing an elegant, light-colored summer suit with broad shoulders and creases and a florid striped necktie and a flashy silk handkerchief and natty two-tone shoes.

He finds a window seat and lights a cigarette and looks at the little illustrations in the compartment showing Dybbøl Mill, Nyborg Castle, the Country Soldier statue in Fredericia, and the monuments at Skamlingsbanken. And he gallantly helps a lady put her suitcase up in the baggage net and squints at her handbag, which she carelessly leaves lying on her seat when she goes out to the platform to buy some refreshing lozenges and a copy of *Family Journal*.

He once traveled this same route as a vacation boy with a bottle of red soda pop and a lunchbox—and fun, tomfoolery, expectations, and high spirits. Later he made the trip in a reserved compartment, accompanied by a husky escort, to the juvenile prison in Nyborg. He can remember clearly that there were pictures of the King's country house in Skagen and bathers on Fanø in the compartment then.

The countryside is green and pretty. Filled with sunshine and summer vacation. Allotment gardens and nurseries and little roosters that crow so loud you can hear them inside the train. You can see the trees on the highway to Roskilde. He traveled along that road once too. In a locked green paddy wagon with no windows and only one small air vent for each tiny little cubicle.

He peers out of the compartment window and looks with interest at a large building passing by. So that's what it looks like from the outside. Circular walls around it and a little spire on the roof and a lot of tiny windows. It actually looks rather nice from the outside. When he was on the inside, it was impossible to get a good idea of the building's layout. Now he can see that it has symmetry and monumentality.

It's only 6:00 o'clock. They're about ready to get up in there. Their beds will be slammed up against the wall and locked in place. And the latrine parade will begin. They'll trudge out on their clattering wooden clogs holding their pots. "Hey! Not so fast! Don't look back!" And if they meet anybody, they have to stand with their faces to the wall. That's the etiquette. Then they'll empty their pots and scrub them and clatter back. And the keys will rattle and iron doors will slam all day long.

Olsen gets all wistful when he sees the place he called home for such a long time. How are they doing in there? he wonders. What are they having for dinner today? Is that fly still alive that was so tame it would come and eat his sugar?

He thinks about the prison guards, who wear white jackets in the summertime. And he thinks about the warden. Olsen is just like somebody who has been separated from his family. But he also thinks about a short, fat deputy warden. Henningsen was his name. Henningsen was afraid of the prisoners, which is why he was brutal and uneasy about his dignity. Maybe he'll meet Henningsen's father today. The holy tailor from Præstø, who is an idealist and works for the Salvation Army and the Prisoners' Aid Society, and who once got Olsen a position as a servant with Squire Skjern-Svendsen at Frydenholm.

Now he knows something about Skjern-Svendsen. And maybe he'll be set up for the rest of his life. Not as a servant, but as somebody who lives off his investments.

If you know something unfavorable about a man and demand money for keeping your mouth shut about it, it's blackmail and against the law. But if you know something favorable about him? If you have information about something nice and good and sympathetic that he has done in all secrecy, well, then it can't be illegal blackmail to want to have a slight consideration to keep your mouth shut, can it?

It's a strange case. It's a strange mission that Olsen has to carry out. He's sitting there fresh from a good night's sleep, feeling quite comfortable, smoking his cigarette, and looking out at the flat countryside between Copenhagen and Roskilde. The countryside is green and fertile and well cared for. The sun is shining wonderfully, and little roosters are crowing.

In the compartment next to his sits a man who is on his way to the same place as Olsen. A tall, thin man wearing a sports suit with a large checked pattern and high riding boots. He isn't looking at the countryside but is reading a thick book about Scandinavian literature. In the baggage net above him he has a suitcase with more books in it. It is his occupation, his trade, to read books. For many years he has been reading constantly, and if for one moment he isn't reading, he feels that he doesn't have any life. When he was in school, he wanted to be a poet. But he only became a reader. Eventually he had read so much that he could write books about the books he had read. That's almost as good as writing poetry yourself. "H.H." is printed on his suitcase.

Olsen hasn't read many books. He is just a weak man, and he has had bad luck and a number of adversities. Not everything that he has been through has been all that pleasant. But he went through it himself. He has his irons in the fire; he has his little gimmicks and tricks. There may be more real life in Olsen, after all, than in the man with the books.

They have to change trains in Køge. The literary man drags along his heavy suitcase with the books that are his life. But Olsen walks along light and unencumbered. Smart and jaunty with his padded shoulders and creases and a flashy tie and an elegant silk handkerchief. On the little private train the two men happen to sit in the same compartment.

Olsen would like to strike up a conversation and offers a cigarette. But "No thank you," says the man of letters. He isn't interested in his vulgar fellow creatures. He has his book about books. And he has to keep on reading it if he wants to feel like a living human being.

They ride through the countryside, which is hilly now and pretty and varied, with woods and fields and gardens and meadows. The little train stops at all the little stations and shifts and shunts. And the man of letters has nothing against Olsen's opening the window so the warm air and flies and bees will come into the compartment. It smells like the country, with hay and elder trees and manure and wood smoke.

The stationmaster's rooster crows when the two men get off. Out in front of the station the yellow bus and a shiny, stylish car are waiting. Pastor Nørregaard-Olsen is standing on the platform bidding welcome to the man in the large-patterned suit. "A most cordial welcome. I'm absolutely overjoyed that you've actually come. We're going to have a very nice time at our old parsonage." And he squeezes and shakes his guest's hand. "Oh, let *me* take your suitcase. It certainly is heavy!"

"It's books," his guest says. "I brought along a few books. There'll be some time to do a little reading down here, won't there? I'm not a human being if I don't have a book in my hand."

"There'll be time for everything you want. I hope you'll make yourself at home and do exactly what you feel like." The pastor introduces his guest to the stationmaster. Loudly and distinctly so everybody can hear who the stranger is: "This is the critic, Dr. Harald Horn. We're old friends and classmates." And even though the people standing on the platform don't know who Harald Horn is, they nevertheless realize that he must be a person of importance.

"You look fit and fresh," the pastor says. "Not at all the way one envisions a bookworm. Ha, ha! Sporty, and I'll be, wearing high boots too. Do you ride?"

"No. But I thought they would be good out here in the country if we're going to go hiking on plowed ground or in meadows. And I feel so comfortable wearing high boots."

"You look dashing, old friend. And my wife thinks you're a pale, quiet scholar. She's got another think coming!" Then the gentlemen get into the car and Pastor Nørregaard-Olsen drives off.

Olsen watches them go from the yellow bus. "Now the pastor's got company," the driver says. "Lord knows who that might be. Say, aren't you Olsen? Have you come back? Are you going to be up at the castle again?"

"No," replied Olsen. "I just have to talk to the squire about something."

"Well, that sounds pretty mysterious," the driver says, a bit put off at not having learned any more than that.

# [ 47 ]

D R. HARALD HORN has been given the guest room in the gable end of the parsonage. A large, bright room with flowered English wallpaper, sun in the morning, and blue-striped curtains.

He can look out across the yard with its large trimmed lawn and blossoming ornamental shrubs, perennial beds, and roses. His room smells of roses, grass, and linden trees.

A vase with wild meadow flowers has been placed on his table. Cornflowers, corn cockles, daisies, and others whose names he doesn't know. Ears of grain and fine silk grass have been stuck in among the flowers. He can feel that he is welcome and that they are trying hard to make him feel comfortable.

He has put his new high boots outside the door so the maid can polish them. He is lying on the soft feather comforters in his bed reading his book while a moth flutters around his reading lamp. And as long as he holds on to his book, he knows that he is alive. But when he lets go of the book, he drifts off into oblivion and unconsciousness.

When he wakes up the next morning, he grabs hold of his book, and as long as he is holding it, he is alive. He carries his book under his arm when he goes down to breakfast in the garden room.

"Look at that," says the pastor, "always with a book under his arm. The true scholar."

"Yes," says Dr. Horn, "I just can't seem to do without it." And he clings to his book in order not to lose his identity and his conscious life.

The room smells of toast and crisp warm rolls and small home-baked buns with caraway seeds. And the coffee is fragrant and is served from the silver coffee service in honor of the doctor's visit.

"Do you prefer tea or coffee?" the pastor's wife asks him.

"Coffee," says Dr. Horn. "I swear by coffee. Voltaire was also very fond of coffee. We literary people have to have something to inspire us and brace us up."

The coffee is strong and good. Since both the ladies of the sewing circle and the YDers bring coffee along when they come, there is always some left over for the parsonage to use.

The soft-boiled eggs, however, have gotten a trifle too hard. This isn't the first time, either, even though the pastor attaches great importance to their being just right. He asks that this error be called to the attention of the maid who boiled the eggs.

"So come out into the garden, old friend, and let's smoke our morning cigars in the fresh air."

"This is a delightful garden you have," says Dr. Horn. "I recently read a book about Danish parsonage gardens. They're really a slice of Danish culture that it would be most unfortunate for us to lose."

"Yes, that's a fact," the pastor responds. "And you see, over there I've had a little gate made to the churchyard so I can take a shortcut when I have to go over to the church. I've changed a lot of things about this garden. I personally feel that it makes quite a fine impression now."

The two friends slowly stroll the length of the garden, thoughtfully puffing on their cigars. As usual the pastor puts a rose in his buttonhole, and he sticks one in Horn's buttonhole too. The doctor sniffs at it and quotes, "O thou most gracious of rosebuds."

From the walkway lined with nut trees they can look out across the fields, where the wheat is standing tall, green, and even. Farther off there is clover where Squire Skjern-Svendsen's cows are standing in long rows grazing. They are fat and shiny and well cared for, and they are tuberculosis-free. Far off they can see the woods and hills and white houses. There is a succulent, rustic smell all around, and the larks are singing up in the sky. Dr. Horn looks at the countryside and thinks about what literary passage it might remind him of. It would almost have to be something from Christian Winther's works. Although the field of clover would really have to be from Poul Martin Møller.

Then the pastor's wife calls out to them that the study has been vacuumed and is ready. The gentlemen can withdraw and talk about the happy memories of their school days. The pastor's wife and children can hear them laughing loudly and heartily in the study. "You must have been a couple of naughty boys," she says jokingly.

"Yes, we were some boys, all right," Harald Horn replies.

They send word to Panty Marius for chickens. The little yellow peeping chicks which arrived on the bus in a cardboard box have now grown big and edible. Panty Marius butchers three young roosters at the chopping block and wipes their blood off his fingers on a piece of newspaper. He mumbles to the maid that the chickens will be a gift to the pastor. He's certainly not about to accept any payment for them. Marius may well be a tight-fisted man, but it will be worth something to have the pastor shake his hand on Sunday and say, "Thank you *very* much for those splendid chickens!" so everyone can hear it.

Word is also sent to the gardener. If Johanne is coming by with strawberries today, would she please bring along a few more than usual because they have company at the parsonage.

Red wine is brought up from the cellar and uncorked and allowed to warm. They're doing their best to make their guest feel comfortable.

"You live well here," says Harald Horn. "It's enough to make a man envious."

"Yes," the pastor says, "I'm doing fine here. I'm satisfied with my calling. I'm happy in the work that I have been charged to carry out. I can feel it growing and thriving beneath my hands. Can a person ask for anything more?"

"No," says Harald Horn. "And what a nice large collection of books you have."

"It's a good thing to feather the nest with books," says Pastor Nørregaard-Olsen. "When you have to live in an out-of-the-way part of the country like this, you must gather a little culture around you. I suppose you noticed that I also have your doctoral dissertation among my books?"

The pastor takes Harald Horn's book about adverbs in Holberg's *Epistles* down from the shelf. "I would really appreciate it if you had a chance to write a few words on one of the first pages," he says.

"It will be a true pleasure," says Harald Horn, taking out his fountain pen. "I really should have sent you the book when it came out. But of course there were so many people I had to send it to. All those people who always send me their books. One has to return the favor, you know."

"Naturally," the pastor says. "I certainly understand that very well. I suppose there are a great many people who want your autograph?"

"It does happen, yes."

"Yes, you've become a famous man, Harald. And you give talks on the radio too. I listen every single time you speak. Your lectures about literature are splendid. Positive and affirmative! They are precisely the words we need to hear in Denmark."

"Of course I always strive to look at literature from a positive, national perspective. Scholarship must never be purely objective. It must be actively affirmative."

"You're the same idealist you were as a young man. Oh, it must be a grand feeling to speak over the airwaves to the entire nation! To make your way into every living room! Into every cottage and castle! I've always wanted so very much to talk on the radio. To speak out across the country. To the sick in their beds and the lonely old people. To the sailor at sea and to our fellow countrymen abroad."

"Yes, why haven't you ever spoken on the radio, actually? I'm sure you'd be very good at it."

"Do you really think so? I've certainly thought about it often. It's my calling to bear witness. And it would be very easy to rewrite a sermon as a radio talk."

"They're actually quite interested in religious lectures in the radio department. Let me take a couple of lectures with me to show them. I'm a regular visitor there, you know, and I might just have some influence, in all modesty."

"Would you really do that for me? I can't express how grateful I would be. Perhaps you might like to see some of the sermons I've written? Then you could tell me if you think they might be used as radio lectures, couldn't you?"

"Yes, let's have a look at them," says Harald Horn. "I'm quite certain that they can be used just the way they are."

# [ 48 ]

OLSEN WALKS UP the old, dark avenue of lindens to Frydenholm. He has been there before and knows the way, and he is not impressed by the red castle or the symmetry of the park. He is wearing a natty, light-colored summer suit and is calm and confident and aware of his own importance.

He does not go up the wide central staircase, but in through the kitchen and servants' entrance, where he meets Lukas.

It's the warmest part of the summer, yet Lukas's face is pale and sallow. He looks at Olsen with his expressionless eyes and shows no sign of surprise or curiosity. "Have you come back? Are you going to be working here again?"

"No," Olsen replies. "This is just a short visit. A quick trip. I have something to talk to the squire about. How are you getting along, Lukas? So you're still holding out here?"

"Yes," Lukas says. "I'm holding out here. Still." He would like to know what Olsen is up to, but he doesn't ask any questions.

"Is he upstairs?" Olsen says.

"Yes. Did he send for you?"

"No, I'm the one who'd like to give my regards to him."

"Do you think he'll see you?"

"Oh, I think so. If you go up and announce me and tell him it's something important."

"Is it something important?"

"Yes. You'd better hurry and announce me upstairs."

Lukas goes upstairs and doesn't ask any more questions, and his face shows no expression. He comes back and says, "Yes, the squire will be happy to see you."

"That was sensible of him," says Olsen.

Squire Skjern-Svendsen is sitting in his study in front of the large portrait of himself. And both the portrait and the flesh-and-blood squire look at Olsen with their gentle blue eyes. The portrait has a lavender background and a very thick gold frame, and Olsen notes that a Knight's Cross has been painted on the portrait since the last time he saw it.

Otherwise the room is unchanged. The squire is a modest
man. He has large offices in Præstø with secretaries and stenog-
raphers. And there it's almost impossible to get into his office
and be able to speak with him. The overseer of the estate has a
modern, impressive office with technical gadgets. And the overseer of the estate has office clerks and assistants.

But at home the squire has only a single servant. He lives in a
castle but he uses only a few of its rooms. And his study gives no
impression of the large operations he directs. In the room there
is only a simple table and one high-backed Renaissance chair.
Wrought-iron candelabras with large altar candles. And inexpensive tapestries from his weaving mill in Præstø. There are old
swords on the walls. And Thorvaldsen's sculpture of Christ in
artificial marble. And in the bedroom next door is the historic
canopy bed that the Swedish king slept in. And there's a little
prayer stool with a naively embroidered white dove on a blue
background. Olsen is familiar with it all.

"Well, Olsen my boy, are you coming back to me? Have you
been homesick?" the squire asks. And his voice is soft and
gentle with its guileless Jutland drawl.

"No," Olsen replies. "I've got to go back right away. This is a
matter that can be arranged very quickly, Squire, if you—"

"That busy? That sounds good. So then you do have work.
It's good to be busy. That's how we avoid bad thoughts. Now
isn't this an amusing coincidence, though? Just today I had a
visit from a good friend of both of ours. It was old master tailor
Henningsen. And we talked about you too. Henningsen has a
good opinion of you, Olsen. He's certain that you're on the
straight and narrow now. And I'm very happy to hear that."

But Olsen doesn't feel like talking about Henningsen and the
straight and narrow. He has come on a special mission and wants
to get right to the point. The last time he was here, he was
cheated out of his pay. Now he actually wouldn't mind getting
what he still has coming to him, and maybe some slight compensation for damages and injury. And if he doesn't get it, he knows
a thing or two about Squire Skjern-Svendsen. So of course it
would be in the squire's best interest to pay Olsen a slight consideration to keep his mouth shut about what he knows.

"I don't think our old friend Henningsen would like to hear

you talking like that," the squire says. And he speaks quietly and gently. He still doesn't know what Olsen is driving at. He realizes that something is making Olsen bold and arrogant. Squire Skjern-Svendsen has his secrets. Both in his business and in his private life there are things best left unknown. The smart thing to do is to gain time and be gentle and quiet and look at Olsen with his kind eyes.

And it's quite true that Olsen does know something. And he wants money for not publicizing what he knows. Brazenly he looks straight at the squire and makes demands and claims in a coarse tone of voice.

"Well, I'm afraid it's blackmail you're up to," the squire says. "So I suppose it will be my sad duty to report you to the police. With your past I'm afraid it will be a very serious matter for you." And the squire sighs and feels sorry for Olsen.

"But what if it's something kind and positive that I know about the squire? Something that will only bring the squire praise and gratitude and fame when people find out about it? Now that can't be blackmail, can it?"

The squire still doesn't know what Olsen is referring to. The two men sit looking at each other. It's so quiet that they can hear a little clock ticking in the bedroom next door. The squire is not angry or upset but looks calmly at Olsen with his gentle eyes.

"It's possible that you think you can make some money on some piece of gossip about me, Olsen," the squire says slowly in his Jutland drawl. "But you can't, Olsen my boy. I ought to report you to the police right away. But I'm actually rather fond of you. You've worked here in my house. And I don't have any children. That's why the members of my staff are like my children. I can't regard you or Lukas as anything other than my big boys. When you came, Olsen, I couldn't help thinking of the story of the prodigal son who returned to his father's farm. I guess I'm a little naive and easy to disappoint. But you *didn't* come here so you could return; you came back to threaten me and extort money from me. I'm not at all curious to find out what you think you know. I don't care to hear about it at all. I think you'd better leave, Olsen. And if you really do want to hurt me, then just go right ahead!" And the squire sighs again.

"I know who Danielsen is!" says Olsen.

The squire gives a start. And his gentle gaze vanishes for a moment. And Olsen sees this clearly.

"I know that you're Danielsen!" says Olsen.

# [ 49 ]

IT'S HAPPENED BEFORE that people have wanted to extort money from Squire Skjern-Svendsen because they knew some of his secrets. But it never worked. The squire is a powerful man who pulls strings and has connections everywhere. He's not easy to get at, even though you might know one or two of his secret deeds.

But this time it's something kind, agreeable, and commendable that he committed in secret. And Olsen is sitting there aloof and confident, looking at him expectantly.

"I know there aren't any newspapers that would dare write about your dirty tricks," says Olsen. "Even if somebody came along with the most airtight evidence and revelations, nobody would risk attacking Skjern-Svendsen. On the other hand, all the newspapers would like to write something nice about Skjern-Svendsen and praise him and suck up to him. They'd all like to write about the noble benefactor who was so modest that he called himself Danielsen when he did his good deeds. This is a revelation you don't have the power to stop!"

"I'm afraid I'll have to have you arrested anyway, Olsen. This is too vile!"

"Newspapers are real curious, you know," says Olsen. "They'd love to write about this mysterious Danielsen. And since I've served in the home of Danielsen himself and know the way things are in his castle, I could probably get a little something for telling the newspapers about him. I couldn't help thinking of Squire Skjern-Svendsen as soon as I read the newspaper stories about the nice little man wearing the old fur coat. After all, I've brushed that fur coat many times and dusted it with naphthalene in the summer. I don't think I can be arrested simply because I feel like saying a few things about the famous, mysterious Danielsen."

"It's blackmail because you want me to pay you to keep your mouth shut. And I see no alternative—it's my unpleasant duty to inform the police. With the past that you have, you'll be arrested on the spot. And it'll be a few years before you'll be able to tell anybody about Danielsen. I feel sorry for you, Olsen, my boy. I thought you were on your way to becoming a respectable person. But I guess you'll have to go through one more ordeal before you can make yourself say goodbye to evil ways." And the squire picks up the telephone to call the police.

"Look, it's like this," says Olsen. "If anything happens to me, the story about Danielsen will be in the papers in a few days. I've deposited a sealed envelope with a reporter. And if I don't get in touch with him within a week, he'll open the envelope. Then he'll read that the mysterious Danielsen who gives away so much money is the well-known Squire Skjern-Svendsen. So if you want to call the police and have me arrested now, things will run their course, and I certainly won't be able to prevent your good deeds from appearing in the press."

"Who is this reporter?" the squire asks gently.

"Uh-huh, wouldn't you like to know!" says Olsen. "And you'll find out, all right, if you wait a week and the story gets printed in the papers. The reporter will simply think he's doing Squire Skjern-Svendsen a big favor by writing about the squire's kind heart. Of course he can't imagine that it's something to be ashamed of."

The squire has gotten up and is pacing back and forth in the room. Occasionally he fiddles with the telephone and every so often he touches one of the old swords hanging on the wall.

"I won't deny that it would be extremely disagreeable to me if my little joke of calling myself Danielsen came out in the papers. It is written that the left hand shall not know what the right hand is doing. And while I'm alive, I don't wish to receive thanks or praise for what I've given away. And you really want to take advantage of that, Olsen? We were really such good friends once, weren't we?"

The squire wanders around the room. Once in a while he touches one of the old swords on the wall. Olsen follows him with his eyes.

"It's wrong of me to do this," the squire says. "It's wrong and reprehensible. But the way things stand, I'll be glad to pay you a sum of money. A small sum to get you started. If, that is, you will refrain from all talk of who this Danielsen might be who once gave away some money."

Olsen nods his head.

"But if I give you a small sum now, you'll come back in a little while with new threats when you've spent the money. That's just the way it is with blackmailers. They keep right at it as long as there's something left to extort. I might know a little something about you too, Olsen. There were a few things back when you were working here. I spared you then, but with your past everything counts. But would that stop you in your greed?"

Olsen says nothing. The squire stops his pacing and stands still in front of his portrait. They hear the clock ticking in the bedroom and they hear other soft sounds. The sun has gone down, and it's starting to get dark.

Again they hear some soft, indeterminate noises. Suddenly the squire spins around and flings open the door. His wife is standing outside.

"Oh!" she says. "Now what kind of behavior is that? Why did you scare me like that?"

"What are you doing out here, Julie?"

"Doing? I'm not the one who's doing something. I'm not holding any secret assignations here! I just this minute got home. And I wanted to come into your study, but then I heard voices and waited a minute so I wouldn't disturb you. I thought the gardener was here. Why are you so nervous? Why do you look so upset?"

"You're the one who's nervous, Julie. You're walking around here like a ghost, like those dead women. Look, it's Olsen who's come for a visit. Don't you remember Olsen?"

"Oh yes," his wife says, nodding her head. "I certainly do. Good evening, Olsen. How are you?"

"Great, thanks," Olsen says.

"I'll be leaving," says the squire's wife. "I certainly don't want to disturb you."

"You're not disturbing us in the least, Julie, my dear," the squire tells her.

"Oh, really? Well, I'm tired after my trip. I'll just have a cup of tea, then I'll go to bed. Good night. And pardon me if I interrupted you two gentlemen." And Julie quietly closes the door and walks out into the long corridor where the shields and suits of armor are on display.

"I didn't know my wife had come home," the squire explains. "I thought there was someone listening. It could have been Lukas, for instance, or one of the maids. My wife is very nervous. She's been to Copenhagen today."

"Yes," Olsen says. "Today is Wednesday."

"Wednesday? Why do you say that?"

"It's on Wednesdays and Mondays that your wife usually drives to Copenhagen in her blue car."

"How do you know that? And what do you mean by saying that?"

"I know a lot of things. I also know Dr. Robert Riege well."

"Where do you know Dr. Riege from?"

"I help print a magazine for him. *Sex News*. It's a pretty racy magazine. I was a guinea pig for the doctor once too, in his laboratory. It was a rough job. Those experiments he conducts are pretty strange."

"I can imagine," the squire says. "What do you know about Dr. Riege and my wife?"

"I'm pretty discreet by nature," Olsen says. "And I don't like to meddle in other people's affairs."

"Now listen, Olsen," says the squire. "I think the two of us could come to an understanding. Let's continue to be friends. The two of us might have some use for each other. We shouldn't be threatening and putting the squeeze on each other. I'll make you a reasonable proposal that you will benefit from. I'm not going to pay you a lump sum. Because you'll use it up too quickly. And then you'll want to have more and more. Instead, I'll give you the *interest* on a sum of money. A pension. A monthly wage. What do you think about that?"

"Maybe," says Olsen.

"I will retain you. You'll be my agent. You'll get me information about certain things. It's easy and convenient work that you can do in your spare time."

"I take it I'll be spying?" Olsen says.

"You were a servant here at Frydenholm, Olsen. And you know the way things are. I won't try to pretend. You know that my wife lives her own life. She has her own rooms, and I have mine. We eat separately and we live separately. We're not like a married couple. This is no secret. And it certainly can't be any secret to the servants of the house."

"No," says Olsen.

"You're smart enough to know what information I would like to have. You know Dr. Riege and you've been his subject. You might be able to get that job again. I'm sure it can be done during the time you're not working at the print shop. I'll give you 150 kroner a month fixed salary as long as you submit regular reports about what you see and hear and find out for yourself concerning Dr. Riege and my wife. We won't say anything more about your little attempt at blackmail. As long as you don't talk about this business of Danielsen to anybody, you'll be employed in my service and get 150 kroner in wages from me each month. For almost no work! If anything should appear in the newspapers about me and Danielsen, naturally you'll have to count on losing your employment with me. And I suppose I'll also find it necessary to inform the police about certain things I happen to know about you. What do you think about that?"

"I don't think 150 kroner is enough," Olsen says.

"That's the interest on 30,000 kroner," the squire says. "That's the interest on a fortune, Olsen, my boy! That's a whole lot of money. And it's something that will last. It's a position for life. A life insurance policy. It's more substantial than black-mail. And if you should happen to bring me extra good information some time, you'll get extra compensation for it. I'm not going to dicker. Do you accept my offer? Yes or no?"

Olsen thinks about it. Matters have taken a different turn than he had imagined. In a sense a fixed salary is better than a lump sum. And without risk. And Olsen has been a spy before. When he was in the penitentiary he spied for the deputy warden and reported what the other prisoners were talking about, and received small favors and extra food in return. The activities of a spy and a rat are not unfamiliar to him. And it won't be hard to find out things at Dr. Riege's if he can come and go in his laboratory as a subject. On top of everything else, he'll get his supper from Riege the whole time.

They negotiate about the payments for a while. Olsen knows Squire Skjern-Svendsen and knows that it doesn't do any good to dicker about his prices. They reach an agreement on a fixed monthly salary of 150 kroner plus extra compensation for especially good information. Olsen is to come to Frydenholm every month and submit his report. The squire opens the door and peeks out to see whether anyone is listening. But the long corridors are empty and deserted with their shields and armor and old halberds on the walls.

It has grown completely dark. There won't be any more buses going to the station tonight. "You can certainly spend the night here with me," says the squire. "You're familiar with the premises after all, Olsen."

"No thanks," Olsen replies. "I've already taken a room at the inn."

"You don't need to be afraid of sleeping here at Frydenholm, Olsen, my boy. I won't do anything to you. Why, we're friends and associates." And the squire looks affectionately at Olsen with his moist, light-blue eyes.

"No thanks. I have to go," Olsen says. He has 150 kroner in his pocket and would rather sleep at the inn.

# [ 50 ]

THE NIGHT IS BRIGHT AND STILL. There's a spicy scent from the sweetbriar and honeysuckle bushes. And hedgehogs come out and walk around, grunting and coughing and drinking dew from the grass.

Olsen is asleep in the historic inn, in a drab room with clammy sheets.

And Mrs. Julie Skjern-Svendsen is asleep in her own wing of the castle. She has locked her bedroom door and has nothing to do with her husband.

A light is burning in the squire's room. He is kneeling on the cushion of his prayer stool with its white dove that his mother embroidered. He is saying his prayers to God. He is praying for forgiveness for things he has done, and he is praying for good luck and success for the projects he has under way. He has annexed new farms to his estate. And he has bought up horses. And he has set up scutching mills for fiber flax. He has purchased hundreds of sheep for his estate in Jutland so he himself can supply the wool to his clothing factory in Præstø. He has a lot of irons in the fire. And he has his secrets too. He believes in God, and there is something he has to ask forgiveness for.

If he gives 20,000 kroner for the prevention of diseases and calls himself Danielsen and doesn't want anybody to know it, he undoubtedly has his reasons. Perhaps he thinks that one act will cancel out another, or that good deeds can neutralize something else that he has done. Perhaps he is afraid that he has cancer himself and would like to do something to speed up cancer research. And when he does die someday, and his estate has to be settled, and it is discovered that he was the charitable Danielsen, maybe people will be inclined to overlook other things that the settlement of the estate will reveal.

After Squire Skjern-Svendsen dies, he wants his castle Frydenholm to become a museum and be the property of the entire nation. A home for the memories of the aristocratic age, even though Skjern-Svendsen himself was no aristocrat. Foundations will be established and sums of money given to charitable causes, guaranteeing him a posthumous reputation. And the powers that see all and know his secrets should be placated by these good works that his fortune is supposed to endow.

But he has a wife who, first of all, is supposed to inherit what he has amassed. And it isn't easy to have a will drawn up against her wishes. She is twenty years younger and has different interests and is not part of the Kingdom of God.

She doesn't talk to her husband and doesn't want to have anything to do with him. She behaves scandalously and is the focus of gossip and rumor. Maybe it would be possible to have her declared insane and have her disappear into a hospital.

His wife gets curious whims; lately her inhibitions have begun to disappear. There is a wooden horse in the castle courtyard. It is an exact replica of the original torture instrument that irreverent peasants burned and destroyed 150 years ago.

One day Mrs. Julie happens to climb onto the wooden horse to find out what it would have been like to sit on. She is wearing a stylish brown suit. She is delicate and aristocratic and she isn't an athletic woman. She gets up onto the tall framework with the greatest difficulty. And once she is sitting up there, she can't get back down and has to cling to the animal and shout for help. Fortunately gardener Holm is just coming into the courtyard and runs over to lift her down.

It is a strange experience for the gardener, who hasn't touched a woman in eighteen years. He can't avoid putting his arms around her and touching her legs and feeling her silk stockings. He is giddy and confused.

"Oh, thank you!" she says with a gasp. "Oh, it was lucky you came along. That was a crazy thing for me to do. I just wanted to

see what it was like to sit on the wooden horse. I wanted to know what they felt like in the old days when they were put up there. Oh, it was terrible! Thank God you came along. I think you saved my life."

And the gardener is standing there red in the face holding on to her. "Shall I carry you inside?" he asks.

"No, no. I can manage all right by myself. I'm really not injured."

"But shouldn't I give you some help, ma'am?"

"No, thank you. That's fine. I can manage by myself now." She straightens her clothes and smooths her hair. "Oh, it was a good thing that nobody else saw that. You won't tell anybody, will you? My husband would be awfully angry if he found out about it. Oh, I'm sure you know that he isn't as mild and gentle as he looks. Promise me you won't tell anybody! Promise me!"

"All right," says the gardener, "I promise." Now the gardener shares a secret with her. He is giddy, and his head is swimming.

Gardener Holm is a gloomy man. He has his problems and troubles. He is a capable gardener, but other people get the credit for his huge squashes and his giant strawberries. He works diligently in his greenhouses. But he doesn't get the profits and the surplus himself. He sends his daughter to the parsonage with vegetables, but he's not on familiar terms with the pastor. He doesn't understand the pastor's breezy manner. He believes in God, but he doesn't know whether he wants to be on God's side. He doesn't approve of the way God runs the world. He has heavy thoughts and misgivings.

He is alone in his own home too. His wife goes around wearing drab black dresses. She's not the sort to make an effort to look attractive. There are no carnal or sensual pleasures between them. The gardener cultivates the fruits of the earth and pollinates melon blossoms and watches them germinate and grow out of the ground. But Mrs. Holm has turned her thoughts away from this world. They sleep separately. And it's been eighteen years since they managed to have a daughter together.

Sometimes the squire's wife comes down to the nursery and looks at the flowers and asks about the plants and is interested in what's going on. She really would have liked to be a gardener and asks whether she still might become an apprentice gardener. "But you wouldn't want me, would you?" she says. She is sitting on a box smiling at the gardener, and he thinks of the angel who sat on the gravestone amid the lilies in the garden.

"You haven't told anybody about the business with the wooden horse, have you?" she asks. "Oh, I'm so terribly embarrassed about it. And I'm still so tender here. I think you saved my life. But don't tell anyone, all right?"

On Sundays Squire Skjern-Svendsen goes to church and sits in his reserved pew alone and listens to Pastor Nørregaard-Olsen's sermon. The pastor's guest is in church too, and after the sermon he is introduced to the squire. "The literary historian, Dr. Harald Horn!—Squire Skjern-Svendsen!" the pastor says loudly and distinctly, so everybody can hear who his guest is.

"What a marvelous sermon!" says Harald Horn. "So alive and topical. Of course it can be used as a lecture on the radio. It doesn't even need to be rewritten. Give me your handwritten copy the way it is. I think I can get it accepted. I have some say in the broadcasting system!"

Harald Horn has had a fine time at the parsonage. The days have passed pleasantly with conversations and reading and good meals and excursions to the surrounding area. The pastor has driven him around in his car, and they have visited Fensmark, Gisselfeldt, and Vester-Egede. And Harald Horn has written a newspaper article about southern Sjælland and Christian Winther. "This area is so Danish," says Harald Horn. "So quintessentially Danish! So soulfully Danish!" He thinks "soulfully Danish" is a good phrase that shouldn't simply be squandered away. And he writes the phrase down and saves it to use later.

Every day the gardener's daughter comes with fresh strawberries, even though the season is just about over. The strawberries taste marvelous with a glass of old sherry. The pastor has good cigars and good red wine. Even though you have to lead an out-of-the-way, rustic existence, life can still be tolerable. And when the pastor is busy with his work and is unable to entertain his guest, Dr. Horn can find himself a book in one of the bookcases and pass the time reading. Or he can turn on the radio. It's amusing to sit in precisely these surroundings and listen to a lecture about memories from old Danish parsonages.

Old tailor Henningsen comes bicycling from Præstø and talks with Pastor Nørregaard-Olsen in his office.

"Do you know who that old man was?" the pastor asks his guest. "That was Henningsen's father."

"Henningsen? What Henningsen?"

"Don't you remember Shorty Henningsen? From our university days. From Walkendorff's dormitory?"

"Oh yes, him! The one who was studying law."

"That's right. And now I talk to his old father fairly often. He's a wonderful man—the evangelical movement out here is greatly indebted to him."

"So whatever became of Shorty Henningsen?"

"I understand he has a very good position. He does something in the prison system. Do you remember how we were always pulling his leg when we were students?"

"Ah yes. But quite frankly he deserved it. He was such a nasty pest. He always had to be borrowing money and sponging off people. I actually think he still owes me 5 kroner," says Harald Horn.

"Yes, that's what he was like," says the pastor. "But his father is all right. I truly appreciate that old man of honor." Neither of the two gentlemen knows how strangely the future will turn out and what Shorty Henningsen will become when the conditions are right for him.

Time passes with conversations about old memories from their university and high-school days. And the men laugh loudly and are once again schoolboys and lighthearted young university students.

Harald Horn has been fortunate with the weather on his vacation. The sun is warm, and the large wheat field behind the pastor's garden has turned yellow while he has been there. Autumn will begin in a few days, and there will be a record harvest this year. There is good reason to be worried and apprehensive because with this surplus of grain and meat and milk, farming won't pay for itself. In all probability, the state will have to step in with help and assistance for the threatened farmers.

A thunderstorm is brewing over behind the woods. The sky is dark and strange while the sun is still shining on the bright field of grain. The thunder rumbles and rolls. The pastor's wife has the maids bring in the lawn chairs and the umbrella, and the pastor shuts the windows in his study. "How small we are compared to the enormous forces of nature," says Pastor Nørregaard-Olsen.

"Yes," Harald Horn replies. "It was a thunderstorm like this that Goethe described with such inspiration in *The Sorrows of Young Werther*. Where they're standing in the doorway and say but a single word: 'Klopstock'!"

Then the sun is gone. The rain starts falling in large drops. And gusts of wind sweep over the yellow wheat field.

Summer vacation is over. The yellow bus is driving the children to grammar school again. They will have to learn about stamens and verbs and square roots and naval battles for six hours a day again. And when they come back home on the bus, they'll have to study their lessons, write compositions, and do their math homework. There won't be any time to play or learn something about life.

It gets dark early in the evening. Panty Marius is restless again and prowls around on the roads so people don't dare let their laundry hang outside. It's a pretty gruesome thing having a man like Panty Marius running around loose. Someday he might commit a murder or some other ghastly crime.

Jens Olsen's vacation girl has gone home to Copenhagen. It was amazing the way she put on weight and got tanned and healthy-looking. They gave her two big baskets of berries and other things, and she didn't forget to thank them politely for her summer. Her mother also wrote to Jens Olsen and thanked him for all the nice things he did.

Dr. Harald Horn has gone home to the capital city too, where the book season is about to begin. A busy time awaits him. Pastor Nørregaard-Olsen has received a letter from the broadcasting system saying that his lecture has been accepted and that they would like to have more of them. It's not only in his own parish that Pastor Nørregaard-Olsen has become a spiritual leader. His words will now be heard over the radio and make their way into every house and cottage and stir up and incite people and work for the Kingdom of God. "You can easily use your old sermons," Harald Horn writes to him, "just as long as you make sure to think up a neutral title so they look like lectures."

The harvest has been brought in. It is the largest harvest that Denmark has ever had. The year 1938 was a year of abundance that will be remembered for a long time.

In the nursery the workers are busy picking fruit and putting it in boxes and storing it in cellars, where it will stay until prices go up. Every day the gardener sends small and large cucumbers to town. The ones that are culled out are sold in the little shop at 3 kroner for a bunch of twenty.

"But they charge 3.50 for twenty small cucumbers in the stores in Præstø!" says the squire. "By God, you'd better pay attention to the price, Holm! It might not matter to you. But I'm the one who gets cheated out of 50 øre for every twenty small cucumbers that are sold at too low a price. It's easy to be extravagant with other people's money." The gardener doesn't make any reply, but he changes the price the way the squire wants it. But there is hatred in his heart, and perhaps the devil is on the verge of gaining power over him. He is silent. He broods and he broods. And he can't sleep at night. His wife is beginning to get anxious about his mind.

There are mushrooms in the woods and blackberries along the fences. In the parsonage garden the goldenrod, asters, and dahlias are blooming. And the leaves are starting to turn yellow on the large linden trees in the avenue leading up to Frydenholm.

Olsen has paid a visit and submitted his report. The squire is satisfied with him. Olsen gets his compensation and a monthly salary and is a well-to-do man without being in trouble with the law.

Damascus notices that Olsen has a lot of money in his pocket. And Olsen is no longer as willing to do his job and refuses to be sent into the city with galley proofs and printed matter. "I wasn't hired as a delivery boy!" he says. He has gotten a new raincoat, and Damascus is worried about what Olsen is up to.

"Olsen's not a bad person, but he is a weak man."

Now Olsen also has a job as a subject with Dr. Riege. After he finishes at the print shop, he goes out to Dr. Riege's laboratory in Sex Park to sit on a chair and get charged up and discharged as the doctor reads the strength of his life-energy in the form of a graph on a rotating cylinder.

Olsen takes a good look around Dr. Riege's clinic. He peers into medical records and asks questions and is interested in special cases. "An intelligent and interesting man!" says Dr. Riege. "Finally a worker who for once seems to understand that sexual liberation is a precondition for political and economic liberation. Unfortunately I must say that the working class has disappointed me. But Olsen is an exception." And the doctor brings Olsen along to his study groups and has him say hello to other believers. "A young worker who has joined us and who has an understanding of sexual-political development."

In Dr. Riege's laboratory there is a round-bottomed flask with a milky liquid in it. Those of his disciples who are allowed to take a look at the flask can distinctly see a tiny, pale, transparent being living in the liquid and emitting small bubbles. Olsen looks at the mysterious being too. "It must be expensive to make something like that. So who is paying all this money?" he asks.

The summer is long and goes on and on. Roses are still blooming in all the gardens in October. Evenings are warm and clear enough to see the stars, and young people in love can walk along the roads.

People were afraid that work on Squire Skjern-Svendsen's burial mound wouldn't be finished before the frost arrived. The squire urged the workers on, impatient and nervous that his grave wasn't going to be ready on time. But the frost didn't come. Now his mausoleum has been completed, and it has become a tourist attraction and a marvel, and people have no idea what treasures have been put into that grave. When they open the grave and take those things out several thousand years from now, they'll see how high our nation's cultural level was in 1938. And the elegant items will be put in a museum and photographed and preserved—if they have museums then. The marble sarcophagus alone, which was executed by a professor at the art academy, is worth a fortune and can hold its own beside the finest sarcophagi of antiquity. And the porcelain tiles with their Biblical motifs are on the same high level as the best church art of the Middle Ages. The bronze doors are Assyrian. The lamp bases are Greek. The lotus blossoms on the flagstones are Egyptian. The wrought-iron gate is French. And the whole thing is covered by an old Norse barrow. A Viking barrow. A chieftain's barrow. Danish and proto-Norse.

There are electric lights in the Greek lamps as well as a lot of other little contraptions and refinements.

On a clear day in October, the mound is consecrated and blessed by Pastor Nørregaard-Olsen. The ceremony is a moving

and solemn one, almost like a funeral. The professor who created the sarcophagus and the artist who executed the ceramics
are here from Copenhagen. They are delighted with each other's
work, and the professor sees to it that the ceramist gets a grant in
recognition of his work, and the ceramist, who is a member of a
foundation, obliges the professor with a prize.

The master craftsmen, the architect, and the engineer who
designed the bombproof reinforced concrete have shown up too.
Rasmus Larsen is present as a representative of the workers.
After the professor and the architect have spoken, Rasmus Larsen takes the floor and delivers thanks to the man who had the
magnanimity and public spirit to set this project in motion,
which provided bread for many mouths as well as animation and
activity to the benefit of the nation and its people. The religious
consecration follows, and after the pastor has finished his consecration, the squire himself speaks, thanking each and every person who assisted in creating this work, which will be preserved
down through the ages as a worthy part of Danish culture. An
expression of what our country is capable of producing today. A
legacy that we hereby bequeath to our posterity.

Short and gray, the squire stands speaking from the middle of
his burial mound. He talks very quietly and gently. His eyes are
blue and kind. This is what he looks like, this authoritative
businessman who created such a grand life's work.

The brief ceremony concludes with everybody singing "A
Mighty Fortress Is Our God."

It is worth noting that Squire Skjern-Svendsen's wife does not
take part in the ceremony. And there is only one sarcophagus
and room for only one person in the burial mound. When the
squire is dead, the mound will be closed. And it won't be opened
for anyone else.

His wife won't be buried in the mausoleum. And people say
that his wife isn't quite sane, and that she associates with occultists and magicians, and that she squanders her husband's fortune on sorcery and black magic.

There are a lot of weird things going on right now. You really
can't blame the squire for wanting to have a wife like that committed to a mental hospital before she manages to ruin him.

# [ 52 ]

A STORM IS RAGING, whipping and shaking the old linden trees around the red castle and making large branches fall down into the park. That's usually how it is: stormy and miserable weather follows an unnaturally long period of fine weather.

The rain is beating against the windows. It's clammy and it feels like a cellar inside Frydenholm's thick walls. Things smell musty and moldy. But Squire Skjern-Svendsen is a frugal man and doesn't want the heat turned on until it's absolutely necessary.

It's only in his wife's living room that a fire has been lit in the fireplace, because she doesn't have her husband's frugal habits. She is delicate and frail and has a cold and can't stand the musty odor.

She has arranged a few matters and has written a few letters. She has packed up some belongings in a flat suitcase. She is nervous and uneasy and apprehensive that something is going to happen to her.

She is afraid of the little gray man with the kind, gentle eyes. She knows that he has great power and can make his fellow human beings do many things, even though these things might be in conflict with laws and regulations.

Mrs. Julie is wandering through the castle's long corridors. She is like those deceased, pale aristocratic ladies who can't find peace in their graves but wander restlessly through the hallways of the castle.

She wants to make a telephone call to a certain person. But the telephone is in the squire's study, and he mustn't hear what she says. The mistress of Frydenholm will have to go out into the storm to ask someone if she can use their telephone. That's how far things have gone. She hasn't even been able to have a telephone installed in her own rooms.

The storm is howling and crashing. This is no weather to go out in, for an aristocratic lady who has a cold and is sickly. The park is wet and deserted, and it smells of fungus and dank earth.

There are no more blossoming flower beds in the nursery. Everything is black; the soil has been turned over for the fall and fertilized and covered up.

But inside the greenhouses, the chrysanthemums are in bloom. Big and Oriental and shaggy. They are magnificent and sumptuous, and each flower is worth a couple of kroner and will make a handsome profit for the squire.

These are the Japanese chrysanthemums called Nogiku, and one of their varieties called Kiku that the gardener of Frydenholm has nursed into especially admirable shapes. They once earned Squire Skjern-Svendsen the Queen's Grand Prize at an exhibition.

The squire's wife comes into the greenhouse where gardener Holm is walking around puttering with the strange Japanese flowers. She is as delicate and pale as a flower herself. And she looks mournful and has red-rimmed eyes. "This is probably the last time I'll be coming here to look at your flowers," she says. "I've been so grateful that you let me take some joy in your flowers."

The gardener sees that she has tears in her eyes, and he is startled and confused.

"I'm a kind of prisoner here at Frydenholm, you know," she tells him. "My family owned this place for several centuries, but I'm just a prisoner here. And they can send me away and shut me up like a wild animal."

She touches the flowers and smells them, even though Japanese chrysanthemums have no fragrance. "I really just wanted to say goodbye to all this," she says.

The gardener is standing across from her and staring, not comprehending anything, and he is full of anxiety and agitation.

"Will you think some kind thoughts about me after I'm gone?" she asks. "Or do you think I'm insane too?"

"No, no!" the gardener says and doesn't know where to look. "Madame isn't! Madame is so—"

"Do you think I'm dangerous and mad and perverted too?" she shouts.

"Oh, no!" the gardener replies. "Certainly not!" And he puts his arm around her because she is crying. She is delicate and slender and strange to the touch. He can smell her perfume.

And he thinks about the time she was sitting on the wooden horse and was so wretched and needed his help so he had to take hold of her and touch her knees and legs and body.

He is holding her very tight. He has strong arms and rough hands and smells of composted earth and sweat. And she is holding on to him tightly. And he feels dizzy.

The rain is beating against the windowpanes of the greenhouse. Things are crashing and clattering in the storm. And amazing and dramatic things are taking place inside the greenhouse, where the squire's wife and the gardener are together among the Japanese chrysanthemums of the Kiku variety.

# [ 53 ]

LATER THAT AFTERNOON Dr. Riege gets a telephone call from the provinces. He has to go to Frydenholm. He has to get a move on and hurry up and do something. It's a cry of distress from a lady who feels that she is in danger and who has such great confidence in the doctor that she credits him with the power and influence to take care of everything. A cry for help from a patient and a disciple who is helping to pay for the production of the costly homunculus in the bottle. Both his patient and his homunculus are in danger.

The doctor says reassuring words over the telephone. It can't be as bad as all that. You can't just have people committed against their will. She should stay calm. Of course he'll come. But he can't do it right this minute. Patients are waiting. But toward evening. Then he'll cancel his study group.

And that evening he starts his little cream-colored sports car and drives to Frydenholm, where he has never been before. He has to put the top up because it's raining and the wind is blowing hard. It's black and dark and difficult for him to get his bearings.

A few hours before Dr. Riege gets there, however, Olsen arrives at Frydenholm. He arrives on the evening bus, and he is the only passenger to get off at the inn. He is wearing a shiny

new black raincoat and he turns the collar up around his ears
when he gets out. "So when does the first bus leave tomorrow
morning?" he shouts to the driver.

"Ten minutes past seven," the driver answers. "That's the
school bus."

"So there aren't any more tonight?"

"No, this is the last one."

"It's dark as hell, and the weather is rotten," Olsen says.

An electric light is burning by the parking lot out in front of
the parsonage. But the avenue up to Frydenholm is pitch dark.
Olsen has to grope and lurch his way along in order not to run
into the trees. And he has to lean into the storm and almost trips
over the branches that have been blown down.

The squire doesn't know that he's coming. So Olsen will just
have to hope that he's home and has time. The agreement is that
he's only supposed to come once a month. And he is not to
telephone or write letters.

It's the 21st of the month. But Olsen needs some extra compensation and has things to report that he feels are probably
worth some money. He is a capable spy but he is disorderly in
financial matters, and there are negotiations and tugs-of-war
about every single payment.

He finds his way to the kitchen entrance and knocks on the
door until Lukas comes. Lukas doesn't ask him any questions
and never looks surprised. "I'll announce you to the squire
now," he says, looking at Olsen with expressionless eyes.

"Just have him come in," the squire says. He is in his study,
busy working with numbers and calculations and new ideas. He
has a lot of projects under way. But he always has time to talk to
Olsen and get his reports.

They are sitting together in the room with the cheap tapestries, the portrait of the squire, and the old swords on the walls.
And Lukas isn't listening at the door and doesn't know what
they're talking about.

A couple of hours later Dr. Riege arrives in his small car.
There are no people out in the bad weather, and there's nobody
he can ask for directions. He stops at the historic inn and gets
hold of the waiter, who explains the way to him. And the waiter
at the inn is the only one who has seen the doctor's car and will

be able to give a description of it later. At this point, the time is
9:30.

Dr. Riege doesn't drive his car up the linden avenue. He
parks it at the inn and walks out into the rain and the darkness.
He has a small flashlight with him so he is able to find his way
with relative ease. If there aren't any vicious dogs, it's not likely
anything will happen to him.

About halfway up the avenue, he meets another person. He
shines his light on him and sees that it is a very tall man with a
drooping mustache. And the man is frightened and runs off into
the darkness. Robert Riege thinks he was holding something
white in his hand.

The main door is closed. And nobody hears his knock. It's
dark and deserted. This is a weird castle, without any doormen
or serving staff. He finds his way to the kitchen entrance and
knocks loudly. He discovers that there's a bell too and rings it.
Then Lukas comes out and looks at him vacantly.

"I'm supposed to meet Mrs. Julie Skjern-Svendsen. Your
mistress is expecting me."

"Whom should I announce?"

"Just tell her that it's the doctor. Your mistress is informed."

Then Lukas disappears. And it takes some time before he
comes back. Dr. Riege stands waiting in a cold, half-dark entry-
way. This is a hell of a way to live in a country manor, he thinks.

Lukas comes back. "This way, doctor," he says. And he leads
the doctor down long hallways and upstairs to the mistress's
apartment. And it's storming so hard and the wind is banging
and howling so much that nobody has heard the doctor arrive,
and the squire doesn't know that his wife has company.

Squire Skjern-Svendsen goes to bed early. He has done so for
many years; it is a habit that he never breaks. "Are you sleeping
at the inn again? Or will you show us the honor of spending the
night here? If so, I'll inform Lukas." Olsen hasn't received the
extra payment that he had hoped for, and he doesn't have a lot of
money in his pocket and is reluctant to go out in the rain. He is
morose and sullen.

The squire rings for Lukas and asks him to show Olsen a
small room where he can sleep that night. "I don't suppose I'll
be seeing you tomorrow morning. I don't get up until 7:30, and

of course you have to catch the bus at 7:00. And next time you don't need to come when you're not supposed to. In the future your report must be far more reliable, Olsen, my boy. The idea is for you to do some work for the money I'm paying you. You're not just supposed to keep on making demands. Things had better be different next time. Good night, Olsen." And the squire's eyes are kind even though he was dissatisfied with Olsen.

At 10:30 the squire goes into his bedroom. Lukas brings him a glass of warm elderberry juice and asks if there is anything else the squire wishes.

"No, you can go to bed, Lukas. But don't go into the pantry and steal the food tonight. Yesterday somebody took some sugar and butter. I checked. Do you understand?"

"Yes sir, Squire."

"Good night."

"Good night, Squire."

Then the squire kneels on the prayer stool with the white dove and says his evening prayers before he lies down in the historic canopy bed where Karl Gustav once spent the night.

At 12:30 Dr. Riege leaves the building. And according to Lukas's explanation, the mistress herself must have let him out. Lukas claims to have been asleep at this point.

Shortly after Dr. Riege has driven off, the squire's wife starts her long blue car. She goes out to the garage carrying her own suitcase to the car. And no one hears her start the engine and drive out into the night.

# [ 54 ]

It's still dark out when Olsen sits down in the bus. It's not raining anymore, but the wind is still blowing and tearing at the leafless trees in the gardens.

Olsen is freezing in his shiny raincoat. He didn't get any coffee and he doesn't have any cigarettes.

The bus is full of schoolchildren who have to be at grammar

school at 8:00. They are talking and bickering and quizzing each other about terrible vocabulary lists and arithmetic problems. It's amazing what those children have to know and how they can keep it all in their heads.

The driver would like to chat with Olsen. But Olsen is taciturn and not in the mood. Last night he was talkative enough. But today he is close-mouthed and somber, and the driver gives up trying to carry on a conversation.

There are a few other adults on the bus. They look at the children's schoolbooks and shudder in amazement. At the inn some packages are brought out to the bus. Then the driver starts up. The bus drives through the village, where there are lights in the windows.

As yet no one knows that Squire Skjern-Svendsen was murdered during the night.

Jenny is the first person who can tell the town about what happened. She comes down the road in her blue hospital dress with her bare arms sticking out and a whole bunch of barrettes in her straight yellow hair. Giggling and feeble-minded. She points her fingers and says, "Now he's dead! Ugh, ugh! He was strangled. Like this. Aeeagh!"

People come out of their houses and stand in the wind talking about what happened and who they think might have done it.

Cars roar in with the police and experts and specialists from Copenhagen. The castle and the park are cordoned off and combed through. The servants are interrogated. The police look for fingerprints and footprints. Pastor Nørregaard-Olsen goes up to the castle and promptly holds a devotional service and talks about the dead squire, who was a good man for the evangelical movement and the Kingdom of God in this parish. The flags are lowered to half-mast and sigh and snap in the wind.

Dr. Riege telephones police headquarters himself when he hears about the murder on the radio and finds out that the police are searching for a little cream-colored sports car. He has to tell the police what he knows about the precise circumstances of his nighttime visit to Frydenholm.

It is somewhat difficult for him. He doesn't dare call the squire's wife his patient, in order not to come in conflict with the quack-medicine laws. He has to say that Mrs. Skjern-Svendsen was his coworker and was interested in biochemical experiments which he is in the process of setting up, and which have already solved the riddle of life and will make it possible to produce an artificial, chemical human being with life-energy and sexual power.

"Did you talk to Squire Skjern-Svendsen last night?" the police ask him.

"No, I only talked to his wife. She has her own apartment in the castle and doesn't live with her husband."

"Did you talk to any of the other people who live in the castle?"

"I was let in by a pale man who I'm sure was a servant. But I didn't talk to him beyond telling him that I wished to see the mistress and that I was expected."

"Haven't you ever talked to Squire Skjern-Svendsen?"

"No. And I've never met him. Mrs. Skjern-Svendsen often visited me in Copenhagen and participated in my experiments and in our study groups. But I wasn't acquainted with her husband at all."

"Why did Mrs. Skjern-Svendsen send for you yesterday?"

"She telephoned me in the afternoon and asked me to come right away. She was terribly upset, and I had the impression that she might have had a scene with her husband. She said that the squire wanted to have her committed to a mental hospital. That he was a monster and a devil. That she was afraid of him. And that he had everybody in his power and it would be easy for him to have her put away."

"And you promised to come at once? You wanted to help her, didn't you? How had you actually thought you would help her?"

"Yes, I promised her I'd come. I felt I had to calm her down and talk to her. I may be her only friend. She was very lonely and somewhat reserved."

"Were you having an erotic relationship with Mrs. Skjern-Svendsen?"

"All people have erotic relationships with each other. All existence consists of an eternal charging, a tension, and a discharging of life-energy, which is the same thing as sexuality."

"Are you trying to say that you were having a relationship with the squire's wife?"

"What do you mean by 'relationship'? Everything of the opposite polarity attracts. The atoms in a mineral are held together
by this attraction. As are the planets and galaxies. Fundamen-
tally, magnetism, or the attractive force, or electricity, or energy
is nothing but sexuality."

"So you don't wish to answer the question? If you're asked to
testify, though, you'll definitely have to do so. What did you talk
to Mrs. Skjern-Svendsen about last night?"

"She talked about her husband and her marriage. As far as I
was able to understand, her husband was a person with pro-
nounced inhibitions and stress brought about by the accumula-
tion of unused sexual energy. As far as it goes, his case is fairly
simple. For instance, he did not smoke. His orality was inhibited, probably as early as in the maternity clinic. And his anal—"

"That doesn't interest us all that much. Wouldn't you tell us
instead what Mrs. Skjern-Svendsen talked to you about?"

"She talked about her unhappy marital situation which made
it impossible for her to reach orgasm, which is the meaning of
life. Her inhibited husband regarded her as insane. He had been
in touch with a number of doctors to have her declared mentally
deranged and a danger to herself and others. She was considering running away from him and asked me for help and advice."

"What did you advise her to do?"

"I advised her to stay at Frydenholm for the time being. I said
I didn't feel that the squire would be able to get the doctors to
obtain her compulsory commitment. I explained to her what the
phenomenon of fear is. The actual fact of the matter concerning
the phenomenon we call fear is that it is the sexual—"

"Thank you. Did you get the impression that Mrs. Skjern-
Svendsen wanted to do away with her husband? Did she say
anything that might indicate that she was tired of him?"

"No. Not directly. She said only that he was a brute, a devil,
and a scoundrel."

"I'd say that ought to be interpreted as a certain dislike for her
husband."

"Yes, I suppose it might."

"Did Mrs. Skjern-Svendsen want to start living with you if
she could get rid of her husband?"

"She wanted to leave with me last night. But I advised her

against it. That would harm her financially and put her in a difficult position in the event of a divorce."

"How was Mrs. Skjern-Svendsen when you left?"

"I attempted to calm her. She seemed to feel that I had let her down because I didn't want to take her with me. She reproached me. But I did have the impression that she was starting to calm down."

"And have you heard from her since?"

"No. I heard on the radio that she had driven off in her car sometime during the night. But she hasn't gotten in touch with me."

"Do you have any idea where she might have gone?"

"No."

"Do you expect her to come to you?"

"She usually comes every Monday and Wednesday. I would be inclined to believe that she will continue to do so."

"But you can't give us any clue about where we can find her now?"

"No. I have no idea at all about where she might have gone."

"Do you have anything else to state that you feel might be of interest to the police in this investigation?"

"No, I don't. — Yes, I do, come to think of it! When I arrived at Frydenholm — it must have been around 9:30 — I met a person in the avenue that leads up to the castle. The weather was horrible, you know, so I was surprised that anybody was out. I had a flashlight with me and happened to shine the light on the man for a moment."

"So it was a man? What did he look like?"

"I saw him only very fleetingly, of course. He was very tall, I believe. And I think he had a mustache. And I think he was holding something white in his hand."

"Something white? What do you think it might have been?"

"I don't know. It could have been a piece of paper or a handkerchief."

"Why do you think that the person you met might have had something to do with the murder of Squire Skjern-Svendsen?"

"I didn't say I thought that. I merely said that I met a man who was prowling around in the dark at Frydenholm. And the man was obviously frightened of me and took off quickly."

"That's really pretty vague. And it's curious that you can't give a description of the man."

"I can't see a man's face in the dark. And I really didn't think anything more about it."

There is nothing more to be learned from Dr. Riege. But the doctor is instructed to remain at the disposal of the police. This simply means that he must not leave the country as long as the investigation is pending.

# [ 55 ]

MRS. SKJERN-SVENDSEN'S CAR has been seen on the Storebælt ferry. The long blue car was ferried across the channel on the first boat of the morning, and it's easy for the police to trace it. They quickly discover that the squire's wife has taken up residence with her brother, Imperial Count Preben Rosenkop-Frydenskjold of Fyn. It will be the local police on the island who will have to conduct the necessary interrogations.

Mrs. Skjern-Svendsen's explanation agrees with Dr. Riege's in all the essentials. She did not talk to her husband after 9:00 in the evening. She did not observe anything suspicious. And she didn't know whether there were any other persons in the castle on the night in question aside from the servant Lukas and the page boy and the maids. Dr. Riege had left around 12:30. And she left immediately after that herself. Naturally she had no idea that her husband was dead at that point.

It is understandable that Mrs. Skjern-Svendsen is greatly shaken by what has happened. Her doctor orders absolute rest and has allowed the questioning only with great misgivings.

Lukas, on the other hand, is interrogated thoroughly and carefully. It comes out that he has been convicted four times. For theft, assault, and fraud. He was taken on as a servant at Frydenholm on the recommendation of master tailor Henningsen in Præstø, who works for the Prisoners' Aid Society and the Salvation Army's Prison Mission.

"Now think very carefully!" Police Superintendent Odense says to Lukas and bangs on the table. "You've got to tell the truth now!"

"I don't have to say anything at all if I don't want to," Lukas says. "If you want to charge me with the murder, first I have to have a public defender appointed and have a chance to talk to him. And I have to be brought before a judge within 24 hours. And you don't need to bang on the table and scream and shout, Mr. Odense."

"You haven't been charged. Not yet, anyway. It's simply in your own best interest for you to testify and tell the truth."

And Lukas tells them that a man wearing a black raincoat arrived and was shown into the squire's study at around 7:30 in the evening. And that the man's name was Olsen, first name Egon, he thought. And that he stayed overnight at Frydenholm in a little room in the attic. And that he left early the next morning with the school bus that leaves the inn at 7:10.

A couple of hours after Olsen arrived, a man came who wanted to talk to the mistress. He didn't want to give his name but said that he was expected and that Lukas should just announce to his mistress that it was the doctor. But Lukas doesn't know how long the stranger remained in the castle. He didn't hear him leave and didn't hear the squire's wife leave either. Besides, it was so stormy that night that you couldn't hear a car start.

Lukas doesn't know anything else. Just because he has been convicted of theft and is known to the police doesn't mean he is a murderer. Lukas is not arrested, but he is requested not to leave Frydenholm.

The police are busy. And the officers from Copenhagen with their windbreakers and bicycle clips on their pants act superior and condescending toward the local policeman. "I bet you've never been involved in anything like this before, Hansen. I bet this is the first time something big has happened in your district."

"No, there isn't that much murdering out here," the local police officer says. His name is Hansen. A number of the officers from the capital were named Hansen once too. But now they're called Odense or Aalborg or Horsens or Aakirkeby.

Hansen is an unobtrusive policeman. It's not his business to create criminals. When one neighbor reports another for illegal hunting or unauthorized fishing or slander or for not keeping his dog on a leash, the policeman naturally has to go out and talk with the person who lodged the complaint. "You don't really want to have a report written, do you?" he says. "Because then there'll be a lawsuit and red tape, you know."

"Oh, no! Let's avoid that, by all means," says the person who filed the complaint. "But now he's been reported at any rate."

"Yep, now he's been reported," the policeman says and drives home.

He knows the people of the area and knows what each one of them just might think of doing. There are so many little conflicts and insults and squabbles that can be taken care of and smoothed over without having to bring the law into it. A local police officer can accomplish a great deal if he takes it easy and knows how to talk to people.

Hansen looks up Panty Marius and asks him discreetly where he was on the night the squire was murdered. Because someone did see him out in the bad weather. What business did he have outside?

Marius squirms and isn't happy about the situation. "I'm not the one who killed him!" he says. But even though he hasn't committed a murder, there is also a penalty for going around trying to get your hands on other people's laundry.

"I'm sorry, Marius," the officer says. "But there's nothing that can be done about it. I'm afraid I'm going to have to arrest you. But just take it easy. You know how it goes, and it's not that bad."

"At least it's a good thing that it isn't right at harvest time," Marius says. "So how long do you suppose it'll take?"

"I don't imagine it'll take too long. It's not really theft that you committed. Just 'unauthorized use.' "

And Marius blows his nose in his fingers and takes a piece of hard candy and offers the policeman a piece.

But Panty Marius probably isn't the murderer. And it gives the people of the area an eerie feeling to have a killer and murderer running around loose. They're terrified, and they lock their doors tight at night and sleep with loaded hunting rifles

beside their beds. And when there's a knock at the door, they jump and break out in a sweat from fear and fright. It's a shocking thing that the police haven't been able to find that murderer yet, so decent people can sleep in peace at night.

# [ 56 ]

OLSEN IS STANDING next to the printing press. He is silent and sullen. Damascus scurries around on his little bare feet looking anxiously at Olsen.

Olsen has studied the morning papers very carefully. And around 2:00 o'clock he goes out to the street to buy the afternoon papers.

"Now they've found the murderer!" Olsen says. "They've arrested a man who was prowling around the castle the night Skjern-Svendsen was killed."

"Oh, they have?" Damascus says. He is both relieved and sorry. "The poor man!"

"He sure wasn't a 'poor man' at all," Olsen says. "He was a real s.o.b., that Skjern-Svendsen!"

"I don't mean Skjern-Svendsen. I mean the poor murderer."

"Oh," says Olsen.

"Let me have a look at the paper too," says Damascus. ARREST IN MURDER CASE, the headline reads. A man from the area. An individual with a previous conviction who can't account for his whereabouts between 9:00 p.m. and midnight on the night of the murder. Seen in the vicinity of Frydenholm Castle just before the murder. His explanations are incoherent and confused. And there's an interview with Police Superintendent Odense, who has stated to the press that he's convinced that they've found the right man. There still hasn't been a confession. But the explanations of the arrested man, Marius Petersen, are so confused and improbable that there's absolutely no doubt that he has something he wants to hide. Marius Petersen has previously been convicted of a hideous crime. He is a cynical, insensitive person who shows no remorse but grins stupidly when questioned. A confession can definitely be expected in the course of the day. "I think," Police Superintendent Odense is quoted as saying, "that I daresay the police have done a splendid piece of work."

Damascus feels pity for the man. Nevertheless, he's strangely relieved. And Olsen isn't silent and gloomy anymore but turns quite cheerful, whistling and humming as he tends to his press.

The idealists come and go in the little print shop. And messengers come with bills. And Damascus reassures the messengers and discusses lofty problems with the idealists. No one any longer suspects him of being an eccentric rich man who goes around distributing fortunes behind his friends' backs. Good relations have been reestablished in the little print shop.

Mr. Sivertsen, B.A., arrives with the manuscript for his magazine GYP, which stands for Geography, Yield, Purchase.

"Here's an editorial with teeth in it! It'll give our political economists something to think about!" And he haughtily discusses things with student Skodsborg, who is editing his *Academic Intelligence Journal*. No one knows what purpose this *Intelligence Journal* is supposed to be serving. But there must be some purpose to it since the student's father is willing to pay for it.

Two gentlemen come up the iron staircase and walk in through the glass door to the little outer office. They don't say who they are and they don't have any bills to present. They continue on into the print shop. Damascus walks over to meet them, probably thinking that they're a couple of idealists who need to have something printed. But Olsen sees the two gentlemen and gets a funny feeling and goes weak in the knees.

The two strangers are wearing windbreakers and have bicycle clips on their pants even though they're not riding bicycles but have their car parked down in the courtyard. They walk right up to Olsen and say, "Well, Olsen! Are you ready?"

"I didn't do anything!" Olsen says.

"Just come along with us and don't make such a fuss," the officers tell him. "You know it won't do any good, Olsen."

"What is it I'm suspected of?" Olsen asks. His voice is very shaky, and he is very pale and on the verge of tears.

"You're accused of murder. Come along."

"But I didn't do it! I didn't do it! It wasn't me!"

"I know that Olsen is a weak man," Damascus says, "but he isn't a bad person. It would never occur to him to kill another human being."

"No, it wouldn't!" says Olsen, close to tears.

"Come on!" the officers tell him. "Let's get a move on!" And they grab hold of Olsen and lead him down the iron staircase and into their car.

Olsen has been arrested before. He knows the routine. He knows what rights a defendant has according to the Constitution. He knows that before the interrogation the police have to advise him that he isn't bound to make a statement and that anything he says might be used against him. So he is silent and impenetrable until a public defender is assigned to him. Within 24 hours he is supposed to be brought before a judge, who will decide whether there are sufficient grounds to jail him. And he is supposed to have permission to talk to his lawyer in private. And before the police can carry out a search of Olsen's lodgings, the judge has to issue a warrant.

But they find nothing of interest in Olsen's room. And Olsen obstinately denies having strangled Squire Skjern-Svendsen.

"GUILT CYNICALLY DENIED!" the newspapers write. "The murderer is apparently totally unmoved by his appalling deed. An insensitive, inaccessible individual whose only response is apathetic sullenness."

The newspapers praise the brilliant job that Police Superintendent Odense has done, which led to the extremely prompt apprehension of the murderer. In a new interview Mr. Odense states that rarely in his long experience as a police officer has he been confronted by someone as obstinate and shameless in his denial of guilt. "Egon Charles Olsen has been convicted several times previously. He is a very dangerous felon who is capable of anything. No confession has been made yet, but the police are holding good cards in their hands."

None of the newspapers writes about Marius anymore. He is no longer accused of murder. But his affairs are going to be looked into very carefully, and he certainly can't be expected to be released right away.

"I just knew it," says the poetess Mrs. Drusse. "I knew that Olsen was a killer. I saw it in my crystal ball, you know. I saw the whole thing the way it eventually happened."

"I didn't think you could remember what you had seen afterwards," says Damascus.

"Oh yes. Now I remember it. I saw the killer in my crystal ball. And I told you too, Damascus, once when you were up in my artist's garret."

"I remember that you said you saw a man with a dagger. And you saw blood flowing. But Skjern-Svendsen wasn't stabbed with a dagger. He was strangled. He didn't bleed at all!"

"Just let them write what they want to in their newspapers! I saw a man being killed. And I saw who the killer was. Whether it happened with one instrument or another seems to me to be so utterly trivial. I abhor pedantry. You mustn't get to be like that pedant Christensen."

"But I just don't think that Olsen did it," says Damascus. "He may be weak, but he's basically good. It's a real shame for Olsen."

"I have always had a feeling that that man was a killer!" says Mrs. Drusse. "I have felt him as an evil and alien element in my aura. As something poisonous. My aura is very large. Whenever I'm in this print shop, I can't avoid feeling all of you within my auric egg."

"Among the adepts they say that the aura can be several kilometers wide," says editor Christensen.

"I don't think my auric egg is *that* big. But it's very large," says Mrs. Drusse. "And it was a chilling and horrible sensation to feel the killer in my egg!"

The terrible murder has created a real stir all across the country. Voices have been heard proclaiming that the time of softness and laxity must come to an end, and that it's time for the death penalty to be reinstated. Well-known Danish men and women have written articles in the newspapers demanding beheadings and an eye for an eye and a tooth for a tooth. Two clergymen, a university professor, and several high-school teachers have joined the newly reestablished League for the Reinstatement of the Death Penalty. They're all idealists.

And while the police are still working on Olsen and waiting

for his confession, a committee has been formed to urge that a monument be erected to C. C. Skjern-Svendsen. They're already at work organizing a fundraising effort for the necessary means to realize their project. Their idea is for the monument to be erected in the part of the country where C. C. Skjern-Svendsen lived and worked to the benefit of Danish economic life. It might, for instance, stand in the old linden-lined avenue leading up to Frydenholm Castle. Or in the little park next to the evangelical meeting house. A monument like that would be especially important for young people because of the example that C. C. Skjern-Svendsen set for youth through a life in the service of his fatherland.

# [ 57 ]

IT's SNOWING A LITTLE, and it's raining a little. It's the dark time of the year, and it's dank and depressing.

Frydenholm stands there empty and sinister among the old black trees. The countryside is wet and black with its autumn fields plowed under, and the sky is gray.

It will soon be the Christmas month. Niels Madsen is force-feeding his geese to get their weight up. His boys who come from the children's home look on enviously. A chocolate camel is on display in the grocer's window. Layers of cotton have been spread out, and tufts of cotton have been hung up on threads to look like snowflakes. And the children can stand there looking at the camel for hours, discussing whether it's hollow or whether it's chocolate all the way through.

It's already dark by 4:00 o'clock in the afternoon. A man is riding his bicycle along the country road. He has turned on his bicycle light because he is a methodical person who doesn't want to risk not complying with the rules and regulations and have to pay a fine. He rides his bicycle into town and stops at Officer Hansen's house. He places his bicycle carefully in the bicycle

rack and locks it before he goes into the policeman's house. He is as pale as a corpse, and his hands are shaking.

It's gardener Holm, who has come to turn himself in for murder.

"Sit down, Holm. Sit down, and let's talk about it calmly," says Hansen. He pats the gardener lightly on the shoulder to calm him down.

"I strangled him," the gardener tells him. "I grabbed him around the throat and squeezed until he fell. I cast him out as Michael cast out the Beast. And no one else should be punished for what I did."

"Why did you do it, Holm?"

"It is written that they should not love their lives unto the death," says the gardener. His eyes are shining. And he looks at the policeman as if transfigured. "I did it because it had to be done. It had to be done for her sake and for the sake of all humanity. Jesus died for humanity and received salvation and eternal hymns of praise for it. But I am giving up my salvation for her sake and for everyone's sake. I say 'No thank you,' that's what I say. I don't want to have any salvation. I won't accept it. 'No thank you,' is what I say!" He is shaking. He has beads of sweat on his forehead. His eyes are shining. And Hansen realizes that he's talking to a madman.

"Try to be very calm. And then tell me how it happened, and why you did it."

But the gardener is unable to tell him anything coherent. He talks about a large squash that he got no credit for. And about a gigantic potato that was in the newspapers. And the squire stole his big potato from him. And the squire was the Devil who wanted to have an angel put away and drive her insane. And she was a prisoner in the estate of her ancestors. But now she has been freed. No one shall do anything to her. She will have his salvation. "Please, here's my place! I'm giving my place to a lady! And the great dragon was cast out. The old serpent, called the Devil and Satan, was cast out unto the earth. And they loved not their lives unto the death. Woe to the inhabitants of the earth! For the Devil is come down unto you. He hath great wrath because he knoweth that he hath but a short time. And when he saw that he was cast unto the earth, he persecuted the woman. And lo, the woman is gone, having driven away in the blue wagon. And her beloved has saved her!"

"There, there! Just take it easy," the policeman says. "Just take it nice and easy, Holm."

"For the accuser of our brethren is cast down, which accused them before our God day and night. And they overcame him by the blood of the Lamb and by the word of their testimony!" says the gardener. His eyes are rigid, and he doesn't see the policeman.

"Lo, I have made a place for her so that she might receive my life. She shall live and smell the flowers, and I have made the way free for her and removed that which persecuted her. And the merchants of the earth shall weep and mourn over the great magnate; for no man buyeth their merchandise anymore and all manner of works of brass and iron and marble and burial mounds and oxen and horses and slaves and souls of men. All things which glisten have departed from thee. And the voice of the bridegroom and of the bride shall be heard no more at all in

thee: for thy merchants were princes on earth; for by thy sor-
ceries were all deceived."

The policeman lets him talk. It is impossible to write a coherent report of what he is saying. It was probably the Revelation of
St. John the Divine and religion that drove him crazy. And the
policeman remembers that people have been saying that there
was something wrong with the gardener's mind. And there
probably was something between Mrs. Skjern-Svendsen and the
gardener. And now he's killed a man.

"And there shall be shouts of halleluia in Heaven! And the
false prophet shall be cast out into a lake of fire!" the gardener
shouts. His voice is hoarse, and his eyes are shining with
madness.

"Yes, yes," the policeman says. He pats him on the shoulder
and waits patiently for him to calm down.

Little by little the gardener does grow calm and collapses
completely. The policeman has plenty of time. "We'd better
have a cup of coffee before we leave, don't you think, Holm?
It'll do you good." He asks his wife to make a pot of strong
coffee and bring it in. "Maybe a couple of slices of bread too,
right, Holm?"

The gardener drinks the hot, strong coffee. Little by little he
recovers some of his strength and leans back in the policeman's
green sofa.

"Just take it easy. There's no hurry. And eat a little something. Wouldn't you like a smoke too, Holm?"

"No, thank you," says the gardener.

"It was a good thing you came and told me. You wouldn't
have been able to stand it anyway."

"No," says the gardener.

They sit together for a long time without saying anything.
Later they go out to Hansen's little car together and drive to the
courthouse in Præstø.

"But what about my bicycle?" the gardener asks.

"I'll make sure it's taken care of. Nothing will happen to it,"
says the policeman.

# [ 58 ]

THE YELLOW BUS is driving through town. It's fairly full because this isn't any weather to be riding a bicycle in. You'd only ruin your clothes. It's snowing and raining at the same time.

The bus stops at people's houses, letting passengers on and delivering packages. It will soon be Christmas, and people are busy. They're talking about everything that has been happening recently. So they've been going and buying their vegetables from a murderer. It's an awful thought. It's enough to make them shake all over. The gardener, of all people. He was such a nice, quiet man. And religious. Why, they say he's insane and he'll probably be put in an asylum. It's supposed to be religion that affected his mind. His head couldn't take it.

They also say that he was going to bed with the mistress up at the castle. So that's what she was like. And she was supposed to be elegant and aristocratic. But things were never really good between her and the squire. Why, anyone could see that.

Gardener Holm probably had some old grudge or animosity toward the squire. One thing led to another. Looking back on it now, there are certainly a lot of things that are easier to understand.

And now a monument is going to be erected to the squire. Lord only knows where they're going to put it. It will probably be next to the evangelical meeting house or inside the park.

But it's not all that certain that the new owner will care to have the monument in the park. It was the squire's wish, of course, that Frydenholm be turned into a museum, but probably nothing will come of it. They say that Mrs. Skjern-Svendsen's brother is going to take it over. He's a count, after all, and is said to do things in style. And maybe things will be like they were in the days of the old count, who rode in a carriage drawn by four horses and everything.

But Mrs. Skjern-Svendsen probably won't be coming to Frydenholm anymore. You wouldn't think that she could ever show her face in public again!

So it was Hansen who brought the murderer in after all, and not those conceited experts from Copenhagen. And that Police Superintendent Odense. He sure was quick to make statements to the newspapers about having discovered who the murderer was. First it was Panty Marius. And then it was Olsen. And then it wasn't either one of them after all. And Panty Marius is free again and is walking around sucking on hard candy with snot in his mustache. But he won't be able to avoid getting a sentence, because he's been swiping other people's underwear again. That certainly is a weird way to behave.

But they're keeping Olsen locked up even though he isn't the murderer. They've found out about a few little things that he's done. If it isn't one thing, it's another. They usually do find something. But the people on the bus don't know that the police up in Copenhagen have good use for a man with Olsen's special talents and would hate to lose him. The time will come when Olsen will be an important man in Denmark.

Little by little the rain changes into snow. And the snow is beginning to stick in the plowed furrows and on the fences. It'll probably turn into frost now too. The unemployed men are standing outside Rasmus Larsen's house waiting. There are a lot more of them since winter began. "It's just no good for people to want to live on relief instead of doing some work!" says Niels Madsen. "Who's helping the farmer? That little bit of emergency aid he gets is neither fish nor fowl!" Niels Madsen has put on his high, shiny boots. They're good to have now that winter is coming. Maybe other people should buy a pair of boots like that.

Jenny is running around on the highway gesticulating with her arms and being of no use to anyone. But there really isn't much room for her at home in the long clay-walled house where the town has placed its homeless families. Homes don't have any influence on young people anymore. Just look at Johanne, who had a Christian upbringing, after all. Why, she's started sleeping with Oscar from the dairy. And they're going to get married too, now that she's turned eighteen. You'd think they might have been able to wait a while. It's certainly a funny time to have a wedding.

And it's probably also a sign of the times that such a ghastly murder could be committed.

The countryside turns white beneath the snow. It will soon be Christmas. The grocer has a Christmas display, and the radio plays Christmas carols all day long. But if you turn the radio dial a little, you hear that there is unrest out in the world.

The countryside lies there white and silent with its church and parsonage and ancient barrow for the dead squire. The houses smell of Christmas baking. They're slaughtering pigs on the farms. And the Christmas geese are being plucked and put in boxes and sent to the city. The bus is full of packages and people. They talk about what has been happening. The murder of Squire Skjern-Svendsen is an important event that will be discussed for a long time.

Later on there may be other events that can be written about someday.

# [ About *Idealists* ]

In his novel *Idealists* Hans Scherfig set out to satirize the foibles of the subculture of scheming charlatans, social outsiders, and guileless altruists that flourished in Copenhagen during the 1930s. The outbreak of World War II, however, caused him to inject a more pointedly political, class-conscious element into his work. The political and social climate in Denmark and the rest of Europe had become so unsettled that Scherfig could not help but comment on what he saw as the growing threat to rational, civilized behavior. The German occupation of Denmark in April of 1940 added a further note of urgency to his project.

The author had hoped to publish *Idealists* in the fall of 1941, but the roundup of Danish communists in June of that year (after Hitler's invasion of the Soviet Union) foiled these plans. Imprisoned briefly in "Vestre Fængsel" (the site of head clerk Amsted's incarceration in *The Missing Bureaucrat*), Scherfig was later transferred to a Copenhagen hospital, where he underwent an eye operation to cure him of his almost total blindness. After his release from the hospital, Scherfig withdrew to the idyllic surroundings of his northern Sjælland home, where he continued work on *Idealists*. He submitted the finished manuscript to his publisher in 1942.

As the novel was being readied for printing, however, the Danish Foreign Ministry confiscated the proofs and subsequently prohibited its publication. For good measure, the Danish government, ever anxious to remain on good terms with the German occupying powers, imposed a writing ban on Hans Scherfig. This proscription did not prevent the author from publishing frequent newspaper polemics under a pseudonym. Nor, ironically enough, did it discourage a Danish representative of a German publishing house from seeking out Scherfig in 1943 to try to arrange a publishing agreement for a German translation of *Idealists*. Out of deference to his still imprisoned comrades, Scherfig respectfully declined the otherwise cordial invitation.

Not long thereafter, however, he entrusted a carbon copy of the manuscript to a friend, who managed to smuggle it to Sweden. *Idealists* finally saw the light of day three years after its intended date of publication, in a 1944 Swedish translation. The Danish audience did not have the opportunity to read the novel until after the liberation of Denmark in 1945.

*Frank Hugus*
December 1990

## [ *About the Translator* ]

BORN UNDER THE SIGN of the Twins in 1941, Frank Hugus first turned his kindly blue eyes toward the works of Hans Scherfig while conducting research in Denmark some twenty years ago. He has been a Scherfig enthusiast ever since. While preparing this translation of *Idealists*, Mr. Hugus made several trips to Denmark to examine material in the archives of Copenhagen's Royal Library. He also visited many of the places described in the novel and interviewed friends and family of the author.

When not translating or writing about Danish literature, Mr. Hugus can be found teaching a variety of courses in the Department of Germanic Languages and Literatures at the University of Massachusetts. He lives in a rambling old three-story house in Amherst with his wife and daughter.

# [ GLOSSARY OF PROPER NAMES ]

Altruist League. The Baltimore address given for international head-quarters is now that of the Enoch Pratt Free Library.

Anthroposophy. An outgrowth of *theosophy*, founded by Rudolf Steiner in 1913. Anthroposophy is more closely linked to Christian theology than is theosophy.

Assistens Cemetery. Perhaps the best known cemetery in all of Denmark. Tucked away in the Nørrebro section of Copenhagen, it is the final resting place of a number of famous Danes: Søren Kierkegaard, Hans Christian Andersen, and Hans Scherfig himself.

Bion research. Scherfig modeled Robert Riege on the Austrian-born psychoanalyst Wilhelm Reich (1897–1956). One of Reich's many exotic ideas was that of the role of "bions" in human sexuality. Reich, who lived in Scandinavia during the early 1930s, also managed a "Sexpol" publishing house.

Blavatsky, Helena Petrovna (1831–91). Born in Russia, she later traveled to America, where she became prominent in spiritualistic circles and founded the Theosophical Society in 1875. Her commanding presence and her apparent miracles gained untold thousands of disciples for the movement.

Brahe, Tycho (1546–1601). Danish astronomer who left Denmark after a dispute with King Christian IV. He was appointed Imperial Astronomer in Prague, where Johannes Kepler was his assistant.

Bruno, Giordano (1548–1600). Italian philosopher, Dominican friar, many of whose ideas (such as *monadism, pantheism*) anticipated those of later thinkers. He was burned at the stake as a heretic.

Christian II (1481–1559). King of Denmark (and briefly of Sweden as well) from 1513–1523. Opposed by the nobility for his support of the commoners, he was forced to flee Denmark in 1523. After an unsuccessful attempt to regain the Danish throne, he was captured and imprisoned until his death.

Christian IV (1577–1648). King of Denmark from 1588–1648. Among his lasting contributions are the many buildings he commissioned in and around Copenhagen, with their characteristic green copper spires.

Copenhagen Industrial Exhibit. The year 1888 marked the centennial of the freeing of Danish peasants from villeinage. One of the many events that year was the Industrial Exhibit—at which the huge Tuborg beer bottle, two stories tall, now gracing the Tuborg Brewery grounds was first displayed.

Cyprianus. Probable reference to the (fictitious?) Saint Cyprian the Magician of Antioch (fl. pre-fourth century A.D.).

Dannebrog. The name given to the Danish flag, according to tradition the oldest national flag in the world, having dropped from the sky during a battle in 1219. The Order of the Dannebrog was established by King Christian V in 1671.

Dybbøl. Town in southern Jutland, site of a major battle in the Dano-Prussian War of 1864, during which the Dybbøl Mill was destroyed.

Esperanto. An artificial language created in 1887 for the purpose of facilitating international communication.

Fælled Park. A large park in the Østerbro section of Copenhagen bordered by many scientific institutes and the National Hospital.

Frue Plads. A square in Copenhagen next to Vor Frue Kirke (the Church of Our Lady), where the oldest part of the University of Copenhagen is located.

Gjønge, Svend (ca. 1600–1676). The legendary "Gjøngehøvding" (Gjønge Chief) popularized by Danish author Carit Etlar (pen name of Carl Brosbøll, 1816–1900) in a series of romantic novels about Danish history. Svend Gjønge, whose real name was Svend Poulsen, did in fact play an important role in the Dano-Swedish wars of 1657.

Gram, Hans (1685–1748). Danish philologist and historiographer.

Holberg, Ludvig (1684–1754). Born in Norway, Holberg was educated in Denmark. He was first a professor of metaphysics and later of Latin at Copenhagen University. In 1722 he penned the first in a series of 26 dramas that are still part of the Danish repertory. They show the influence of Shakespeare, Molière, the *commedia dell'arte*, and Danish folk humor.

Jungshoved. Peninsula in southern Sjælland. Jungshoved Castle was torn down around 1700.

Karl X Gustav (1622–60). King of Sweden from 1654–60.

Klopstock, Friedrich Gottlieb (1724–1803). German poet who was the court poet of Denmark between 1751 and 1770.

Krishnamurti, Jiddu (1895?–1986). Hindu religious philosopher, regarded by many as the Messianic Buddha. He established his "Star in the East" in 1911 but dissolved it in 1929.

Lullus, Raimund (ca. 1229–1315). Born in Spain, he became a monk and set out without the Pope's blessing to Christianize the Moors of northern Africa. His repeated efforts failed, and he died a martyr's death. He was never canonized, probably due to his interest in alchemy, about which he wrote several treatises.

Luna, Johannes de (fl. late 16th–early 17th centuries). Supposed author of a treatise on coercing spirits to do one's bidding; also purported to have been the disciple of Christoph Wagner, who was Johan Faust's famulus.

Middelgrund. Located in Øresund (the Sound) to the northeast of Copenhagen harbor, Middelgrund has the largest marine fortifications in the world.

Montvoisin, Madame (d. 1680). The fortune-teller Catherine Deshayes, known as the "Widow Montvoisin" or "La Voisin," implicated in the "Chambre Ardente" affair (a tribunal set up by Louis XIV to investigate poisonings among the French nobility—including a suspected attempt on the Sun King's own life). La Voisin was charged with having gotten rid of 2,500 unwanted babies, many of whom were said to be buried in a Paris suburb. Testimony during the affair indicated that Black Masses were performed by several of the accused, during which babies were sacrificed—often over the bellies of naked women. Although horribly tortured, La Voisin refused to confess. She was nevertheless convicted and burned at the stake.

Møller, Poul Martin (1794–1838). Danish author and professor.

Neophit. Probably a reference to Neophytus, a 13th-century writer on theological subjects.

Nostradamus, Michael (1503–66). French physician and astrologer, best known for his prophecies. His *Centuries* were written in 1555.

Novial. An artificial language created in 1928 by the Danish linguist Otto Jespersen (1860–1943). It employs more Germanic roots and grammatical structure than does Esperanto, which is largely based on the Romance languages.

Nyborg. Town on the Danish island of Fyn where the ferry from Sjælland lands. Its castle dates from around 1100.

Oxford Movement. Conservative Protestant religious movement, founded in 1921 in the United States by Frank Buchanan. The Oxford Movement was widespread in Scandinavia in the 1930s.

Paracelsus, Philippus Aureolus Theophrastus Bombastus von Hohenheim (1493–1541). Swiss physician, founder of the modern science of medicine. He also delved into spiritualism and alchemy (writing on sylphs, salamanders, and nymphs). He visited almost every country in Europe and went to the Middle East. He died under mysterious circumstances.

Rosenroth, Knorr von (1636–1689). German scholar and poet. He was greatly interested in the kabbala and alchemy.

Roskilde. This city, located some 20 miles west of Copenhagen, is the site of an imposing brick cathedral, the final resting place of all Danish monarchs and many other prominent members of the Danish Royal Family since 1536. The Peace of Roskilde (1658) saw Denmark cede large areas of Sweden and Norway to the Swedish crown.

Skagen. A small town on the absolute tip of northern Jutland, renowned for its wonderful light and its colony of artists in the late 19th and early 20th centuries.

Skamlingsbanken. A hill in southern Jutland, since 1843 a place for large, open-air meetings of a political, patriotic nature.

Sosigenes of Alexandria (fl. first century B.C.). Egyptian astronomer and mathematician at the court of Cleopatra, he was commissioned by Julius Cæsar in 46 B.C. to devise a more accurate calendar.

Steiner, Rudolf (1861–1925). Austrian philosopher and pedagogue, he founded anthroposophy and the Rudolf-Steiner (or Waldorf) Schools.

Storebælt. The channel between the islands of Fyn and Sjælland.

Strindberg, August (1844–1912). Swedish author whose dramas are world-famous. He also dabbled in alchemy and the occult.

Svaning, Hans (ca. 1500–84). Danish historian, best known for his unflattering portrayals of Christian II.

Tatwa stream. A reference to Tatwic Yoga ("the science of breath"). The Tatwas are the five elementary principles of nature, the five essences of the human being. Knowledge of the Tatwas is said to confer wondrous powers. (From Sanskrit *tattva*, "that-ness" or "essence".)

Theosophy. A religious movement founded in 1875 in the United States by Madame Blavatsky, which preached the universal brotherhood of humanity and sought to unify all religious experience. It was tinged with occultism and mysticism.

Thorvaldsen, Bertil (1770–1844). Danish sculptor who drew inspiration from classical Greek and Roman art.

Thy. The western part of the northern tip of the Jutland peninsula.

Trekroner. Harbor fortification in Copenhagen, closed down in 1922.

Villoms, Sigbrit (d. ca. 1531). Originally from Amsterdam, she and her daughter Dyveke met the future Danish king Christian II in Bergen, Norway. Dyveke became the king's mistress. Mother and daughter followed the king to Copenhagen, where Sigbrit exerted a "strange" influence over Christian. Dyveke died in 1517, doubtless poisoned. Sigbrit remained with Christian. She is said to have met Paracelsus when he was in Denmark.

Walkendorff's Dormitory. Founded in 1588 by Christoffer Valkendorf (1525–1601) to provide free lodging to twenty students of the University of Copenhagen, this dormitory is still in use.

Winther, Christian (1796–1876). Danish poet, known for his nature and love poems as well as his epic *Hjortens flugt*, 1855 ("The Flight of the Hart"), a tale of knights and ladies set in medieval Denmark.

# Forthcoming translations from Fjord Press

*Pelle the Conqueror, Vol. 2: Apprenticeship* by Martin Andersen Nexø
Translated from the Danish by Steven T. Murray & Tiina Nunnally
$9.95 paper, $19.95 cloth

*Love & Solitude: Selected Poems, 1916–1923* by Edith Södergran
Translated from the Finland-Swedish by Stina Katchadourian
$9.95 paper, Third bilingual edition

*Night Roamers and Other Stories* by Knut Hamsun
Translated from the Norwegian by Tiina Nunnally
$9.95 paper, $19.95 cloth

## Titles now available:

*The Missing Bureaucrat* by Hans Scherfig
Translated from the Danish by Frank Hugus
$8.95 paper, $17.95 cloth

*Stolen Spring* by Hans Scherfig
Translated from the Danish by Frank Hugus
$7.95 paper, $15.95 cloth

*The Faces* by Tove Ditlevsen
Translated from the Danish by Tiina Nunnally
$9.95 paper, $19.95 cloth

*Katinka* by Herman Bang
Translated from the Danish by Tiina Nunnally
$8.95 paper, $17.95 cloth

*Niels Lyhne* by Jens Peter Jacobsen
Translated from the Danish by Tiina Nunnally
$19.95 cloth

*Peasants and Masters* by Theodor Kallifatides
Translated from the Swedish by Thomas Teal
$8.95 paper, $17.95 cloth

*Another Metamorphosis and Other Fictions* by Villy Sørensen
Translated from the Danish by Tiina Nunnally & Steven T. Murray
$8.95 paper, $17.95 cloth

*Pelle the Conqueror, Vol. 1: Childhood* by Martin Andersen Nexø
Translated from the Danish by Steven T. Murray
$9.95 paper, $19.95 cloth

*Laterna Magica* by William Heinesen
Translated from the Danish by Tiina Nunnally
$7.95 paper, $15.95 cloth

*Witness to the Future* by Klaus Rifbjerg
Translated from the Danish by Steven T. Murray
$8.95 paper, $17.95 cloth

*Please write for a catalog:* Fjord Press, Box 16501, Seattle, WA 98116